EDUCATION *for* Development

A TEACHER'S RESOURCE FOR GLOBAL LEARNING

SUSAN FOUNTAIN

Hodder & Stoughton

A MEMBER OF THE HODDER HEADLINE GROUP

Order queries: please contact Bookpoint Ltd, 39 Milton Park, Abingdon, Oxon OX14 4TD. Telephone: (44) 01235 400414, Fax: (44) 01235 400454. Lines are open from 9.00 - 6.00, Monday to Saturday, with a 24 hour message answering service. Email address: orders@bookpoint.co.uk

British Library Cataloguing in Publication Data
A catalogue record for this title is available from The British Library

ISBN 0 340 61904 X

First published 1995

Impression number	12	11	10	9	8	7	6	5	4	3
Year	2004	2003	2002	2001	2000	1999	1998			

Typeset by Wearset, Boldon, Tyne & Wear.
Printed in Great Britain for Hodder & Stoughton Educational, a division of Hodder Headline Plc, 338 Euston Road, London NW1 3BH by Scotprint Ltd, Musselburgh, Scotland.

EDUCATION *for* Development

A TEACHER'S RESOURCE FOR GLOBAL LEARNING

Contents

Acknowledgements

The idea of producing a resource manual for teachers on global learning, organised around the five concepts elaborated in this book, originated in the work of Nóra Godwin and Andrés Guerrero of the Education for Development Section, UNICEF New York and Geneva. Their guidance and support was essential at every step of the writing, piloting, and revising process, and is gratefully acknowledged.

The author would also like to acknowledge the other individuals and organisations who made this book possible, in particular: David Adams of Wesleyan University and UNESCO for permission to reprint the text of *The Seville Statement on Violence*; Oliver & Boyd for permission to reprint the cartoon on page 189, which first appeared in *Making Global Connections* by David Hicks and Miriam Steiner (1990); Quaker Peace and Service, London, for permission to reprint the cartoon on page 31.

Some of the activities in this book have been adapted from other sources:

Activities 5, 13, 44, and 51 were based on material which appears in *Global Teacher, Global Learner* by Graham Pike and David Selby (Hodder and Stoughton, London, 1988). Activity 4 was based on material which appears in *Tomorrow's Woods* by Sue Lyle (Greenlight Publications, Carmarthen, 1987).

The UNICEF photo library supplied the photos used in Activities 17 and 18. Individual photo credits are as follows: (Activity 17): Ethiopian orphans: UNICEF/3240/89, Edith Simmons; Workers in Chad: UNICEF/4421DZ/90, Maggie Murray-Lee; Children in Peru: UNICEF/Photo 18: PERU 3363, Fran Antmann; Mother and child in Zimbabwe: UNICEF/3140/89, Carolyn Watson; (Activity 18): Social worker and children in Mexico: UNICEF/3831/89, Francene Keery; Guatemalan woman: UNICEF/4047/90, Jorgen Schytte; Child in Thailand: UNICEF/1920/86, Sean Sprague; Library in Sri Lanka: UNICEF/1629/86, Carolyn Watson; Nutritionist and child in Sudan: UNICEF/1178/85, Maria Antonietta Peru.

All other photographs in the book were taken by Nicole Toutounji.

Finally, on behalf of the Education for Development Section of UNICEF, the author wishes to thank the following education officers and teachers from around the world. These individuals field-tested and evaluated the activities in this manual, and in some cases allowed their classes to be photographed as well:

AUSTRALIA

Andrea McGinlay, Education Officer, UNICEF Committee of Australia; Heather Angus, Yarrabah State School, Yarrabah, Queensland; Bernadette Willans, Lourdes Hill College, Hawthorne, Queensland; Neville Blampey, Caversham Primary School, Beechboro, Western Australia; Ronis

Chapman, One World Learning Centre/Quakers, Gundaroo, New South Wales; Sheryl Morgan, Margate Primary School, Margate, Tasmania; Sandra Walker, Richmond Community Primary School, Richmond, Victoria.

AUSTRIA

Ernst Popp, Austrian Ministry of Education; Dr Klaus Edel, Hayonrealgymnasium, Vienna.

BELGIUM

Yves Willemot, Information Officer, Véronique Meunier and Mia Versmissen, Education Officers, Belgian Committee for UNICEF; Paul Demonie, Ecole Communale d'Estaimpuis, Estaimpuis; Marie-Paule Corbeel, Ecole Ste Jeanne de Chantal, Brussels; Georges Clément, Ecole Communale, Verviers; Danny Declerck and Damiaan Jacobs, Gemeentelijke Basisschool, Kalmthout; Liliane Juffrouw and Diane Spinnael, St. Lutgardisinstituut, Etterbeek; Ghislaine Tilleux, Collège Notre-Dame de la Paix, Erpent; Eric Vanhelsuwé, Zeelyceum, De Haan.

CANADA

Lori Latchman and Priscilla Slocum, Education Officers, Canadian Committee for UNICEF.

COLOMBIA

Vicki Colbert de Arboleda, Regional Advisor, Education, UNICEF Regional Office for the Americas and the Caribbean.

FINLAND

Ulla Pehrsson, Education Officer and Liisa-Maija Susiluoto, Finnish Committee for UNICEF; Riitta Cederqvist, Ritva Kae-Järvinen, Marja-Leena Kanervisto, Jaana Lemminkäinen and Ilkka Talasranta, Lotilan ala-aste, Lahti; Maiju Hemminki, Kurikan yläaste, Kurikka; Ritva Jäättelä, Espoon Kauppaoppilaitos, Espoo; Annukka Kavanne and Pirjo West, Helsingin I Normaalikoulu, Helsinki.

GERMANY

Marianne Müller-Antoine, Education Officer, German Committee for UNICEF; Professor Asit Datta, University of Hannover, Faculty of Education, Department of School Education.

GREECE

Ilias Liberis, Information and Education Officer, Hellenic National Committee for UNICEF; Neta Chioni, Elementary School of Perahora,

Loutraki; Andreas Morikis, Lyceum of Athens College; Kostas Papadonopoulos, Gymnasium of Athens College; Professor Stamelos, University of Athens; Vassilis Siamos, 78th Elementary School of Athens; Aristea Vavouyiou, 6th Gymnasium, Kalamaria, Thessaloniki.

KENYA

John O. Shiundu, Basic Education Resource Centre, Kenyatta University, Nairobi.

THE REPUBLIC OF KOREA

Okja Im, Education Officer, Korean Committee for UNICEF; Suk-Joo Kwon, Kangnam District Education Board, Seoul; Man-Gon Kim, Korea Federation of Teachers' Association, Seoul; Hyung-Shin Baik, Shin Wha Elementary School; Seung-Joo Baik, Machon Elementary School; Mi-Sook Cha and Chung-Hee Park, On Soo Elementary School; Soon-Hee Chang, Koo-Am Elementary School; Choon-Ja Choi, Daedong Elementary School; Jung-Ja Choi and Sung-Ae Yoon, Moon Baik Elementary School; Eun-Mi Chung, Chongryangri Elementary School; Kyung-Sook Chung, Kong Yeon Elementary School; Yang-Jae Chung, Il-Won Elementary School; Mi-Kyung Hahn, Yale Elementary School; Sung-Ye Hong, Hong Je Elementary School; Young-Lim Kang, Kyungbok Elementary School; Chan-Soo Kim, Do Bong Elementary School; Il-Soo Kim, Kaebong Elementary School; Jae-Soo Kim, Dae Hyun Elementary School; Jung-Sun Kim, Si Heung Elementary School; Young-Bong Kim, Woo Myun Elementary School; Sung-Wook Koh, Kye Sung Elementary School; Joong-Wook Kook, Mookdong Elementary School; Dong-Kwan Lee, Hong Ik Elementary School; Ji-Young Lee, Choong Hyun Elementary School; Sung-Ok Lee, Soosaek Elementary School; Young-Ja Lee, Won-Dang Elementary School; Chai-Soo Lim, Bang San Elementary School; Mi-Sook Sohn, Moon Le Elementary School; Kook-Sung Woo, Dong Won Elementary School; Byung-Ho Yeom, Young Do Elementary School (all schools are in Seoul).

NAMIBIA

Professor Donton S. J. Mkandawire, Faculty of Education, University of Namibia, Windhoek.

NEW ZEALAND

Pamela Glading, New Zealand Committee for UNICEF; Alyce McMaster, Wellington College of Education, Wellington.

SWITZERLAND

Elsbeth Müller and Michael Herzka, Education Officers, Swiss Committee for UNICEF; Christian Graf, Executive Director, Hannes Kurz and Trix Dörig, Forum Schule für eine Welt, Jona; Kurt Weiss, Marcel Meier and Ursula Weiss, Zug; Andrea Iten and Thomas Dobler, Baar; Bruno Nussbaumer, Unterägeri; Claudia Wehrli, Horgen; Peter Marty, Schwyz.

UNITED KINGDOM

Heather Jarvis, Education Officer, United Kingdom Committee for UNICEF; Pat Francis, Hampshire Development Education Centre; Romsey Youth Theatre; Roger Aldridge, Andrew Alexander, Steven Anson, Edwin Gruber, Jonathan Hart, Tony Hazzard, Alexandra Reeves, Betsy Reid and Janice Watson, St Christopher School, Letchworth; Beverley Hawker and Kay Read, Oak Lodge School, Southampton.

UNITED NATIONS INTERNATIONAL SCHOOL (NEW YORK)

Joseph Blaney, Director General; Mary Blake, Radha Rajan and Ray Taylor, principals; Tony Doyle, Urella Edwards, Jane Kaminski, Susan Knox, Steve Korolczuk, Peggy O'Brien, Maureen Overall, Adina Vanderpuye, Anne Zacharia and Phyllis Murray.

UNITED STATES

Elisabeth Schalk, Education Officer, US Committee for UNICEF; Chris Morton, Putnam/Northern Westchester BOCES; Heidi Carr, Jonathan Goldberg and Pat Snodgrass, Carmel High School, Carmel; Sue Cooper, Mary Costello, Peggy Dwyer and Elizabeth K. Hill, Westorchard School, Chappaqua; Michael Milove, Increase Miller Elementary School, Goldens Bridge; Margaret Podesta and Pat Robison, Furnace Woods School, Peekskill; Karen Sconce, Pound Ridge Elementary School, Pound Ridge; Eric Tomlins, The Randolph School, Wappingers Falls; Fran Varady and Cathy Windrum, Carrie E Tompkins School, Croton-on-Hudson (all schools are in New York).

What is Education for Development?

The complex challenges of the 21st century can only be met by people who are willing to be active global citizens. Education for Development is an approach to learning which aims to build global citizenship. UNICEF defines Education for Development as a process which:

> '... promotes the development, in children and young people, of attitudes and values such as global solidarity, peace, tolerance, social justice and environmental awareness, and which equips them with the knowledge and skills which will empower them to promote these values and bring about change in their own lives and in their communities, both locally and globally.'
>
> UNICEF, 1992

Education for Development has its origins in two movements, which began in the industrialised and developing countries respectively. In the 1970s, non-governmental organisations and aid agencies involved in development issues began producing teaching materials which encouraged awareness and advocacy among young people in industrialised countries. This area of study became known as Development Education.

During the same period, many community educators in developing countries began to look at strategies for local organising that could help people address problems such as poverty, ill health, and illiteracy. This movement encouraged the development of skills that empower individuals and groups to create change.

These two initiatives formed the roots of Education for Development. It has grown further in the 1980s and 1990s for three main reasons.

IDEAS ABOUT WHAT CONSTITUTES 'DEVELOPMENT' ARE CHANGING

> 'Development in the 1990s should be judged by human indicators, not economic variables.'
>
> James Grant, *1990 UNICEF Annual Report*

Economic growth has, in the past, frequently been given priority over such concerns as health, education, and environmental quality. It is increasingly clear that short-term sacrifices in these areas undercut the long-term human potential of a country, an outcome which is neither sustainable or morally acceptable.

THE NATURE OF GLOBAL ISSUES IS CHANGING

Global issues are increasingly complex, having social, economic, political, cultural, technological, and ecological dimensions that must be understood before solutions to contemporary problems can be found. Global issues are universal – no part of the world is free from environmental concerns, issues of justice, or conflict. The possibilities for making progress on these issues at the level of only one country or region are limited.

EDUCATIONAL VALUES ARE CHANGING

> **'. . . the education of the child shall be directed to . . . the development of respect for human rights and fundamental freedoms . . . the development of respect for . . . civilizations different from his or her own . . . the preparation of the child for responsible life in a free society, in the spirit of understanding, peace, tolerance, equality of sexes, and friendship among all peoples . . . the development of respect for the natural environment.'**
>
> Article 29, *The Convention on the Rights of the Child*, 1989

Curricula which are primarily nation-centred, focusing on a country's own (often military) history and economy, and emphasising the contributions of a few dominant cultures, will leave children ill-equipped to take an active role in an interdependent world. And schooling which encourages only a competitive, me-first mentality in both content and learning processes fails to prepare children for the cooperative efforts needed to address global issues. Education can play an active part in not only the transmission of knowledge, but the promotion of the attitudes and values of global citizenship.

Education for Development prepares students for a rapidly changing, interdependent world by addressing **five global concepts**, and by using a particular **learning process**.

Five global concepts

There are five global concepts that are basic to Education for Development, and that are equally relevant to learners in both industrialised and developing countries. These concepts are not new subject areas, but can be thought of as lenses through which information can be examined.

INTERDEPENDENCE

No matter where we live, we are all linked to other parts of the planet. In our increasingly global society, places, events, issues and people are connected in a complex and delicately balanced web of relationships. An understanding of interdependence allows students to perceive the systemic nature of the world we live in.

IMAGES AND PERCEPTIONS

Images refer to *what* we see – the ideas about other people and places that are conveyed through photographs, television, films, and printed and spoken words. Perceptions refer to *how* we interpret those images. All too often, young people's perceptions of persons who are 'different' – in terms of country of origin, race, gender, age, or physical ability – are based on stereotypes and prejudice. Learning about images and perceptions helps young people to become more aware of and sensitive to the effects of bias.

SOCIAL JUSTICE

Social justice refers to the widely-held notions of fairness and human rights that can either be denied or promoted, on individual, local, national, and global levels. It is only in the presence of justice that individuals can develop to their full potential, and that the conditions for lasting peace can exist. An understanding of these issues will enable young people to work for greater justice in their own countries and abroad.

CONFLICT AND CONFLICT RESOLUTION

Conflict resolution is the exploration of the ways in which conflict and controversy may be handled. For many young people, conflict is synonymous with violence. But violence, is, in fact, only one of many possible responses to conflict. The skills of non-violent conflict resolution can be learned and applied constructively to disputes on a personal, intergroup, community, national or global scale.

CHANGE AND THE FUTURE

The world is changing as a result of actions that have been taken in the past. And it will continue to change in the future as a result of actions taken today. But this does not mean that the future is predetermined. Many different futures are possible. Young people can learn to examine the processes which bring about change and use them consciously to create a better future.

The learning process

Education for Development involves more than organising knowledge around a set of global concepts. It is also a methodology, with learning processes that are distinct from those often used in the traditional subject areas of the curriculum.

THE CYCLE OF LEARNING

The process of Education for Development can be thought of as a three-step cycle, consisting of an **exploration** phase, followed by a **responding** phase, and leading ultimately to an **action** phase (UNICEF, 1991). Each phase of this cycle is of equal importance to the learning process.

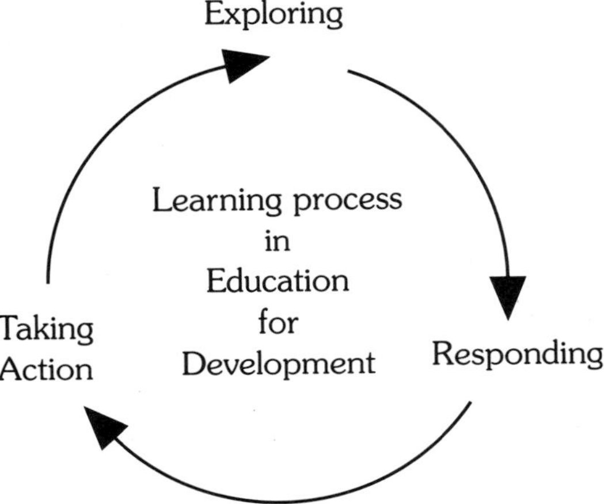

The cycle of learning

The exploration phase is primarily a cognitive one. Students collect, analyse, and synthesise information on a particular topic or issue. They develop the understanding and awareness that will form the basis for the responding phase.

During this second step, students develop a personal response to the material studied. They become familiar with a range of perspectives on an issue, and form their own perspective or point of view. They become aware of the human dimension of the topic. They develop empathy, as well as a sense of involvement and commitment.

The action phase then follows naturally. Learners explore practical actions that might address the issue in question. It is crucial that real opportunities for involvement are provided. This is not only a logical outcome of the learning process, but a significant means of reinforcing new knowledge, skills, and attitudes.

The activities in this manual cover each of the three phases of the learning cycle; the use of action projects in the third phase of the cycle is discussed in special detail in the final chapter of this manual.

LEARNING STRATEGIES

In all parts of the three-step learning cycle of Education for Development, interdisciplinary learning, cooperative learning, and participatory and experiential methods are used.

Interdisciplinary learning

Learning approaches that integrate a number of curriculum areas (English, mathematics, science, humanities, the arts) are highly effective at helping students grasp complex concepts and issues such as those described above (Jacobs, 1989). Interdisciplinary methods take a problem-centred approach that helps students see the contribution of the various subjects in addressing real global concerns. This is of special value at a time in which many students fail to see the relevance of the curriculum to the world outside the classroom.

Cooperatively-structured learning

Cooperatively-structured learning promotes the attitudes needed for global citizenship. The consistent use of cooperative learning groups helps to break down barriers of prejudice, and to increase liking among children who differ in race, ethnicity, gender, and physical ability (Johnson and Johnson, 1983). And complex concepts (such as those basic to Education for Development) are more fully understood when cooperative, rather than competitive or individualistic learning methods are used (Johnson and Johnson, 1975).

Interactive, participatory, and experiential methods

> **. . . Interactive and participatory communication offers the only means for any real possibility of accomplishing behavioural change.**
>
> *The Future Role of UNICEF External Relations*, 1990

These methods include group discussion, debates, role plays, and simulations. They are effective in bringing abstract concepts alive, and making apparently far-away issues seem less remote and more personal. They encourage the sharing of perspectives that brings about a holistic understanding of issues, and the appreciation of diversity.

TYPICAL EDUCATION FOR DEVELOPMENT STRATEGIES

There are a number of types of strategies that are frequently used in Education for Development work. Some of these are described below.

Small group work

Small groups encourage participation by all students, the exchange of perspectives, and cooperative teamwork. When beginning small group work, assigning clear roles may be helpful. For a group of four, suggested roles might be:

Resource person – responsible for seeing that everyone in the group has the materials needed to carry out the group task.

Recorder – writes down any notes, discussion, or statements of position that result from the group's work.

Facilitator – makes sure that everyone in the group gets a turn to speak, keeps the group focused on the task or questions, and keeps track of time.

Spokesperson – responsible for reporting back to the class.

Regardless of role, each person in the group contributes to the discussion. With groups smaller than four, two of the roles can be combined. The teacher should ensure that over time, each student has the chance to try out different roles.

The jigsaw puzzle format is another type of small group work that builds cooperation. In groups of four, each student is assigned a number from one to four. All the number ones in the class then meet together to research and become experts on a given aspect of the topic being studied; all the number twos meet separately to research a different aspect, and so on. When their research is complete, they return to their original groups, and are responsible for teaching the rest of the group about their area of expertise.

Discussion techniques

Group discussion requires students to clarify and articulate their points of view, as well as to listen to other perspectives. Helpful strategies for large groups include:

Magic microphone The group sits in a circle. An old microphone from a tape recorder (or a similarly-shaped object) is passed around the circle. Only the person holding the microphone is allowed to speak; the others are to listen to and look at the speaker. When the speaker is finished, the microphone is passed to the next person in the circle. This is effective with younger students, or groups that have difficulty in listening.

Concentric circles The class divides into two equal groups. The first group stands in a circle facing out. The second group stands in a circle facing in, so that everyone is facing a partner. The class is asked a question, which the students discuss in pairs. After a few minutes, the outer circle rotates to the left, so that each student is facing someone new. The process is then repeated, with either the same question or a new one.

PROMOTING A POSITIVE CLASSROOM CLIMATE: GUIDELINES FOR GROUP DISCUSSIONS

- Only one person at a time talks, and the others look at and listen to the speaker.
- Refrain from making judgmental comments to the speaker, and from any form of ridicule.
- Talk from your own perspective and experience, rather than trying to generalise about others'.
- Remember that there may be more than one 'right' answer.
- Agree to maintain confidentiality when talking about sensitive issues.
- Everyone has the right to be silent and not take part in discussion on a particular issue, if they so wish.

Continuum A line is made across the classroom floor with chalk or tape. One end of the line represents strong agreement with a position, the other end represents strong disagreement, and gradations of opinion are represented by points in between. A statement on a controversial issue is read aloud. Students are asked to stand at a point on the line that represents their position. The teacher then breaks the line into two segments with equal numbers of students. The two halves of the line are matched up with each other so that students at the extreme ends are facing someone with a more moderate position. The students are asked to share their points of view with each other. They may then choose to regroup along the line.

Brainstorming

Brainstorming is the first step in problem-solving. It stimulates creative thinking and generates a number of alternatives. When brainstorming, students are asked to think of as many possible ideas or solutions as they can. It is essential that *all* thoughts are recorded, and that no judgements are made at this stage as to how practical they might be.

Once an exhaustive list has been made, students review the options and discard any which seem unworkable, ultimately deciding upon one or two possible best solutions.

Ranking

Ranking is a way of stimulating deeper discussion of an issue, and clarifying priorities.

Ladder ranking Eight to ten statements (or pictures) on a topic are written on cards. In small groups, students work together to place the statements in a vertical column, in order of their importance (see diagram below). The most important statement is placed at the top of the ladder, the second most important statement just below it, and so on.

1
2
3
4
5
6
7
8

Diamond ranking Nine statements are written on cards. The group negotiates a diamond-shaped arrangement with the most important statement at the top. Two statements of equal but lesser importance are placed below the first. On the third level are three statements of moderate importance, followed by two statements of relatively little importance. On the bottom level (the lowest point of the diamond) is the statement which has the least importance for the topic under discussion.

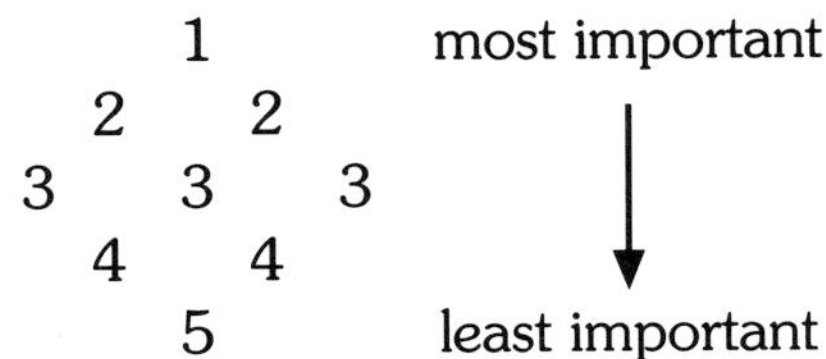

Role play

Role play exercises increase students' ability to take other perspectives, and develop problem-solving or conflict resolution skills. Individual scenes may be only a few minutes long. Teachers can use the following guidelines in organising a role play session:

Set the scene Describe the setting and characters clearly, but in a way that still allows for individual interpretation.

Casting In general, it is best to allow students to volunteer for the roles they wish to play.

Preparation Each actor should have a minute or two to think about the part. Avoid over-preparing; emphasise the informal nature of the role play.

During the role play Make a note of any actions that cause a change in the course of the scene, and why a solution was reached or not reached. Students who are observing should watch for similar points. Instruct students not to make comments which would distract the actors.

Coming to an end Stop the action when a solution has been reached, if the action seems to be slowing down, or if the actors begin to have difficulty staying in their roles. Give the actors a chance to relax, move around, or break the mood in some way.

Discussion Allow the actors to express their feelings. Then encourage them to evaluate what took place: what feelings arose during the scene, the effect that various actions had, their level of satisfaction with the ending. Observers may also share their perceptions, or suggest other ways the situation could have been handled.

More advanced role play techniques include:

Freeze Call out 'Freeze!' during a moment of intense involvement in the role play. Then ask the actors to describe their emotions at that moment.

Role reversal Halt the action without warning in the middle of the role play. Ask the two actors to reverse roles, and continue the role play from that point.

Alter-ego Have an observer stand behind each of the actors. Halfway through the role play, halt the action. Ask the two observers to state what they think their respective actors are feeling and thinking, and why. This may help the actors clarify their own positions and consider alternatives.

Simulations

Simulations can be thought of as extended role plays involving the whole class simultaneously. They deal with complex issues affecting various people or groups, which are played by individuals or small groups in the class. Simulations require students to be familiar with the background issues. This information is usually supplied on role cards. In some simulations, new elements are interjected during the course of the action, for example, a dramatic environmental change. Students must then adapt their responses accordingly.

A thorough debriefing must follow any simulation. Students should discuss their feelings, why they chose to take the actions that they did, any injustices they perceived, and how acceptable they found any resolution that was achieved. They must be helped to draw parallels between what they have experienced and actual situations in the world. Otherwise, they may view the experience as simply a game.

After a simulation, it may be desirable to change the pace with an activity that will re-unite the group, and help them to leave their roles behind.

Decision-making strategies

These techniques build skills which are useful for future democratic participation.

Direct voting Direct voting is useful when making decisions of major importance on which the input of each student is desired. Each student votes on the choices, either by a simple show of hands or by secret ballot.

With younger students, it is helpful if voting is made concrete and visual. The different options are written along one side of a large grid. Students write their names on cards and paste them onto the grid next to their choice. The result is the majority decision shown in graph-like form.

Priority voting This works well when the students must reduce their choices from among a large number of possibilities. Students are allowed three votes each. They may cast one vote for each of three different possibilities, cast all three votes for one, or split their votes between two. The number of votes cast for each choice is then totalled to determine which are the top three priorities in the group.

Representative democracy The class elects a small number of persons who are given the responsibility to make certain decisions without consulting the class as a whole. This is a useful strategy when, for example, the class is running a complex project which requires a large number of decisions to be made frequently, as it greatly speeds the decision-making process.

Consensus Consensus decision-making is used when it is important that everyone's ideas are considered. It develops high levels of communication and negotiation, and promotes a sense of unity in the class. It is possible to arrive at consensus through discussion with the whole group. Alternatively, students may work in pairs to come to an agreement that is acceptable to both. Then two pairs can join to form a group of four, share their decisions, and come up with a new position that all four are satisfied with. The groups of four can then join to form groups of eight, repeat the process, and so on.

Reporting and presentations

There are a number of ways for small groups to report on their work to the whole class.

Plenary A spokesperson from each small group describes its results to the class, and takes questions.

Paired sharing Each small group (or pair) joins with another group, and shares the results of its work. The combined group may attempt to arrive at a consensus which takes into account the viewpoints of both groups.

Circus A spokesperson from each small group is positioned somewhere in the room with the group's product – perhaps a group drawing, a brainstormed list or a flowchart. The rest of the class moves freely around the room, looking at the other groups' work and asking questions.

Using this book

Education for Development is an approach to learning, not a new subject to be squeezed into an already overcrowded curriculum. It is an approach that embraces many previously existing educational initiatives, such as peace, development, human rights and environmental education.

The concepts and learning strategies of Education for Development can be incorporated into more traditional subject matter. This is perhaps easiest to do in the humanities. For example, the curriculum for a certain age level may call for teaching about the geography, history and exports of Latin America. Teachers might use this as an opportunity to introduce issues of conflict and conflict resolution in the region, Latin America's interdependence with other parts of the world, or common media images of Latin American peoples.

But Education for Development can be infused into other subjects areas as well. Work on interdependence that explores relationships in the ecosystem can be used in a biology lesson. Examining the way visual images are cropped to create differing impressions can be done in the context of an art period. A mathematics class can become a lesson in social justice when statistics on the availability of health care in different countries are used. Role playing different solutions to a conflict depicted in literature can be done in an English class. Exploring global issues through a variety of disciplines can give students a fuller understanding of their significance.

Throughout this manual, learners are referred to as students. But this is not meant to suggest that the activities are only suitable for school use. Many of the learning strategies are effective in youth groups as well.

Similarly, the use of the word 'teacher' is not intended to exclude youth group leaders, who may also be in a position to introduce young people to Education for Development.

THE ACTIVITIES

The next five chapters contain activities organised around the five global concepts. Each activity is laid out under the following headings:

Objectives

This describes the knowledge, skills, and/or attitudes which students are expected to develop during the course of the activity.

Age level

Activities are designed for three age levels:

- Level I: 7–11 years;
- Level II: 12–15 years;
- Level III: 16–18 years.

However, these age levels are suggested as *guidelines* only. Older students who have little familiarity with a particular concept may benefit from beginning with activities one or even two levels below their chronological age. Younger students who show a strong grasp of the particular concept may be able to progress to activities from the older age levels. The judgement of the teacher or youth group leader should be the ultimate guide, and adaptations can be made in order to suit the needs of each group.

Materials

This section lists all supplies necessary for the activity. Some activities include worksheets for use by students. These may be freely photocopied.

Procedure

In this section, the actual process of the activity is described as a series of steps. Most activities can be done in a single class period (approximately 45 minutes). When an activity involves many steps that would be best done over several consecutive days, this is noted in the text. In the case of the simulations, a double period is generally necessary.

Variations

This is a description of possible ways to adapt the activity to the age level, abilities, or interests of the group.

Follow-up

Ideally, the activities in the manual should be used not as isolated experiences but as a way of stimulating further study and research, or as an opportunity for taking meaningful action in the students's own environment. This section suggests options for extending students' learning beyond the activity.

In the curriculum

This indicates the types of academic skills which are developed during the course of the activity. Many of these skills are applicable to other subject areas as well. This section also suggests subject areas in which it would be appropriate to incorporate the activity.

Education for Development: A Teacher's Resource for Global Learning is not intended to be a comprehensive or prescriptive curriculum. It is a resource book, and need not be read from beginning to end in order to be of use. Some teachers may wish to concentrate on activities from only one chapter, building them into a clearly defined unit of study. Others may pick and choose activities from various chapters which are relevant to their ongoing classroom work in different subject areas. Teachers should feel free to combine activities in new ways, and to adapt them to changing circumstances and different cultural contexts.

Why teach about interdependence?

At one time, students were taught to see the world as a collection of nation states whose concerns only occasionally touched upon or collided with concerns of other nation states. But for today's young people, an understanding of interdependence is essential.

Interdependence involves seeing the world as a system, understanding the web of relationships in that system, appreciating the delicate balance between the parts of the web and realising that changes in any one part of the system will have effects on the whole.

For example, environmental pollution spreads without regard to national borders, affecting food chains in neighbouring countries, and thus the health and livelihoods of their citizens. A 'local' conflict in an oil-producing country can affect oil supplies around the world, and initiate changes in energy policies of countries thousands of miles away. All parts of the world are linked in ways which are sometimes obvious, sometimes subtle.

Not only places, but also issues are interrelated. For example, poverty may be due to a number of factors: lack of education, poor medical care, environmental degradation and discrimination, to name but a few possibilities. Attempting to eradicate poverty by providing only education and job training may yield at best partial results. Lasting solutions come from understanding the interdependence of all the contributing factors.

Interdependence is not a new phenomenon, unique to the latter half of the twentieth century. Whenever people have come into contact with each other – through exploration, colonisation, migration or trade – links have been created. Ideas and values have been exchanged, cultural elements have been borrowed, products and technology incorporated into ways of life.

But interdependence has become a critical issue at this point in history because:

- dramatic changes in transportation and communication technologies have occurred;
- this has caused increased movement of peoples around the world, increased cultural diversity, and a complex system of global trade;
- there has been a proliferation of multinational corporations and international organisations, which have forged and reinforced global connections.

Interdependence is not only a characteristic of global systems. It can also be seen at national and local levels. Indeed, younger students can be introduced to this concept by examining interdependence in family roles, within a school, between workers in a business, in the community and between regions of a nation.

But interdependence is more than an area of content in Education for Development. It is also basic to the learning process. Activities in this chapter, and throughout the manual, are structured cooperatively. They require students to function in an interdependent way in order to complete specific tasks.

Some key concepts

SYSTEMS

Systems refer to the arrangement of parts into a unified whole. The loss or malfunctioning of one part has an effect on all of the others, and may even cause the system to cease functioning altogether. There are simple mechanical systems, such as a bicycle, and more intricate human systems, such as a small business. There are systems which encompass human and non-human elements, such as a regional ecosystem. And there are complex global systems, such as global trade networks, which are made of many smaller systems.

SYMMETRICAL INTERDEPENDENCE

When all parts of a system are functioning cooperatively, that is, working together for a common mutually beneficial objective, the system is in a state of symmetrical interdependence.

ASYMMETRICAL INTERDEPENDENCE

This term refers to the links in the world's systems that are *not* mutually beneficial. Such imbalances can often be seen in the relationships between industrialised and developing countries. For example, developing countries are sometimes encouraged to grow cash crops for export. When market prices for those crops fall, industrialised countries benefit from the availability of cheap products, while the nations which produce them find they have less income, less land available to grow food, and less money available for purchasing the food they require. Such a relationship puts the developing countries at a severe disadvantage.

Teaching about interdependence: Aims and objectives

Knowledge	*Skills*	*Attitudes*
• Knowledge of the systems which affect the learners' daily lives. • Understanding the world as a system in which all elements – people, events, trends, places – are interconnected. • Awareness that issues are also inter-related. • Knowing that some world systems operate in ways that favour certain groups or countries, while placing others at a disadvantage. • Understanding the global implications of local decisions and actions.	• Ability to cooperate and work effectively in groups to achieve a common goal. • Being able to evaluate the effectiveness of cooperative versus competitive approaches to different types of tasks. • Capacity to analyse events or trends to see both their many layers of causes, as well as their many potential impacts.	• Respect for the needs and contributions of all members of a system, whether it is in the classroom, the local or global community, or the ecosystem. • Positive valuing of the ways in which individuals can support and benefit the whole, and vice versa. • Willingness to cooperate with others in order to solve problems for the benefit of all.

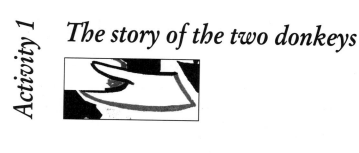

Activity 1

The story of the two donkeys

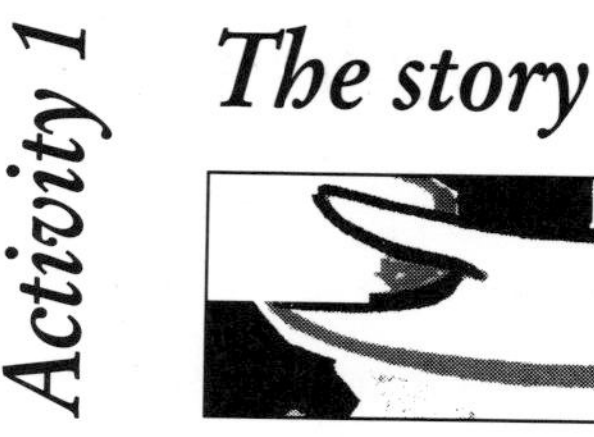

Age level 1: 7–11 years

OBJECTIVES

To help students examine cooperation, a basic skill for living in an interdependent world, as an alternative to competition.

MATERIALS

A copy of the **Two donkeys** cartoon (on page 31) for each pair of students; the six sections of the cartoon should be cut out before starting the activity. A large sheet of paper and a glue stick for each pair of students.

PROCEDURE

Step 1

The students form pairs; each pair is given the six sections of the **Two donkeys** cartoon. They are to place the pieces in order so that they tell a complete story. When this is done, they glue them down on a sheet of paper.

Step 2

Each pair then joins with another pair and tells the story of the two donkeys as they see it.

Step 3

As a class, the students discuss the following questions:

- What was the donkeys' problem at the beginning of the story?
- What did they try to do about their problem at first? Did this work? Why not?
- What did they do to solve their problem?
- Did both donkeys get what they wanted?
- Have you ever solved a problem with another person by cooperating? Tell the class about it.

VARIATIONS

1 Teachers give students only the first four pieces of the cartoon and have them devise their own ending.

2 Students write a story to describe what is happening in the cartoon, or act it out.

FOLLOW-UP

1 Students create their own cartoons about conflicts, real or hypothetical, which can be solved through cooperation. These can be compiled into a class book.

2 As actual conflicts arise in the classroom, school or community, students brainstorm cooperative solutions, in which both parties have their needs met.

IN THE CURRICULUM

The activity involves analysing images, sequencing, and problem-solving. It can be used as part of an English or drama lesson.

Two donkeys

Reproduced by permission of Quaker Peace and Service

Activity 2 Systems that work

Age level 1:
7–11 years

OBJECTIVES

To introduce the concept of interdependence by examining the parts which must work together to make simple mechanical systems function.

MATERIALS

Drawing paper and pencils for each pair of students.

PROCEDURE

Step 1

Working in pairs, students think of a familiar machine which is made up of several parts. Some examples might be: a bicycle, a car, an electric fan, a cart, a telephone, a lamp, a tin opener, a clock or a computer.

Step 2

After deciding on a machine, the pairs draw it on their paper, leaving out of the picture one of the machine's parts.

Working cooperatively to draw a simple machine

Step 3

When each pair has finished its drawing, it joins with another pair. They exchange pictures, and guess what the machine is, what part is missing, and what the effect of the missing part would be on the whole machine.

Step 4

The group then discusses the following questions:

- What examples of machines did you think of?
- How did having one part missing affect your machine? Could it still function in some way? Or was it totally unable to function?

VARIATIONS

1 In groups of four to six, students decide on a machine that they can mime for the rest of the class, who then try to guess what they are. Each student should have a specific part to play in the working of the machine.

They can also act out a situation in which one part of the machine stops functioning, and all the other parts are affected.

2 As a group, the students brainstorm as many parts of the human body as they can think of. They then describe what would happen to the body if one of these parts was missing.

FOLLOW-UP

The class brainstorms a list of situations where human groups or individuals are dependent upon one another, and tries to highlight the specific functions of each group or individual that enable the situation to work smoothly. Are the students themselves involved in any of these situations as part of a group, or as an individual?

IN THE CURRICULUM

The activity requires analysing images, anticipating consequences and cooperative decision-making. It can be integrated into a science, art, or drama lesson.

Activity 3 Who helps?

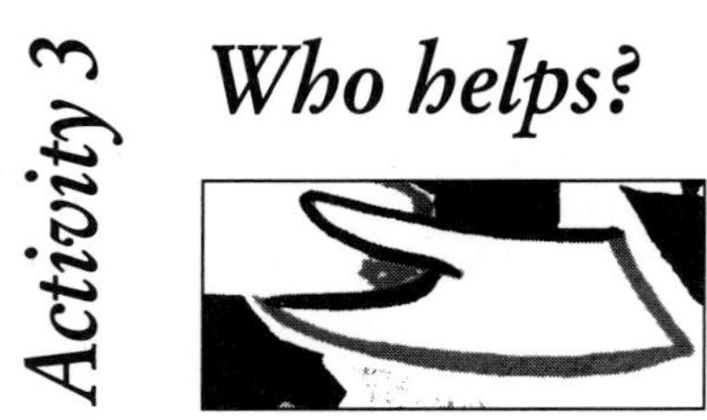

Age level 1:
7–11 years

OBJECTIVES

To encourage students to see the interdependencies which exist between groups or individuals in a situation in which they are involved.

MATERIALS

Index cards, A4 paper and pencils, large sugar paper (optional).

PROCEDURE

Step 1

The students brainstorm all the different roles which exist in their school. These are grouped into types of workers: head teacher or principal, teachers, cleaners, kitchen workers, playground supervisors, special subject teachers, nurse, etc. (Roles will vary with each school.) Students should include themselves as a group. The name of each role is written on a card.

Step 2

The students form pairs. Each pair is given a card with one of the roles named in the brainstorm. (More than one pair may receive the same role, depending on the numbers of students in the group.)

Pairs then work together to list all the ways that the person or persons whose role is named on their card helps other members of the school community. For example:

The playground supervisors:

- help the teachers by watching the students during lunch;
- help the students by planning games for them;
- help the cleaners by keeping the playground free from litter; etc.

The nurse:

- helps the students by looking after them if they get hurt;
- helps the teachers by calling a sick child's parents; etc.

The students:

- help the kitchen staff by bringing their plates back to the kitchen;
- help the teacher by completing work that can be put on display;
- help the cleaners by picking papers up off the floor; etc.

Step 3

Still working in pairs, the students devise one or more brief role plays based on their list, one playing the role of the helper, and the other taking the role of the person being helped.

Pairs then take turns performing their role plays for the rest of the group, without revealing the identity of the helper. The rest of the class tries to guess who the helper is.

Step 4

Following the role plays, the group discusses the following questions:

- What did you learn about relationships between different groups in the school?
- Are there certain groups or people who give help more often than they receive help? Who are they and why?
- What roles do students play in the school community?
- Is there anything about the roles of students that you would like to be different? What is it, and why?

VARIATIONS

1 Students follow the same procedure to explore interdependence in another group or situation, such as their family, their youth group, a local business or in their village, town or city.

2 Students make a mural to depict the relationships between members of these interdependent groups.

FOLLOW-UP

Students interview various workers in the school to learn more about how they depend on others, and how others depend on them.

IN THE CURRICULUM

The skills of cooperation, seeing relationships, and anticipating consequences are involved. The activity can be used in a humanities class on roles in the community.

Activity 4

The web of life

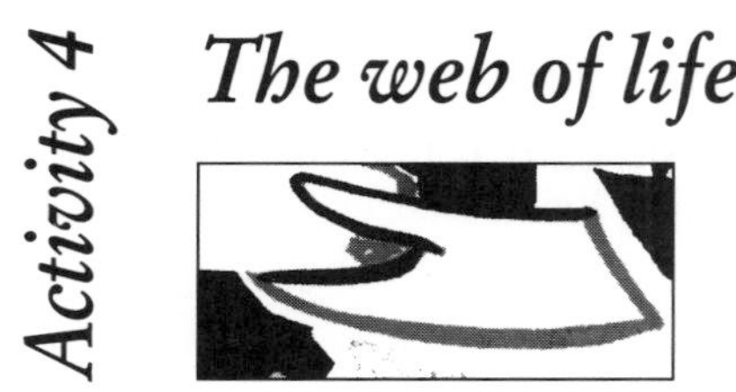

OBJECTIVES

To demonstrate interdependence in the ecosystem, and to show how changes in one part of the ecosystem affect other forms of life.

Age level 1: 7–11 years

MATERIALS

Several balls of wool, scissors; one of the ***Web of Life*** cards (pages 39 and 40) for each student. (Twenty-four cards are included; in a group of more than twenty-four students, extra cards for green plants and insects may be made.)

PROCEDURE

Step 1

The teacher explains to the group that it is going to be learning about food chains by taking on the role of one part of the chain. She then distributes one ***Web of Life*** card to each student. They read these over, and ask questions if they don't understand their card. Students who have a blank space on their card can write in the name of one local mammal, bird, plant, or insect which fits the description.

Step 2

The group clears a space in the centre of the room. A student is chosen to read his card aloud. The others listen and decide if they are linked to the first student – either because they consume the living thing described or are consumed by it. They demonstrate this link by giving one end of a length of wool (about one or two metres long) to the first student, and tying the other end around their waists.

Step 3

A second student is asked to read her card aloud, and the same procedure as in Step 2 is followed. The activity continues until all the students in the group have joined in the web; some students will have more than one piece of wool attached to them.

Step 4

The teacher then explains a scenario in which there is an environmental problem. For example:

> **'A nearby factory is polluting the air. Because of this pollution, acid rain is falling on the land, causing the soil to be too acidic, and killing off green plants.'**

All students who are standing in the web and are affected by this situation (in this case, the green plants) must then sit down, to indicate that they can no longer survive. Then all the students who are directly dependent on the green plants, as indicated by the connecting piece of wool, must also sit down, demonstrating the secondary effect of acid rain. Each student who is connected to someone who is sitting down must also sit, until the chain of effects is completed.

Other environmental scenarios which might be used include:

> **'A farmer who is concerned about insects eating her crops uses a strong insecticide. The insecticide kills many of the other insects living in the area.'**

> **'A logging company decides to clear an area of all of its trees so that it can sell the wood and make a lot of money.'**

Step 5

As a group, the students discuss the following questions:

- What did the completed web tell you about the ecosystem?
- Were there any other living things that should be included in the web?
- What parts of the web were affected by environmental problems? Were there any parts that were not affected?
- What other kinds of environmental problems do you know about? What parts of the ecosystem do they affect?
- Is there anything you can do about these environmental problems?

VARIATIONS

1 A similar activity could be carried out using another ecosystem as a model, for example a lake or river. Students determine what the different members of the ecosystem might be, and make their own set of cards.

2 Students may map the web of relationships in the ecosystem on paper, drawing arrows between members that are dependent on each other.

FOLLOW-UP

1 Students visit an outdoor education centre or natural area to observe food chains first-hand.

2 They look into setting up and maintaining a wildlife area or garden near their school.

3 They investigate situations in which environmental damage is being done in their own community, and consider possible actions to take in response – letter-writing, petitioning, boycotting certain products, etc.

IN THE CURRICULUM

The activity involves seeing relationships and understanding consequences. It could be integrated into a science class.

Web of life cards (1)

For a class of 24, make one copy of this sheet

worksheet

I am a human being. I eat meat that comes from large mammals and birds. I also eat grains, fruit, and vegetables.	I am a bird, a __________. I eat grains, seeds, and insects. Sometimes human beings use me for food.
I am a bird, a __________. I eat grains, seeds, and insects. Sometimes small mammals use me for food.	I am a bird, a __________. I eat grains, seeds, and insects. Sometimes small mammals use me for food.
I am a large mammal, a __________. I eat grasses and grains. Sometimes human beings use me for food.	I am a large mammal, a __________. I eat smaller mammals, and some fruits and grains. When I die, bacteria and moulds help my body decay and turn into soil.
I am a small mammal, a __________. I eat grains, seeds, fruits, insects and birds. Larger mammals eat me, and bacteria and moulds help my body decay and turn into soil when I die.	I am a small mammal, a __________. I eat grains, seeds, fruits, insects and birds. Larger mammals eat me, and bacteria and moulds help my body decay and turn into soil when I die.

worksheet

Web of life cards (2)

For a class of 24, make two copies of this sheet

✂

I am a tree, a __________. I need sun, healthy soil, and clean water to grow. Insects, birds, and small mammals make their home in me, and eat my seeds and fruits.	I am an earthworm. I eat decaying plants, and help turn them into healthy soil.
I am a bacteria. I feed on decaying plants and animals, and help turn them into healthy soil.	I am a mould. I feed on decaying plants and animals, and help turn them into healthy soil.
I am an insect, a __________. I eat plants. Birds and some small mammals use me for food.	I am an insect, a __________. I eat plants. Birds and some small mammals use me for food.
I am a green plant, a __________. I need sun, healthy soil, and clean water to grow. Birds, small mammals, and some large mammals eat me (or my grains, seeds, or fruits).	I am a green plant, a __________. I need sun, healthy soil, and clean water to grow. Birds, small mammals, and some large mammals eat me (or my grains, seeds, or fruits).

Activity 5 Where does it come from?

Age level 1:
7–11 years

OBJECTIVES

To heighten students' awareness of the links between their community and the wider world.

MATERIALS

A large world map, push pins, string or wool.

PROCEDURE

Step 1

Ask students to keep a diary of the foods they eat at home during the course of a day, and note down the country each one comes from. Explain that most packaged foods list the country of origin on the label and that they must read carefully to find the country name.

Step 2

In class, the students then locate on the map the countries which produce foods they commonly eat. They place pins on those countries, or use string to show a link between the exporting country and the students' country.

Step 3

The group then discusses the following questions:

- Is most of your food produced in your own country, or does most of it come from other countries?
- Were you surprised to learn where your food comes from?
- Are there any countries or parts of the world from which you do not receive food? Why might this be?
- Pick one of the countries on the map that exports food to your country. Can you imagine anything that might happen in that country that would make it difficult for you to continue buying that food at home?

Where does it come from?

VARIATION

The activity can be carried out by asking the students to examine and plot on separate maps the following:

- sources of their clothing;
- sources of their toys;
- origins of films, music, videos, or other forms of entertainment and media.

They can then be asked to compare the different maps they have created. What sorts of patterns emerge?

FOLLOW-UP

1 Students research an item which has more than one country of origin, such as an automobile or a piece of clothing. What countries provided raw materials, parts, or labour to produce this item? Why might this be?

2 Students visit local supermarkets or greengrocers to enquire about why they purchase foods from particular countries.

IN THE CURRICULUM

The activity involves reading comprehension and map skills, and would be appropriate for a history or geography class. In mathematics, graphs could be prepared to show the differing amounts of exports from various parts of the world.

Activity 6

Global news/Local news

OBJECTIVES

To examine the ways that far-away places, events, and trends affect one's local community.

MATERIALS

Current local newspapers; a photocopy of a world map, mounted on a large sheet of sugar paper, and a glue stick, for each group of four.

PROCEDURE

Step 1

Students form groups of four. They look through several local newspapers, and cut out any articles which indicate that another part of the world is having an impact on the local community, or that their country is affecting another. Some examples might include articles about:

- economic or political problems which are causing migration between their country and another;
- pollution in another country which is affecting their country, or vice versa;
- an exchange of music, food, or fashion between their country and another;
- a reduction in tourism to or from their country due to a conflict in the host country;
- a disruption in the import/export of food or raw materials between their country and another because of trade issues, drought, or political conflicts;
- military action between their country and another;
- trade competition between their country and another country.

Step 2

Students paste these articles onto the large sugar paper, surrounding the map of the world. They draw lines from each individual article to the country it refers to.

Step 3

Students classify the articles under headings they devise, to indicate the types of links between their community and other parts of the world. The headings may include trade, military contact, cultural exchange, migration, tourism, the environment, etc.

Step 4

When the groups have completed these steps, they discuss the following questions:

- What parts of the world did you find the most links to?
- Were there any parts of the world to which you found few or no links? Why might this be so?
- What types of links were most common? Why?

VARIATION

Students compare the amount of column space given to news which has a purely local focus, news which deals with international events, and news which has both local and global impacts. Is it possible to make these types of firm distinctions when reading the newspaper?

FOLLOW-UP

Students could visit the office of a local newspaper to interview editors about how decisions are made as to how much local news and how much international news will be covered. They may also want to suggest types of global issues they feel should be addressed in the newspaper.

IN THE CURRICULUM

The activity involves reading comprehension, mapping and classification. It can be used in an English or geography class.

Activity 7

The hobusing project

OBJECTIVES

To explore interdependence in a local community by considering the impact of a specific change on its various members.

MATERIALS

A copy of the **Housing project description** (see page 47) for each pair of students; a set of **Housing project role cards** (see pages 48 and 49).

Age level 2: 12–15 years

PROCEDURE

Step 1

Students form pairs; each pair is given a copy of the **Housing project description** and *one* of the **Housing project role cards**. They read these over together.

Step 2

The pairs then take approximately ten minutes to list all the benefits and problems they can think of relating to the proposed new housing project. They must do this from the point of view of a person in their role only. They then decide whether they would favour or oppose this project.

Step 3

The teacher tells the class that they are now taking part in a city council meeting. Each pair in turn presents to the group its position on the proposed new housing project. If they oppose it, they must explain their reasons. If they favour it, they must list what actions, if any, should be taken in and around the neighbourhood to ensure that potential problems are addressed.

Step 4

The students vote on whether or not to carry out the project.

Step 5

They then discuss the following questions:

- Are there any other groups in the community whose opinions should have been consulted?
- How was your opinion on the project affected by the opinions of the other groups?
- Would concerns raised by any one group have an effect on other groups? For example, would inadequate transportation between Riverbank and the rest of New City affect factory owners who might provide jobs for residents? Would inadequate sanitation services cause illnesses, leading to increased pressure on workers at the health clinic? Would lack of recreation facilities lead to an increase in crime?
- Are there some groups whose opinions deserve to be given more weight in this planning decision than others?
- In real planning decisions, do you think the opinions of all groups are given equal weight? Are there groups whose opinions are seldom or never heard?

VARIATIONS

1 Older students can role play a discussion between someone opposed to and someone in favour of the housing project.

2 Students look for newspaper accounts of local development projects being considered – the building of a factory or road, laying a new pipeline, creating a playground, etc. They collect newspaper articles which describe the reactions of various segments of the community.

FOLLOW-UP

The students invite a person who is responsible for making planning decisions in their community to visit the class and talk about the points of view taken into consideration prior to any new development project.

IN THE CURRICULUM

The activity involves understanding different points of view, seeing relationships, anticipating consequences, and decision-making. It could be incorporated into a humanities or drama class.

Housing project description

A housing project is being considered for the Riverbank neighbourhood of New City. Five thousand people live in Riverbank. It is a poor part of the city and few people have jobs. Those who have jobs work in shops and factories in other parts of New City. Few people have cars. There is only one bus line from Riverbank into the centre of New City.

Riverbank has several streets with a few grocers, clothing shops, and chemists. There is one primary school, one health clinic, and one small park.

Most of the houses in Riverbank have three floors. They were once owned by single families. Now they have been turned into flats, with three to five families in each house. The people who live there complain that the houses need repairs, and that there is not enough heat.

The new housing project would replace the old houses in Riverbank with high-rise blocks that are safer and healthier places to live.

When the project is completed, there will be housing for approximately 12,000 people in Riverbank. Unemployed and homeless people in other parts of New City will be able to move there. So will many of the 3,000 people from a nearby country who have recently come to New City to find jobs. They do not speak the local language and have had difficulties finding places to live.

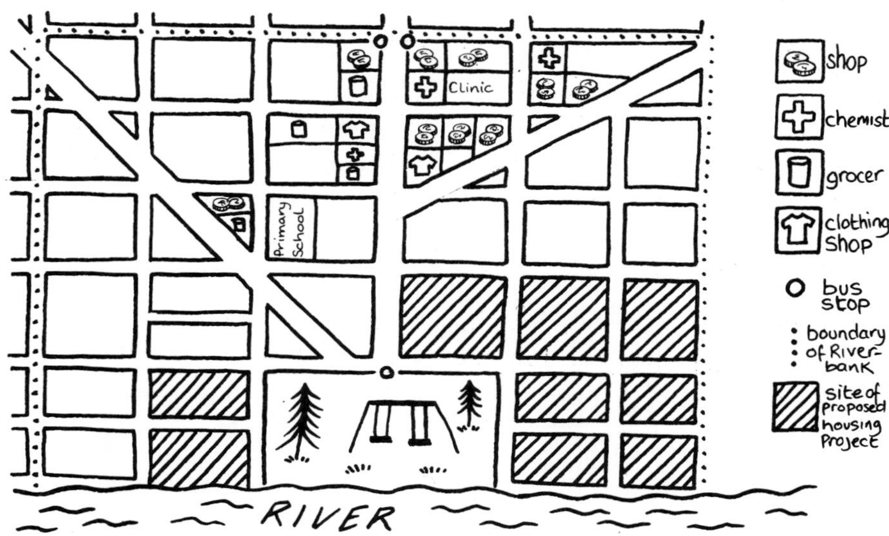

A map of Riverbank

worksheet

worksheet

Housing project role cards (1)

You are teachers in the Riverbank school. Your classes are very crowded, much more so than in schools in the rest of New City. You have read about the plan for the new housing project. Can you think of reasons why it is a good idea? Can you think of any problems it will cause?

You have recently moved to New City from another country. You are learning to speak the language, and are looking for a job and a place to live. You have read about the plan for the new housing project. Can you think of reasons why it is a good idea? Can you think of any problems it will cause?

You are the owners of small shops in Riverbank. You barely make enough money to keep your business going. You are worried that there is more crime in Riverbank. You have read about the plan for the new housing project. Can you think of reasons why it is a good idea? Can you think of any problems it will cause?

You work at removing rubbish in New City. Your department does not have enough workers. People in neighbourhoods like Riverbank complain that rubbish is not removed frequently enough. You have read about the plan for the new housing project. Can you think of reasons why it is a good idea? Can you think of any problems it will cause?

Housing project role cards (2)

You work for the only health clinic in Riverbank. It is difficult for your clinic to take care of all 5,000 people in Riverbank. You have read about the plan for the new housing project. Can you think of reasons why it is a good idea? Can you think of any problems it will cause?

You work for the New City bus company. You are a driver on the only bus line that goes to Riverbank. The bus is always very crowded because people from Riverbank go to other parts of New City to work. You have read about the plan for the new housing project. Can you think of reasons why it is a good idea? Can you think of any problems it will cause?

You are the owners of a large clothing factory in New City. You want to build a bigger factory. You will need more workers, and more people to buy the clothes you make. You have read about the plan for the new housing project. Can you think of reasons why it is a good idea? Can you think of any problems it will cause?

You are young people who live in the Riverbank neighbourhood. You go to the local school. The only place you have to play is in a small park. There is rubbish and broken glass everywhere, and some of the equipment is broken. You have read about the plan for the new housing project. Can you think of reasons why it is a good idea? Can you think of any problems it will cause?

worksheet

Activity 8

Breaking the cycle

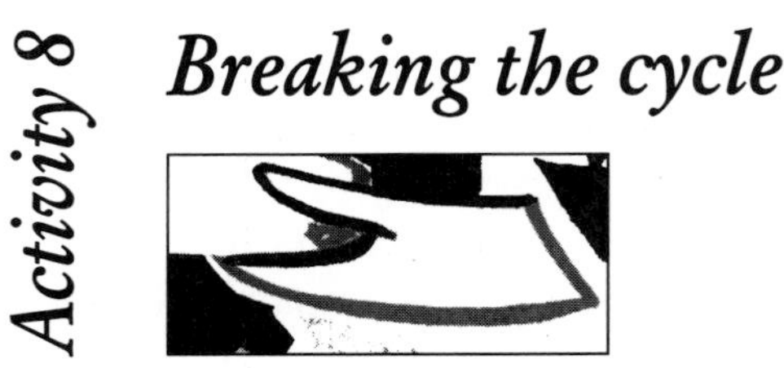

Age level 2: 12–15 years

OBJECTIVES

To explore the interdependence of several different factors in creating poverty; to encourage students to consider ways in which the cycle of poverty could be broken.

MATERIALS

For each group of four, a large sheet of paper, glue, felt-tip pens, and a set of the **Breaking the cycle** cards (on page 52), cut out individually.

PROCEDURE

Step 1

The students form groups of four. Together they read their set of **Breaking the cycle** cards. Then they arrange them on a large sheet of paper in a circle. The card headed 'Poverty' should be at the top of the circle, and all the others should follow it in a clockwise order. The arrangement should show how each condition is created or caused by the one which precedes it.

When the group has agreed on their arrangement, it glues the cards onto the paper, and draws arrows from the 'Poverty' card to the next step in the cycle, and so on until it returns to the 'Poverty' card.

Step 2

In their small groups, the students discuss what steps would have to be taken to break the cycle of poverty. Possible steps might include: creating a programme that provides a basic level of food for all students living in poverty; creating free health care services for the poor; providing more funding for education in low-income areas; setting up adult education and job training programmes.

Step 3

Once students have decided on a way in which they could intervene, they write what this action would be on the large paper next to the step in the poverty cycle to which it corresponds. From that point in the cycle, they write a new sequence of steps, showing how the action taken could affect the poverty cycle.

Step 4

When all groups have completed their work, they exhibit their papers around the room. Together they discuss the following questions:

- What are some of the factors which contribute to poverty? Are there other factors which were not included on these cards?
- Why is it that poverty often continues as a cycle?
- What steps did your group propose to break the cycle?
- Would one intervention be sufficient to break the cycle, or would a number of different types of intervention be necessary?
- Which of the proposals would actually be easiest to carry out?
- What would be required to carry out these proposals?
- Do you know of any similar programmes being carried out in your country or in other countries?

The teacher should ensure that students understand that the cycle of poverty exists not only in developing countries, but in industrialised countries as well.

VARIATION

Students dramatise or write stories about the steps in the cycle, and the effect of breaking the cycle.

FOLLOW-UP

Students collect newspaper articles that show examples of how the cycle of poverty is being broken in countries around the world.

IN THE CURRICULUM

The activity requires young people to use skills such as cooperation, sequencing and anticipating consequences. It would be appropriate for a humanities class.

worksheet

Breaking the cycle cards

POVERTY

An estimated 25 per cent of the world's children live in poverty.

HUNGER

Children who live in poverty often don't get enough food to eat, or don't eat enough nutritious foods.

MALNUTRITION

Children who do not get enough food to eat can, over time, become malnourished, and fail to grow and develop.

HEALTH

Children who are malnourished may become ill more often because their bodies are not strong enough to fight off infections.

SCHOOL

Children who are often ill may find it harder to learn, and may miss a lot of school.

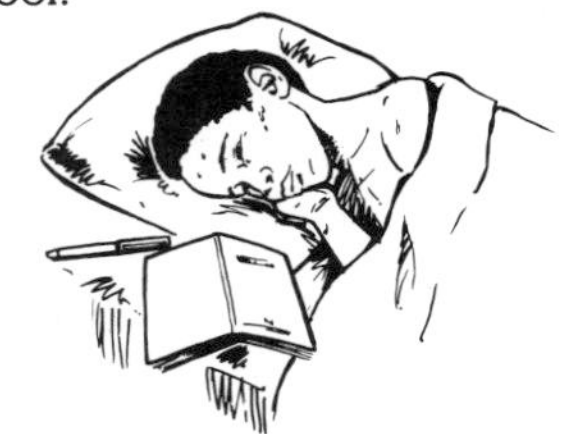

WORK SKILLS

Children who have had difficulties in school, missed a lot of school, or dropped out of school may not learn skills that they will need in jobs – reading, writing, or counting.

UNEMPLOYMENT

When children grow older, they look for work. If they have not learned basic skills in school, they may have trouble finding a job or finding a job that pays them enough.

NOT ENOUGH INCOME

People who have no work, or too little work, cannot earn enough to pay for their basic needs – food, clothing, shelter. Their children are born into a situation of poverty.

Activity 9 The chain game

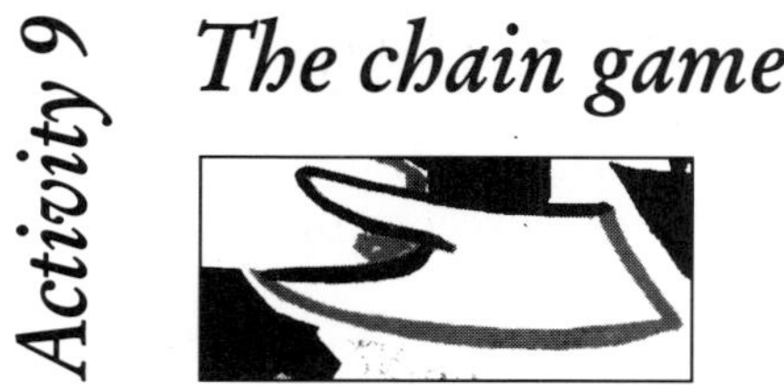

OBJECTIVES

To help students understand interdependence in trade between countries which have different resources; to allow them to experience the injustice that results from unequal distribution of resources.

MATERIALS

Age level 2: 12–15 years

Newspapers, coloured construction paper (or coloured newspaper supplements), scissors, glue, staplers, pencils, rulers, distributed among the groups according to the plan described below. (Staplers are held back by the teacher until the last step in the Procedure, described below.)

PROCEDURE

Step 1

The students are divided into five groups, with approximately five students in each. Every group is given a box containing materials for the simulation as follows:

Group 1 – One sheet of newspaper, one sheet of coloured paper, five pairs of scissors, five glue sticks, five pencils, five rulers.

Group 2 – Four sheets of newspaper, one sheet of coloured paper, three pairs of scissors, three glue sticks, three pencils.

Group 3 – Six sheets of newspaper, two pairs of scissors, two glue sticks, two rulers.

Group 4 – Ten sheets of newspaper, one ruler, one pencil.

Group 5 – Fifteen sheets of newspaper, eight sheets of coloured paper.

The groups are told that they each represent a different country. Their task is to make a product, in this case paper chains of five links each, which can be sold on the world market. They will earn five units of currency for each chain. These are sold to the teacher, who represents the world market for these chains.

Each link in the chain must be made from a strip of newspaper exactly 20 cm long and 3 cm wide. The links are made by overlapping exactly 2 cm on each end and gluing them together. The teacher should make clear to the students that links which do not meet the world market standard – which are too long, short, wide, thin, or irregularly cut – will not be accepted. As the chains are sold, the teacher keeps a record of how much each group earns on the chalkboard.

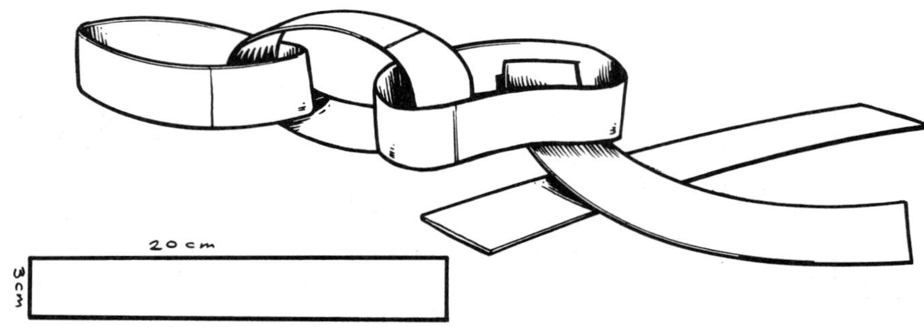

Paper chain dimensions

The teacher should not explicitly point out that the groups are receiving unequal resources. If students argue that it is unfair, the teacher can reply that this is simply the way that materials have been divided up for this game; however, the groups are free to negotiate trading of resources. They may also purchase resources with their earnings, but must notify the teacher, who will subtract the amount spent from their total earnings.

Step 2

Once the instructions have been given, the teacher allows the students to trade and make chains for ten to 15 minutes. After this time, she announces that because there are so many chains of high quality on the world market, the price is going down to three units of currency per chain of five links.

Step 3

After five more minutes at this price, the teacher announces that so many newspaper chains are now on the market that the price has dropped to one unit of currency per chain of five links. However, chains made of coloured paper are increasingly desirable, and can be sold for five units of currency per chain of five links.

Step 4

After five more minutes of play, the teacher announces that a new technology for making chains has been developed which produces a superior product; this involves stapling the links together rather than gluing them. Chains made of stapled links will earn the current world market price *plus* 15 units of currency per chain of five links (i.e., 16 units for a newspaper chain of five stapled links, 20 units for a coloured paper chain of five stapled links).

Five staplers are available, and may be bought from the teacher; a price should be set which would allow only the wealthiest groups to have the possibility of buying them.

Step 5

Once the staplers have been sold, the teacher should allow work to continue for another five to ten minutes. Then the game can be halted, and each group can tally its earnings.

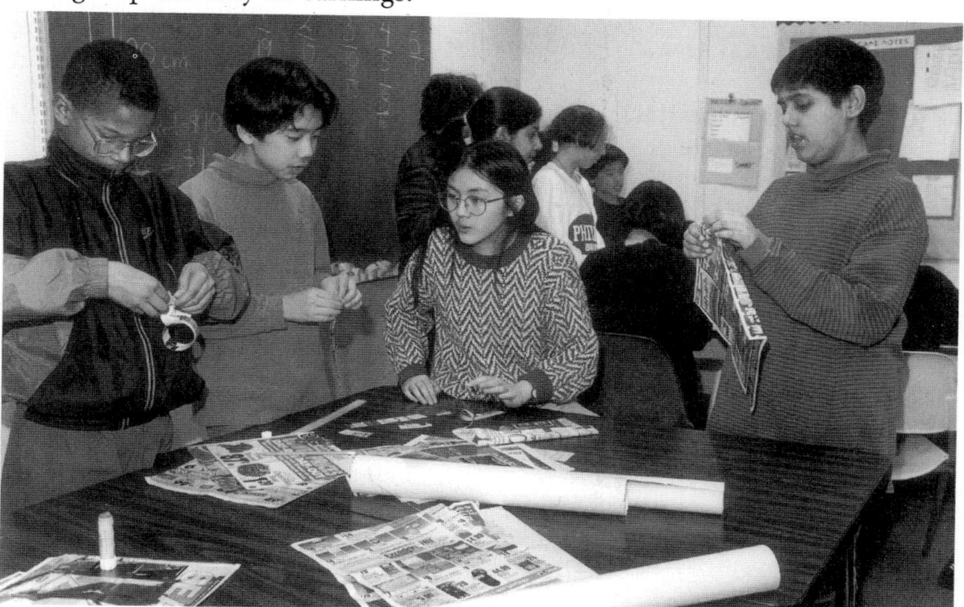

Simulating world trade through The Chain Game

Step 6

The class discusses the following questions. The teacher should attempt to draw parallels with global trade throughout the discussion:

- Which group earned the most money? Which group earned the least? Why?
- What sorts of trades were negotiated? (Exchanging raw materials such as paper, for technology such as rulers and pencils; exchanges of technologies, such as scissors for rulers, etc.)
- What sorts of interdependencies, or divisions of labour, were worked out within the groups?
- Were any cooperative arrangements negotiated between the groups?
- What was the effect on the wealthier groups of the falling world market price for chains? What was the effect on the poorer groups?
- Which groups were able to purchase the new technology, i.e. the stapler?
- Why did the development of a new technology allow the wealthy groups to get wealthier, while the poor groups got poorer?

VARIATION

Distribution of resources, and introduction of new technologies, can be varied in order to more closely simulate world trading conditions.

FOLLOW-UP

1 The students research the origins of products they commonly use at home or school to discover the sources of the raw material and labour; they may find that many products have multiple origins.

2 They can also research inequalities which presently exist in international trade. What countries are involved? What countries benefit from such imbalances?

IN THE CURRICULUM

The activity requires cooperation, decision-making and computation skills. It can be done as part of a humanities, economics, or mathematics class.

Activity 10 Development that works

Level 3 Activities

Age level 3: 16–18 years

OBJECTIVES

To help young people examine various interdependent factors which influence decisions about development projects, and contribute to their success or failure.

MATERIALS

For a group of 32: 32 copies of the **Plan for a hydro-electric plant** sheets (on pages 59 and 60); eight copies of each of the sheets headed **Infrastructure**, **Women**, **Environment**, and **Justice** (on pages 61–64).

PROCEDURE

Step 1

The participants are divided into four groups of eight. In these small groups, they are given copies of the **Plan for a hydro-electric plant** sheets to read. They are told that they are citizen advisors to a national planning commission that is proposing to fund the building of this plant. Projects of this type in this country have failed in the past. Their job is to learn about a specific aspect of the development process, and to decide if they approve of the project, based on their specialist knowledge.

Step 2

After they have had the chance to read the plan, two students from each small group are put in charge of finding out about infrastructure issues with regard to this project; two are in charge of women's issues (these may be either girls or boys); two are in charge of environmental issues; and two are in charge of justice issues.

Step 3

Students then form new groups. All the students who are in charge of infrastructure issues meet together, all those responsible for women's issues meet together, etc. In these new groups, each person is given a copy of the information sheet with the appropriate heading. They read this together, and discuss ways in which their particular issue might be taken into consideration in the planning process.

Step 4

Students then return to their original small groups. Each pair presents to the small group a brief position paper based on the points discussed in their issue groups.

Step 5

After each pair's report, the small group draws up a recommendation to either build or not build the plant, giving reasons for its decision. If it decides to go ahead with the construction, its recommendation should include a list of the main considerations necessary to ensure the success of the project for all the people who will be affected by it.

Step 6

The whole class comes together to discuss its results. The following questions can be raised:

- Are there other factors that should be considered in development planning besides the ones on the sheets?
- Which issues seemed most important in thinking about the construction of the plant? Why? Would this change if the proposed development project was a different one?
- Which issues seemed least important in thinking about the construction of the plant? Why? Would this change if the proposed development project was a different one?
- Were any of these issues related to each other? Which ones? How?
- What were participants' reactions to the process of the activity?

VARIATION

Students can research an actual development project, in their own country or abroad, and decide on what the critical issues are. In small groups, they can then write their own summaries of each issue and use these in the course of the activity.

FOLLOW-UP

Students can interview planners of development projects in their own country to find out more about the issues they take into consideration.

IN THE CURRICULUM

The activity uses skills in reading comprehension, anticipating consequences, decision making, and consensus-building. It could be used in a history or geography class.

Note that three of the four development issues were based on information in the *State of the World's Children Report*, 1989, UNICEF.

Plan for a hydro-electric plant (1)

The village of Prima lies along a river in Terrania, a developing country.

Most of the women in Prima work as farmers. The food they grow is the basis of the villagers' diet. Some of the men in the village work at fishing. The fish caught in the river adds to the diet of the people of Prima. A few fish are also sold in markets in neighbouring towns and villages. This provides a small but much-needed source of income.

Prima has a small primary school. Most of the children in the village start school but not all of them finish, as they are needed to help with farming, fishing, and housework. At this time, about 70 per cent of the boys and 30 per cent of the girls finish primary school. The number of girls finishing school is gradually increasing. Prima has a small health clinic. Treating water-borne diseases is a major part of the clinic's work. Both the school and the clinic have a telephone and electricity.

Homes in Prima are built from local materials. Most lack telephones, electricity, running water and sanitary facilities. People use the river for drinking, washing, and disposal of waste. The primary fuel for cooking is wood, which is collected by the women from nearby forests.

The government of Terrania has decided that the standard of living in Prima could be raised by a project to build a new hydro-electric plant along the riverbank. The construction and running of the plant would provide paying jobs for the men of the village. The plant would also allow every home to have electricity.

Any extra electricity produced could be sold to neighbouring towns and villages and the profits would further benefit the people of Prima.

Some flooding of low-lying flat lands on the riverbanks and near the village will occur as a result of the hydro-electric plant's operation. An artificial lake will be created upriver from the plant. The river will continue to flow in its present course below the plant, but the flow will be regulated by the plant's operation. The plans for the plant are sound from an engineering point of view.

Most of the funding for this project is coming from an aid organisation based in an industrialised country, and a loan from another industrialised country. Some money is also being given by the government of Terrania.

worksheet

Plan for a hydro-electric plant (2)

AREA WHERE FISH SPAWN
FARMLAND
DIRT ROAD
AREA OF FUTURE ARTIFICIAL LAKE
SITE OF PROPOSED PLANT
VILLAGE CHIEF
CLINIC
KIOSK
SCHOOL
DOCKS
DIRT ROAD
RIVER
FARMLANDS
TO CAPITAL CITY

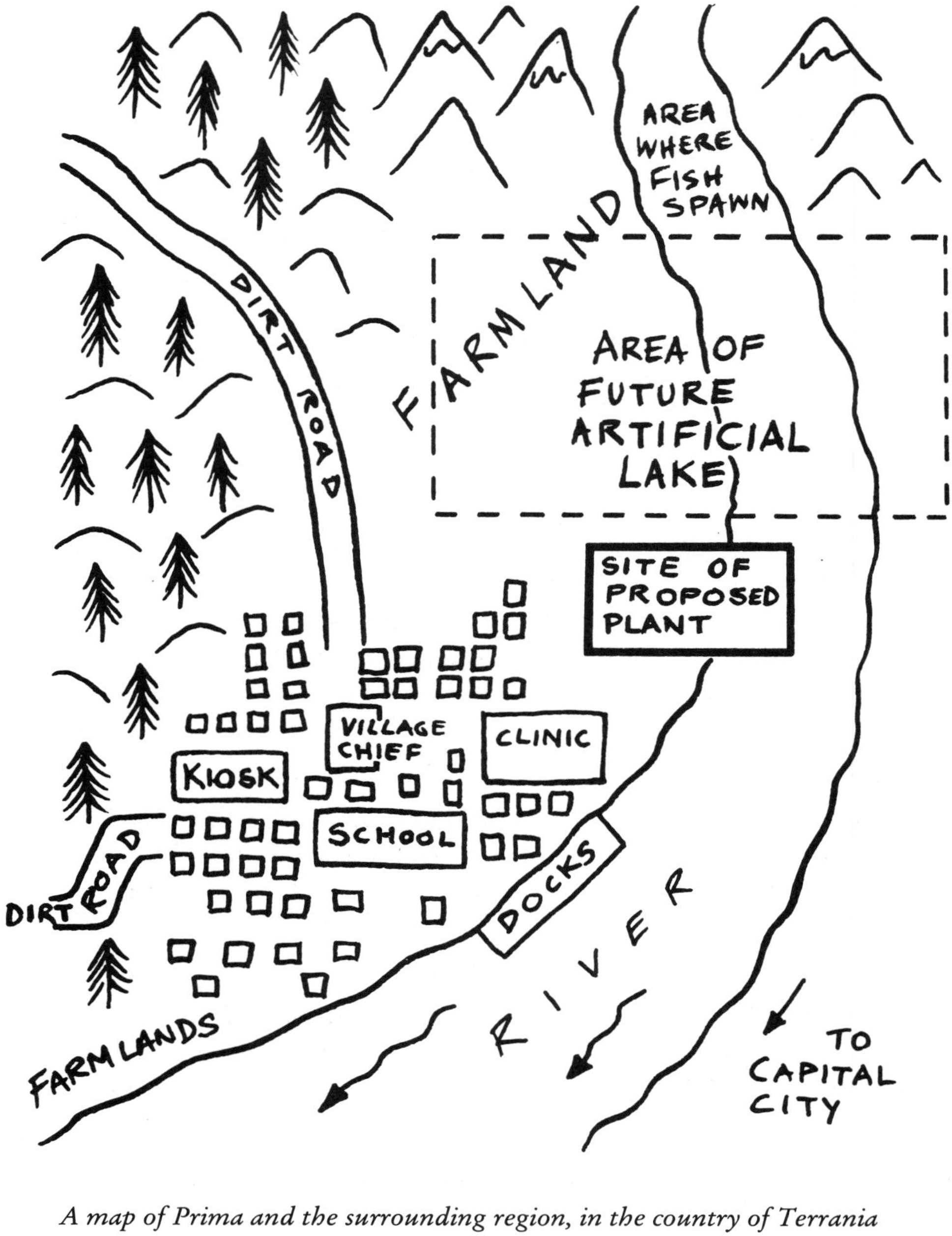

A map of Prima and the surrounding region, in the country of Terrania

Infrastructure

Terrania's capital city is 200 kilometres downriver from Prima. It is located on the coast, where the river which passes through Prima reaches the sea. The capital city is home to all the major construction companies, and Terrania's only airport. All supplies for the construction project would have to pass through the capital in order to reach Prima.

There are only two dirt roads across rough terrain which connect Prima to the nearest towns and villages. At present, these roads are not maintained well enough to transport heavy machinery and equipment. For the construction to begin, it would be necessary to clear some of the trees in the hilly regions surrounding the village and widen the roads.

The main way to reach this village is to travel on the river. The river is easily navigable as one travels from the capital city to Prima, until approximately 10 kilometres before reaching Prima. At this point, the river is extremely wide but shallow, only 3 to 4 metres in depth. This can make it difficult, if not impossible, for large cargo ships to reach Prima. Prima has a small docking area which is used by fishing boats.

Telephone and electric services are present in the village, but on a limited basis; the school and clinic have phones and electricity, as well as the village chief and the owner of a kiosk. The lines are above ground, and are often out of service due to heavy rainfall during three months of the year. Repairs can be slow, owing to the conditions of the local roads.

What infrastructure issues must be taken into consideration if the construction of the hydro-electric plant is to proceed successfully?

worksheet

Women

Women grow most of the foods that are eaten in Prima. The land is not fertile enough to produce extra crops for local sale or export. The women have few tools or equipment which would make their work more efficient, and increase the amount they grow. The women of Prima use the river water to irrigate their crops.

By tradition, women usually do not fish. They rely on the men of the village to add to the family diet with fish. There are few other job possibilities for men in the area, so most men spend at least some time each day fishing.

The women also use the river for washing clothes, and as a place to collect drinking water. Because the village is located on the river, they presently need only walk a short distance in order to carry out these daily tasks.

There are several forest areas located 2 to 3 kilometres from the village. The women walk there each day to collect wood for cooking fuel. These trees are near the two dirt roads which lead to Prima. Construction of these roads destroyed some of the trees. While there are still enough trees, the women are increasingly aware of the need to protect the supply of wood which remains.

Women in the village are also aware of how water-borne diseases affect the health of their children. They are organising to look into ways of ensuring that safe, clean water supplies can be made available in village homes.

Recently, the government and non-governmental organisations have worked to increase the number of girls who go to primary school and help them stay in school longer. Adult literacy programmes are also becoming extremely popular among the women of Prima; 15 per cent of the women are now literate.

What issues pertaining to women must be taken into consideration if the construction of the hydro-electric plant is to proceed successfully?

Environment

The river which flows through Prima has its source in a mountainous region upriver from the village. The water is clean and safe for drinking until it reaches Prima. There, the habit of using the river for waste disposal and for washing clothes causes an increase in the levels of bacteria and parasites, as well as some chemical contamination.

worksheet

The flat lands on the banks of the river are the ones which are used by the village for farming purposes. Because they are so close to the river, they are easily irrigated.

A limited number of trees grow in the hilly regions outside the village. Many of these trees had to be cleared to build the two roads which lead to the village. As these trees are a source of fuel, they are gradually being used up. As more trees are cut, a great amount of erosion on the hillsides is occurring. Erosion is causing some of the soil from the low-lying farmlands to wash into the river.

The river is home to a number of species of fish. These fish live most of their life cycle in the parts of the river around Prima and downriver. Once a year, however, some species swim up the river toward its source to spawn in the region of the foothills of the mountains. The fish are sensitive to changes in their river environment such as increased pollution levels, temperature changes, etc. As the population of Prima grows rapidly, resulting in increasing levels of contamination in the river, a small but significant drop in the number of fish caught has been noted by the fishermen.

What issues pertaining to the environment must be taken into consideration if the construction of the hydro-electric plant is to proceed successfully?

Justice

A number of groups within Terrania are interested in the proposed hydro-electric plant in Prima.

Terrania's main power company is eager to begin producing electricity in Prima, and supplying it to towns and villages in the region, as this will greatly increase its profits.

The construction companies in the capital city are competing for the contract to build the plant. At least one of these companies plans to use workers from a neighbouring country which has high levels of unemployment. These workers will accept lower wages than workers in Terrania.

Construction companies in two industrialised countries are also competing for the contract. One of these is in the country which is loaning money for the project, and the other is in the country which is home to the aid agency which is providing part of the funding for the plant. Because they have more modern equipment, they are offering to do the job for less than the construction companies in Terrania can.

Many people who live in the towns and villages around Prima are looking for jobs. Believing that construction of the hydro-electric plant will start soon, some families have moved to Prima and are living in temporary dwellings. They hope to be offered jobs when construction begins. It is expected that once approval is given for the project, migration of job-seekers to Prima will increase.

There are signs that these newcomers are being met with hostility by residents of Prima, who feel that they should be the first to be offered any available jobs.

Opposition to the plant is also coming from some residents who fear that the flooding caused by the plant will destroy the village's farmland and fishing waters. They are currently in conflict with others who feel that the plant will provide jobs and facilities which will raise the standard of living in the region.

What justice issues must be taken into consideration if the construction of the hydro-electric plant is to proceed successfully?

Activity 11

Population growth

Age level 3: 16–18 years

OBJECTIVES

To familiarise young people with some of the factors that may influence population growth in developing countries, and to encourage them to do further research into the interplay of those factors.

MATERIALS

A set of the **Population growth** cards (on pages 67 and 68) for each small group; large sugar paper and glue.

PROCEDURE

Step 1

The young people form groups of three to four. Each group receives a set of the **Population growth** cards, cut into individual sections. They are given several minutes to read all the cards.

Step 2

Students then arrange the cards in a diamond ranking according to their significance to the issue of population growth. The most significant card should be placed at the top level of the diamond, followed by two cards of high significance. The third level contains three cards of some significance to the issue, the fourth level has two cards of lesser significance, and the bottom of the diamond has the card the group judges to have the least significance:

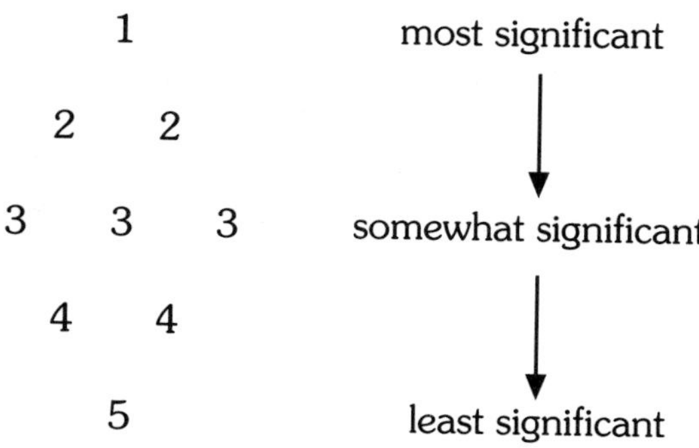

It should be made clear to the young people before beginning that there is no one right answer to this activity and that the cards do not represent a definitive list of all the factors influencing population growth. Once the group has agreed on its arrangement, it glues its cards onto a large sheet of sugar paper.

Step 3

Small groups then come together to discuss the reasons for the various arrangements. The following questions can be raised:

- Did any of the factors affecting population growth surprise you?
- Were there any other factors which you felt should have been included?
- Was there general agreement on which factors were most and least significant? Why or why not?
- Which factors seem most strongly inter-related? Why?

VARIATION

Instead of making a diamond ranking, the small groups use the cards to form a flow chart. They do this by laying the cards on the large sugar paper in a way that shows the relationship of the various factors – sequencing them, clustering them, etc. Lines or arrows can be drawn between the cards to show further how they affect each other.

FOLLOW-UP

1 Groups research countries which are effectively controlling population growth. They can also research the relationships between infant mortality, life expectancy, and population growth rates. Useful sources of statistics are annual publications such as the *State of the World's Children Report* (UNICEF), the *World Population Data Sheet* (Population Reference Bureau), and the *World Development Report* (World Bank).
2 After doing such research, students repeat the ranking activity, possibly adding cards representing other factors, to see how their ideas may have changed.

IN THE CURRICULUM

The activity requires students to see relationships, understand cause and effect, anticipate consequences and make decisions. It could be used in a history or geography class in which conditions in developing countries are being considered. If the statistics are explored in depth, it could also be incorporated into a mathematics class.

Population growth cards (1)

LAND REFORM

When land is redistributed so that the people who farm it own it (rather than wealthy landlords or multinational companies), the living conditions of the low-income farmers are improved. As poverty is reduced, people can have better health care and education: this leads to more babies surviving, so couples can have fewer children. The birth rate goes down in countries where the standard of living improves; so measures such as land reform, which reduce poverty, can contribute to population control.

DEBT REDUCTION

A major cause of poverty in developing countries is debt owed to industrialised countries; poverty in turn is linked to the conditions which encourage higher birth rates. If industrialised countries are serious in their concern over population growth, they should take the initiative by easing or eliminating debt. They should also encourage developing countries to produce the food they need to feed their people, rather than produce crops like cocoa and coffee for export.

HEALTH CARE

Some parents in developing countries are afraid their children won't live to be adults. So they have many children, hoping that some will survive. Research shows that when deaths of infants and children are reduced, the birth rate eventually drops. Providing good health care and sanitation to all, therefore, can influence control population growth.

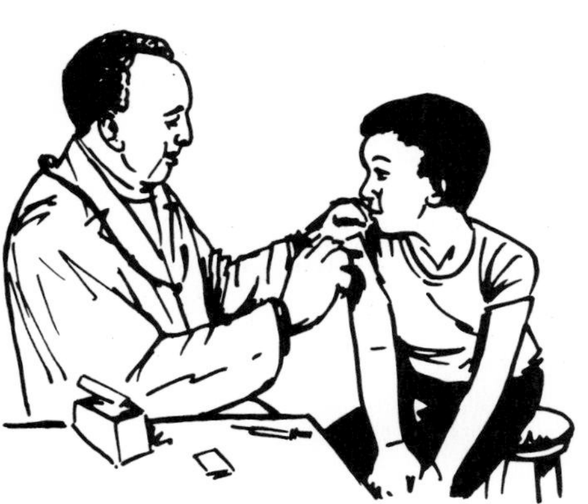

EMPOWERMENT OF WOMEN

Providing equal opportunities for women can help slow population growth. When women feel they have a choice of roles in their lives, both within and outside the family, they often decide to have fewer children.

Population growth cards (2)

APPROPRIATE TECHNOLOGY

In developing countries, rural families need to have many children who can help out with farm work. If appropriate technology could be developed to reduce the amount of labour required, parents could choose to have smaller families.

EDUCATION

In countries where girls and women are better educated, the birth rate drops. Girls who receive education know more about health practices and family planning, and have more employment options. Improving education can influence population growth.

CARE OF THE SICK AND ELDERLY

People in developing countries have many children because they need someone to take care of them when they are elderly or ill. Countries should be encouraged to develop social security systems, whereby the elderly can be assured of pensions and health care. This alone would enable parents to have smaller families.

FOOD DISTRIBUTION

The world has enough food to support a population far greater than the one which presently exists. The real issue is not reducing the birth rate; it is ensuring that food resources are distributed to those who need them most.

FAMILY PLANNING

In order to reduce overpopulation, family planning information and services must be made available to all couples in developing countries.

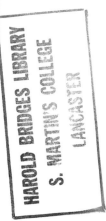

Activity 12 The coffee game

OBJECTIVES

To enable young people to experience, through a simulation, the effects of asymmetrical interdependence between industrialised and developing countries, in this case with regard to the orientation of an economy towards cash crops.

MATERIALS

For each farmer: a pencil; an **Information for farmers** sheet (page 74); a **Typical neffan farm** sheet (page 76); and a **Farmer's tally sheet** (page 77).

For each pair of representatives of the multinational food corporation: pencils; an **Information for representatives of a multinational food corporation** sheet (page 75); several copies of the **Neffan currency** sheet (page 78); a **Corporation's tally sheet** (page 79).

Calculators, if available, will be helpful in completing tally sheets for both farmers and representatives.

PROCEDURE

Step 1 (approximately 15 minutes)
The class is divided into roles as follows:

Farmers in a developing country: four groups of four people each.
Representatives of a multinational food corporation: four groups of two people each.

The farmers and corporate representatives should read over their information sheets, and follow the instructions on them.

(Note: Farmers complete tally sheets individually; the corporate representatives do their tallies as a pair.)

The teacher plays the role of the Controller during the simulation. The Controller reads each of Steps 2 to 6 aloud, and monitors the progress of the groups.

As the simulation progresses, the calculations done by both farmers and corporate representatives become increasingly complicated. In order to assist the teacher in monitoring their work, sample tally sheets for farmers and representatives have been completed, and can be found on pages 80 and 81. The sample farmer's tally sheet is based on the assumption that the farmer has given two acres of land to coffee-growing each year, and has borrowed no money. Should the farmer make different decisions, the tally sheet will differ from the sample.

Step 2 (approximately 10 minutes)
The Controller reads the following:

'As you understand from your information sheets, you, the farmers of Neffa, are looking for ways to improve your economic situation, while, you, the representatives of Bev-Mart, wish to expand your company's operations to Neffa. Please take this opportunity to meet together to discuss whether you can come to an agreement that benefits you both.'

The Controller then matches each pair of representatives of the corporation with one group of four farmers, and allows them to negotiate.

Step 3 (approximately 15 minutes)
The Controller reads the following:

'Congratulations to those of you who reached an agreement. Let us now imagine that a year has passed. Bev-Mart has helped Neffan

'Farmers' and 'multinational corporations' negotiate over growing cash crops

farmers start growing coffee, and the farmers have just harvested their first crop. Representatives of Bev-Mart, it is now time for you to pay each farmer 150 neffs per acre given to growing coffee, as promised. When this is done, farmers and corporations should fill in the "End of Year" column on their tally sheets.

Then ask yourselves – has the coffee-growing project been a success for you? If so, I recommend that corporation representatives suggest to farmers that they give two additional acres to growing coffee in the upcoming year. Farmers, consider how you might benefit from this offer, and decide how much coffee you will grow next year.'

Step 4 (approximately 15 minutes)
The Controller reads the following:

'Let us now image that we have come to the end of the second year of growing coffee. Unfortunately this year there was a drought in Neffa. The coffee crop survived because Bev-Mart saw to it that the coffee fields were irrigated. But your food crops suffered. You were only able to grow half as much food as you did last year: 50 neffs worth on each acre of land. Fortunately, if you have been growing coffee, you now have money in the bank so that you can survive a bad year by buying the food you need. You may have to use up all your savings, but at least your families won't starve.

Once you have filled in the column on your tally sheets under "End of Year 2", consider the fact that the drought is coming to an end. Next year you could be earning a good amount of money again. Representatives of Bev-Mart can suggest that if the Neffans give over two more acres to coffee-growing, they may be able to recover the loss which occurred due to the drought.'

If the farmers want to use their savings to buy food, the Controller should act as the 'market', taking their money and giving them imaginary food in return.

Step 5 (approximately 15 minutes)
The Controller reads the following:

'It is now the end of the third year of growing coffee. Happily for the Neffans and for Bev-Mart, the drought has ended. The land on which the farmers are growing food is now producing a full 100 neffs worth of crops again.

However, there have been some changes on the world coffee markets. Because so much more coffee is being grown, the price is dropping. Bev-Mart now receives only 600 neffs for the coffee produced by one acre of land. So they can only pay the farmers 75 neffs per acre this year.

This may present a temporary hardship to you farmers. Some of you may not be able to provide 100 per cent of the food your families need this year. However, Bev-Mart is prepared to loan money to those of you who need help in meeting your families' food needs. Bev-Mart representatives would also like to speak to you about giving two more acres of your land over to growing coffee. If you had grown this additional amount of coffee this year, you still would have earned enough money to feed your families. As you fill in your tally sheets under the column headed "End of Year 3", consider the extra income and security that more land given to coffee would bring in the years to come.'

Step 6 (approximately 15 minutes)
The Controller reads the following:

> 'It is now the end of the fourth year of growing coffee. The good news this year is that the world market price of coffee has remained stable – Bev-Mart can again pay Neffan farmers 75 neffs per acre of land given over to coffee.
>
> However, it may be a hard year for the farmers again. Because so much Neffan land is now used for growing coffee, there is less food being produced. Since food is scarce, the prices have doubled. The food you produce on each acre of your land is now worth 200 neffs, rather than 100. But the food you must buy also costs you twice as much.
>
> But help is at hand. Bev-Mart can loan you money. Or, Bev-Mart can buy some of your land, at a price to be agreed upon by yourselves. Then you can work on the land as an employee of Bev-Mart, and be paid a regular wage.
>
> Unfortunately, you cannot easily convert your land from growing coffee to growing food. Four years of coffee-growing has depleted the soil, and it will no longer support food crops.
>
> However, I trust that once you have all filled in your tally sheets under the column headed "End of Year 4", you will be able to negotiate a workable agreement.'

Allow ten to 15 minutes for negotiations between the farmers and the representatives of the corporation, then stop the simulation.

Step 7

Students who played the role of the corporate representatives can be asked to explain what their financial situation was before coffee-growing started, and what it is now, after five years.

Students who played the role of the farmers then do the same. The teacher should be sure that these points are made:

- some farmers may now be in debt;
- and most will be suffering from malnutrition.

Step 8

Then discuss the following questions:

- How were the two groups – farmers and corporations – interdependent?
- Did their interdependence benefit both groups equally?
- Why is it that growing a cash crop seemed to be a good idea at first?
- What were some of the unforeseen economic changes that occurred to make the production of coffee a disadvantage for the farmers?
- What might have to be done at this point to help the farmers (financial assistance from other countries, food aid, private fund-raising)?
- How could the farmers of Neffa be helped to become self-sufficient again?

Discuss parallels between the simulation and actual relationships between industrialised and developing countries. It should be pointed out to the students that the simulation is unrealistic in some ways; for example, multinational corporations have assets far greater than those in the simulation; farmers in developing countries may not own as much as ten acres of land. These factors would cause the gap between the two groups to be even greater than it was in the simulation.

FOLLOW-UP

Students research countries which are dependent on cash crops to find out more about their economies.

IN THE CURRICULUM

The simulation involves skills in role playing, computation, examining different perspectives, anticipating and analysing consequences. It would be appropriate for a history or geography class, and could also be adapted for use in a mathematics class.

worksheet

Information for farmers

You are farmers in Neffa, a developing country. Each of you owns 10 acres of land. On your land, you grow grain and vegetables. Each acre of land produces food worth 100 neffs, the local unit of currency.

Each of you has a family to support. You need food worth 1000 neffs to feed your family for a year. At this time, you are producing just enough food to feed your family. You eat everything you grow, and have nothing left over to sell. You have no money in the bank.

You know that as a subsistence farmer, you are at the mercy of many forces you cannot control such as the weather, or insects. A drought, or a new variety of insects could destroy your way of life.

You would like to know about ways that you could earn more money from your land, so that your family's lives could be more secure. You know that having some money in the bank would give you greater protection against natural disasters.

You would also like to see your children have a better standard of living than you do. You believe, therefore, that your children must get an education. You have completed primary school yourself, and you know how important being able to read, write, and do mathematics has been in enabling you to run a successful farm. If your children could go to secondary school, or even university, they would have more opportunities. But further education costs money; you want to find ways to earn more money from your land.

Representatives from the Bev-Mart Corporation will be coming to speak to you about growing coffee on your land. While you are very knowledgeable about your land and your crops, you know nothing about world markets. However, this may be the opportunity you have been waiting for to earn extra money from your land.

Before beginning the simulation, you should be sure you have the sheet of paper headed **A typical Neffan farm**. Each of the ten boxes on this sheet represents once acre of your land, on which you are currently growing food. If, after meeting with the representatives from Bev-Mart, you decide to grow coffee, draw an X through one of the boxes for each acre of land you grow coffee on. You should also have a **Farmers' tally sheet**, and you should fill in the column labelled 'Before growing coffee' right now.

worksheet

Information for representatives of a multinational food corporation

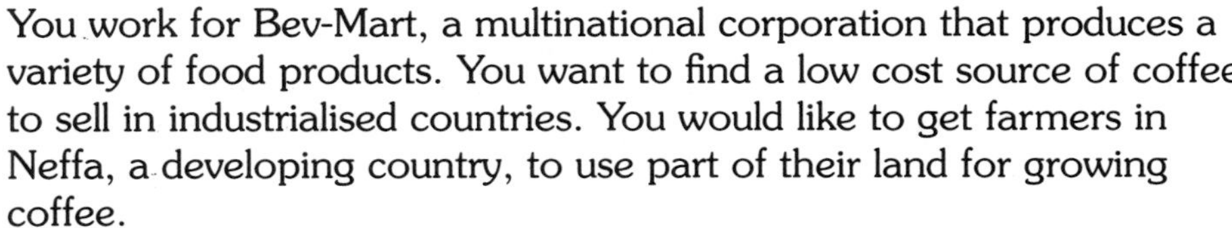

You work for Bev-Mart, a multinational corporation that produces a variety of food products. You want to find a low cost source of coffee to sell in industrialised countries. You would like to get farmers in Neffa, a developing country, to use part of their land for growing coffee.

You are interested in starting business in Neffa because many of the farmers there are living at a subsistence level. When droughts occur, or insects destroy the food crops, famine affects huge numbers of the farmers, causing poverty, illness, and death. The farmers lack the education and training to find other jobs, and may become refugees. But by growing coffee, farmers would have a regular income; they would be able to save money; they would be able to provide education for their children, a high priority among the Neffans. The government of Neffa supports Bev-Mart's investment as a way of raising the standard of living.

Because Bev-Mart anticipates that coffee-growing in Neffa will be profitable for the corporation, you will supply the farmers with the seed, fertiliser, equipment, and technical advice that they will need in the first year to start producing coffee.

You will meet some farmers and try to convince them each to give two acres of their land to growing coffee. Tell them that they will be paid 150 neffs, the local unit of currency, for the coffee that is produced by one acre of land (i.e., they will earn 300 neffs in the first year if they grow two acres of coffee). Though they won't have as much land to grow food, they will make enough money to buy any extra food they need, and to put some money in the bank as well. (Currently, each acre of land produces food worth 100 neffs; each farmer owns 10 acres of land, and the food they grow is just enough for their families to survive on. They do not have any food left over to sell for a profit.)

When you sell the coffee in industrialised countries, you will receive the equivalent of 750 neffs for the coffee grown on one acre of land. Your profit will be 600 neffs per acre given to growing coffee.

Working with your partner, plan what you will say to convince the farmers to grow coffee. Working as a pair, you should also fill in the boxes on the **Corporation's tally sheet** in the column labelled 'Before growing coffee' right now. Your company has 10,000 neffs in a Neffan bank at the start of the simulation. Make sure you have some of the sheets headed **Neffan currency**. You may fill in the necessary amounts as the simulation progresses.

worksheet

A typical Neffan farm

Farmers: Each of these boxes represents one acre of your farm land. Each time you give an acre over to growing coffee, draw an X through one of the boxes.

Farmer's tally sheet

	Before growing coffee	*At the end of year 1*	*At the end of year 2*	*At the end of year 3*	*At the end of year 4*
A Number of acres for coffee					
B Amount of money earned (row A × Bev-Mart price)					
C Number of acres for food					
D Cash value of one year's food for your family					
E Cash value of food grown					
F Amount of money spent on food					
G Total of rows E and F					
H Percentage of family's food needs met (ratio of row G/row D)					
I Money in the bank (subtract row F from row B)					

If at any point you need to borrow money, note the amounts here:

worksheet

worksheet

Neffan currency

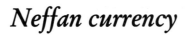

neffs	neffs
neffs	neffs
neffs	neffs
neffs	neffs
neffs	neffs

Corporation's tally sheet

	Before growing coffee	*At the end of year 1*	*At the end of year 2*	*At the end of year 3*	*At the end of year 4*
A Total number of acres for coffee					
B Total amount of money paid to farmers					
C Amount of profit you earned this year					
D Amount of money in the bank (add total from previous year)					

If at any point you loan money to the farmers, note the amounts here:

worksheet

worksheet

Sample farmer's tally sheet

	Before growing coffee	*At the end of year 1*	*At the end of year 2*	*At the end of year 3*	*At the end of year 4*
A Number of acres for coffee	0	2	4	6	8
B Amount of money earned (row A × Bev-Mart price)	0	300	600	450	600
C Number of acres for food	10	8	6	4	2
D Cash value of one year's food for your family	1000	1000	1000	1000	2000
E Cash value of food grown	1000	800	300	400	400
F Amount of money spent on food	0	200	700	450	600
G Total of rows E and F	1000	1000	1000	850	1000
H Percentage of family's food needs met (ratio of row G/row D)	100%	100%	100%	85%	50%
I Money in the bank (subtract row F from row B)	0	100	0	0	0

Amount borrowed: 0

Sample corporation's tally sheet

	Before growing coffee	*At the end of year 1*	*At the end of year 2*	*At the end of year 3*	*At the end of year 4*
A Total number of acres for coffee	0	8	16	24	32
B Total amount of money paid to farmers	0	1200	2400	1800	2400
C Amount of profit you earned this year	0	4800	9600	12,600	16,800
D Amount of money in the bank (add total from previous year)	10,000	14,800	24,400	37,000	53,800

Amounts loaned: ?

Why teach about images and perceptions?

Before they are two years old, children are aware of racial differences. By the age of three they may attach value judgements to those differences. Between the ages of four and six, they show gender-stereotyped behaviours, and may reject children who differ from themselves in terms of race or physical disability.

How do stereotypes come about at such an early age? The first influences are the attitudes of immediate family members, often acquired unconsciously. Later, children absorb stereotypical messages from books, television, movies, magazines, and newspapers. Even the absence of certain people (racial and ethnic groups, the elderly, the disabled) from the media conveys to children a sense of the diminished worth of those groups in society's eyes.

By the age of ten, students hold stereotypes about persons from far-away countries. An important source of these ideas is television news. Television producers rely heavily on sensational stories, often disaster-oriented, to attract and hold the attention of viewers. Such stories leave students – and adults – with the impression that developing countries in particular are mired in problems, and never make progress.

The advertising of aid agencies, devised with the positive intention of fundraising for projects in developing countries, may also reinforce stereotypes. Agencies show images of pathetic children, and reassure potential donors that even small sums of money can work miracles in the lives of these tragic victims. The implied messages are that all children in developing countries are starving and dirty, that people in those countries are incapable of helping themselves, and that only the aid of rich Western countries can save them.

Stereotyping harms *all* members of the world community. Individuals who belong to groups which are commonly stereotyped are often denied education, employment opportunities and housing. They may be the targets of ridicule, harassment, and violence. And these images harm the stereotypers as well. They develop unrealistic views of themselves, which can interfere with their ability to work and communicate effectively in an increasingly diverse world. Their biases rob them of the chance to share the knowledge and experience of other cultures.

A number of initiatives in multicultural education have attempted to promote understanding between groups, and to reduce stereotyping. But despite these worthwhile aims, some multicultural work has unintended effects. By focusing on exotic elements of a culture – such as festivals, clothing and food – in a superficial way, stereotypes can be reinforced rather than broken down. Some multicultural materials focus on aspects of life which are more a part of a country's past than its present, when in fact all cultures are continually adapting to new circumstances. Other multicultural materials simply attempt to substitute positive stereotypes for negative ones, still failing to give students a well-rounded picture of life in another country.

For multicultural education to be effective, it must emphasise the internal consistency of a culture, and the fact that culture is a logical adaptation to local circumstances. It can help students see that no culture is homogeneous, that diversity exists within all cultures. And it must convey the essential dignity of people and their ability to cope with the challenges they face.

However, for real attitudinal change to occur, students need more than information *about* other cultures and groups. They need to address the roots of prejudice, become aware of their own stereotypical beliefs and understand where these come from. Then, they need to work to eliminate stereotypes that they hold, develop skills for dealing with bias in the community at large, and make a personal commitment to equality and justice.

Some key concepts

PREJUDICE

Prejudice is a negative personal attitude or opinion about a person or group which is not necessarily based on knowledge of that person or group.

STEREOTYPE

An oversimplified, generalised attitude about a group of people is a stereotype. Stereotypes are often, but not always, negative. They may be based on prejudice; they may also be derived from contact with one member of a group, if an impression of that person is assumed to be true for all who belong to that group.

RACISM

Racism describes attitudes, actions, or institutional practices based on the assumption that certain people have the right to power over others solely because of their colour. Racism has been described as 'prejudice plus power'.

SEXISM

Attitudes, actions, or institutional practices which subordinate people because of their sex are sexist.

While racism and sexism are widely known types of social oppression, groups of people are also discriminated against on the basis of age, class, occupation, income and physical ability, to name but a few characteristics.

These oppressions can occur between individuals. They also operate at an institutional level when discriminatory practices become implicit or explicit organisational policies.

Teaching about images and perceptions: Aims and objectives

Knowledge	*Skills*	*Attitudes*
• Knowledge of one's own culture, heritage and world view. • Knowledge of the cultures of others, in one's own community and in different parts of the world. • Understanding that world views are not internationally shared, and that different perspectives have their own logic and validity. • Knowledge of the common stereotypes about others which exist in one's own culture. • Understanding the sources of these stereotypes. • Knowing about techniques used in print and visual media to create, alter or manipulate images.	• Being able to detect biases, stereotypes, and egocentric attitudes – one's own and others'. • Ability to perceive differing perspectives in speech, print, and audiovisual media. • Ability to think critically about images and information received from a variety of sources. • Ability to use knowledge and imagination to develop insight into the ways of life, attitudes and beliefs of others. • Ability to challenge stereotyping when encountered in the media, in institutional practices, or in interactions with individuals and groups.	• Positive valuing of cultural diversity, alternative points of view, equality and justice. • Respect and openness towards those who may appear to be different. • Appreciation of the commonalities which exist between peoples. • A thoughtful and informed scepticism about images that are presented in text and media. • A willingness to find out more information about the images one is presented with.

Activity 13 Who's in your group?

OBJECTIVES

To help students see that they are members of many different groups; to encourage them to find things that they have in common with their peers which they may not previously have been aware of.

MATERIALS

None.

PROCEDURE

Step 1

The teacher calls out a series of characteristics, one at a time. After each one, the students move around the room to form small groups with others who have the same characteristic.

For example, if the characteristic is 'favourite colour', the students walk around quietly saying their favourite colour. When two students with the same favourite colour find each other, they move around together looking for others with the same response, until small groups are formed. They spend a minute in this group discussing the characteristic they have in common, and then move on to group themselves according to the next characteristic.

Other characteristics that might be used are:

- favourite television show;
- number of siblings;
- favourite school subject;
- job you do at home;
- favourite season of the year;
- favourite food;
- ideal future occupation;
- a person you admire.

The aim of this activity is to help students discover things that they have in common with those who are different from themselves in terms of gender, race, ethnicity, and social class. Therefore, it is important to *avoid* using characteristics that will cause students to group themselves along these lines. Examples of such characteristics to be avoided could include:

- language you speak at home;
- neighbourhood you live in;
- religion;
- favourite place to go on holidays.

The teacher should be aware of other characteristics which could be sensitive ones in her class.

Step 2

Students discuss their feelings about the activity:

- Did anyone find themselves in a group with someone they did not expect to have anything in common with? Why was this a surprise?
- What new things did they learn about their peers?
- How did it feel to be part of a large group? How did it feel to be alone?

We all belong to the same group!

VARIATION

Students can do parts of the activity non-verbally, for example by pantomiming the job they do at home or their favourite season of the year. (Characteristics can be added or changed according to the interests and age level of the class.)

FOLLOW-UP

Students can be asked to think about other ways in which they might classify themselves. Each new characteristic can be written on a separate slip of paper (without the student's name). All the slips of paper can then be pasted on one large sheet of paper, to form a word picture of the class.

IN THE CURRICULUM

The activity develops skills in categorising and grouping. It can be used in a humanities class as a way of exploring different groups that make up the community. It can be used as part of a mathematics lesson by recording the results in the form of graphs.

Activity 14

All children . . .

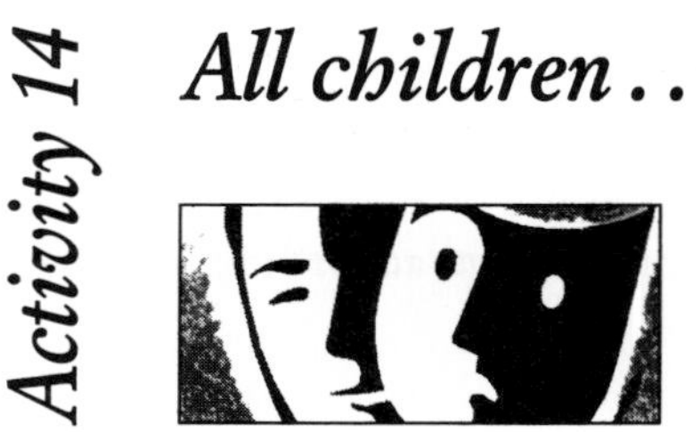

Age level 1: 7–11 years

OBJECTIVES

To introduce the students to the concept of stereotyping by showing them how it applies to themselves.

MATERIALS

Paper and pencils for each pair of students.

PROCEDURE

Step 1

The students form pairs. Explain that they are going to be thinking about stereotypes, and ask the class if they know what a stereotype is.

> A stereotype can be defined as a generalised idea or point of view about a whole group of people.
>
> Stereotypes may be formed when someone meets only one person from that group, does not get to know them very well and then assumes that all people from that same group have the same characteristics. Stereotypes are *not* based on facts that are true for everyone in that group.
>
> Sometimes stereotypes are formed just by listening to or reading about what other people have to say about members of that group, without actually ever knowing those persons. Some stereotypes are so widely believed that they are assumed to be true, and are very difficult to detect.

Step 2

Working with a partner, the students list as many stereotypes as possible that they think adults might have about children. Using a format like 'Many grown-ups think children are . . .' may help them get started.

Teachers should be aware that in a multi-ethnic class, there may be considerable cultural differences in the way that children are viewed.

Step 3

The whole class then discusses the activity:

- What stereotypes about children were most common?
- Are there different stereotypes about girls and boys?
- Why do adults have these ideas? Are they fair?
- How can these ideas be harmful to children?
- Do any of these ideas benefit children?
- What are some examples of children who do not fit these stereotypes?
- What can students do to counteract these points of view?

Same grownups
think children
are noisy
only like to play
makea mess

Stereotypes about children

VARIATION

After completing the discussion of stereotypes that adults have about children, the students can be asked to use the same process to examine stereotypes that they may have, or have heard expressed, about adults, parents, or elderly people. Where do these stereotypes come from? Are the images of women and men different? How do they benefit or harm adults? How do they benefit or harm the young people who hold them? What are some examples of adults who do not fit these stereotypes?

Again, there may be a great deal of diversity within the class in terms of the way that adults and the elderly are viewed in different cultures.

FOLLOW-UP

Students can make a list of stereotypical remarks about other groups of people that they have heard. This can be done without identifying the person who made the remark, so as not to place blame on anyone. What are the types of stereotypes which are most commonly held by people in the school or community? How can you know if a remark is a stereotype? (Hint: Listen for phrases like 'Those people are *all* . . .' or 'They *always* . . .' or '*Everybody* from . . . is . . .')

IN THE CURRICULUM

The activity involves analysing, recording, comparing, consensus-building and critical thinking. It can be used in a humanities class as an introduction to the images students bring to the study of *any* group of people. It could be used in an English class to examine how the qualities of a character are conveyed in literature. It could also be incorporated into a unit on media studies.

Activity 15

What's the message?

OBJECTIVES

To heighten students' awareness of stereotyping, especially with regard to gender.

MATERIALS

A set of sentences about people in non-traditional gender roles (see pages 93 to 95). Each sentence is cut in half so that one part contains information about the role, and the other indicates the gender of the person.

Age level 1: 7–11 years

PROCEDURE

Step 1

Each student receives a slip of paper with a sentence fragment. They move around the room and attempt to find another student whose fragment completes the sentence.

Step 2

When all students have completed their sentences, they read them aloud to the rest of the class. As a class they then discuss the activity:

- Was it easy or difficult? Why?
- Was there anything surprising or unexpected about the completed sentence?
- Where do our ideas or stereotypes about gender roles come from?

VARIATIONS

1 Sentences can be cut into three pieces to make the activity more challenging for older students.

2 Sentences can be created to challenge commonly held images the students may have about older people, physically disabled people, or members of various nationalities or ethnic groups.

FOLLOW-UP

Ask the class to watch a television programme or advertisement and look for examples of gender stereotyping. What types of stereotypes are most common?

Did any student watch a television programme that showed women or girls in non-stereotyped roles? If so, what was their reaction? How might other people react to the same programme?

IN THE CURRICULUM

The activity requires reading comprehension and interpretation skills. It can be used as part of an English lesson, in a humanities class on community roles, or as an introduction to gender issues in a personal and social education class.

What's the message? (1)

worksheet

The girls liked to

play football on the weekends.

After the nurse helped with the operation,

he washed his hands.

The firefighter

put on her helmet.

The boy changed his clothes before going

to the dance class.

worksheet

What's the message? (2)

The surgeon put on a mask before

she began the operation.

The babysitter read a story to the children

before he put them to bed.

The construction worker never felt afraid when

she worked on high buildings.

The father made a

snack for the children when they came home from school.

What's the message? (3)

The police officer was sure that

she knew who the thief was.

Before he went home, the

secretary made sure that all the letters were typed.

The prime minister

worked to improve the schools in her country.

The teacher thought that helping students learn to read was the

best part of his job.

Activity 16 Corners

Age level 1:
7–11 years

OBJECTIVES

To introduce some basic facts about developing countries, and to counter stereotypes about these countries which are commonly held by students in Western industrialised countries.

MATERIALS

Two large signs, saying 'True' and 'False', hung in opposite corners of the room.

PROCEDURE

Step 1

The students stand in the centre of the room. The teacher reads a series of statements about a developing country (see the box on page 97 for examples), one at a time. As each statement is read, the students take a position in one of the corners of the room, depending on whether they think the statement is true or false. Students who are uncertain may remain standing in the centre of the room.

Step 2

Students are asked to explain why they think the statement is true or false. Then the teacher tells them the correct answer.

Step 3

The class discusses where the images they have about developing countries might come from. It should be made clear to the students that the aim of the activity is *not* to prove that developing countries have no serious problems. Developing countries *do* face many challenges in the areas of economics, health and social welfare (as is indicated in some of the answers to the statistical questions). Rather, the intent of the activity is to use facts and statistics to challenge some of the overwhelmingly negative images of these countries which are conveyed through a number of different media.

VARIATION

Statistics from different countries or regions of the world may be substituted in order to address specific stereotypes held by the students, or to augment the study of a specific country by the class.

FOLLOW-UP

Students look for outdated or distorted images of different countries in library books, comics, or television programmes.

IN THE CURRICULUM

The activity involves evaluation and decision-making skills. It can be done in a history or geography class as an introduction to a study of a developing country. It could also be used in the context of media studies.

Sample statements for 'Corners'

Most children in Africa are starving.

False. Less than one third (31 per cent) of the children in sub-Saharan Africa are malnourished. (Malnutrition rates range from a high of 49 per cent in Niger, to a low of 12 per cent in Zimbabwe.)

Most people in India don't have clean water to drink.

False. 86 per cent of the people in India have access to clean water.

In South America, most adults know how to read and write.

True. In South American countries, between 80 per cent and 96 per cent of adults know how to read and write.

Most of the children who start primary school in China finish.

True. 85 per cent of Chinese children finish primary school.

Most children in east Asia are not vaccinated against measles.

False. 89 per cent of these children are vaccinated. (Vaccination rates range from a high of 99 per cent in the Democratic People's Republic of Korea, to a low of 20 per cent in the Lao People's Democractic Republic.)

Age level 2:
12–15 years

Activity 17 Portraits

OBJECTIVES

To help students become more aware of stereotypes they hold about developing countries.

MATERIALS

For each pair of students: drawing paper, coloured pens or crayons, one **Story Starter** (page 101), one corresponding photo (pages 103–6), and one photo description (page 102).

PROCEDURE

Step 1

The teacher should distribute only the **Story starters** and the drawing paper and pens at this stage. In pairs, students read their **Story Starters.** Using the drawing paper and pens, they draw a picture of what they think the people in the **Story Starter** might be doing on a typical day in their country.

Step 2

Students then complete the story starter, writing a paragraph or two on what they think these people would say about their life.

Step 3

Pairs who had the same story starter join together to compare their portraits, and to read their stories aloud to each other.

Step 4

When all stories have been read, the teacher distributes the appropriate photo and description to each small group. Students compare their portraits and stories with the photos of real people in each of these countries. They note the differences; then they make a list of what stereotypes their portraits revealed.

Step 5

The students walk around the room and view each others' work. The whole class then discusses the following questions:

- How did they decide what their portrait was to show, and what to put in their story?
- How did they feel when they saw the photo?
- What kinds of stereotypes about each of the four countries did they have before the activity?
- Where do these stereotypes come from?
- Have those stereotypes changed in any way?

I am a man from a village in Chad. Today, some of the other men in the village and I are hunting on the ground for bugs to eat. We can barely afford food, and we don't have a house. We would like to go hunting for lions and zebras, but we are very poor and can't afford a gun.
We live in the desert. It could be a jungle or a desert, but probably it's a desert. It's very hot here. We ride on donkeys or camels.

We didn't know that people in a village would know about solar power.

We thought they were all poor, but they are wearing good clothes.

We were surprised because they look like they are healthy.

Undoing stereotypes: students' ideas about life in an African country are challenged by a photo (step 2, top, and step 4, bottom)

VARIATIONS

1 Students draw the portraits individually, rather than in pairs.

2 Younger students may simply draw a picture, rather than write a story; older students may wish to eliminate the drawing and move directly to writing a story.

3 Students collect photos from newspapers or magazines which challenge common stereotypes. The same method can then be adapted to address gender stereotypes, or images of the elderly, the disabled, etc.

FOLLOW-UP

1 Students research the countries mentioned in this activity. They can also find out about UNICEF's work in those countries.

2 They look for examples of stereotypes of developing countries in magazines, newspapers, library books, and on television.

IN THE CURRICULUM

The activity requires visualisation, creative writing, the ability to make comparisons and critical thinking. It can be used as an introduction to the study of a country, as part of a media studies lesson, or in an art class.

Story starters

worksheet

1 We are three orphans in Ethiopia. Today we are . . .

2 I am a man from a village in Chad. Today, some of the other men in the village and I are . . .

3 We are students from a small town in Peru. In our town today, we are . . .

4 I am a woman from Zimbabwe. My baby and I are . . .

worksheet

Photo descriptions

1 During the 1984–85 famine in Ethiopia, many people living in the severely affected northern regions were moved to the more fertile provinces in the south-western part of the country. Later the government set up a programme to bring together families who were separated by the move.

These three young orphans, whose families did not survive the famine, play in a field of teff, Ethiopia's staple grain. The region, which was once arid and parched, now promises the best harvest in a decade.

2 These workers install solar energy panels to produce electricity for the refrigerator in the health clinic in Linia, Chad. Refrigeration is necessary to keep vaccines cold in warm climates. Chad has expanded its immunisation programmes, and is vaccinating larger numbers of children every year.

3 About 3 million children die each year because they have not been immunised against diseases such as measles, tuberculosis, and polio. Here, schoolchildren in Peru are part of a campaign to inform the public about the importance of immunisation, and to let people know about immunisation days that will be held in their town.

4 The government of Zimbabwe has set up classes for pre-school children and to train teachers. This woman, whose child is in the Early Learning Centre in Chitungwiza, participates in the class once a week to learn how to stimulate her child's development and learning.

Photo 1

Photo 2

Nacimos para vivir!
Protégenos Ahora!
Lote 20
DOMINGOS 22 DE MAYO 10 DE JULIO

Photo 3

Photo 4

Activity 18

The whole picture

OBJECTIVES

To help students understand how the cropping of images may distort or manipulate one's perception of reality; to make them more aware of the importance of seeing the whole picture (literally and metaphorically) before making a judgement about it.

Age level 2: 12–15 years

MATERIALS

Two photos for each pair of students, one of which shows a detail of a scene, while the other shows more of the background surroundings (see samples on pages 110–19); a copy of the corresponding photo description for each pair (see page 109).

PROCEDURE

Step 1

Students form pairs. Each pair is given one copy of a photo showing a fragment or detail of a scene. Based on this detail, they draw what they think the rest of the picture shows.

Step 2

Pairs are given the second photo, which includes the detail of the first, but shows the context in which it is set. They also receive a copy of the description of the photo. They write a paragraph describing their reaction to the complete photo.

Step 3

Both photos and reactions are displayed around the room. Students circulate and look at each others' work.

Step 4

Pairs then report back to the whole class on their reactions to the activity:

- Did their first impression of the photo differ from their reaction to the second photo? Why?
- Were any stereotypes revealed?

- What techniques can be used to change the way a viewer perceives an image?
- What reasons might there be for people who edit and publish photos to want to provoke a particular type of reaction on the part of the viewer?

VARIATION

After looking at the photo fragment, students write a story telling what they think the whole picture is about, rather than draw their ideas.

FOLLOW-UP

1 The class collects photos from magazines and newspapers which can be used in the same way as in the activity.

2 They may also wish to examine images of other countries on television. What questions are raised by these newscasts and stories? What additional information would they like to receive about these countries? If possible, a visit to a television studio to compare finished news stories with the uncut footage they are based on would help students understand how editing changes the final image.

IN THE CURRICULUM

The activity uses observation, visualisation, writing, comparing, analysing and critical thinking skills. It can be used in a media studies or art class. It an also be used in an English class to raise the issue of how we interpret both visual and print media. It could be used in a humanities class to explore images that students have of developing countries.

Photo descriptions

worksheet

1 In Mexico, programmes are being set up to help children who live on the streets. Here a social worker plays with some children who work in the market; by making friends with them, she is better able to find ways to help them.

2 In Guatemala, this woman proudly shows her diploma. She has just completed a course teaching women how to take action to start development projects in their communities.

3 As part of a health care programme in Thailand, a student at school is being given a vaccination.

4 In Sri Lanka, the government has set up mobile libraries. These libraries visit slum areas so that children there can borrow books.

5 In Sudan, the government is working to provide nutritional assistance to people affected by the drought. Here, Nutritionist Fatma Jibril measures the height of a child.

Photo 1

Photo 2

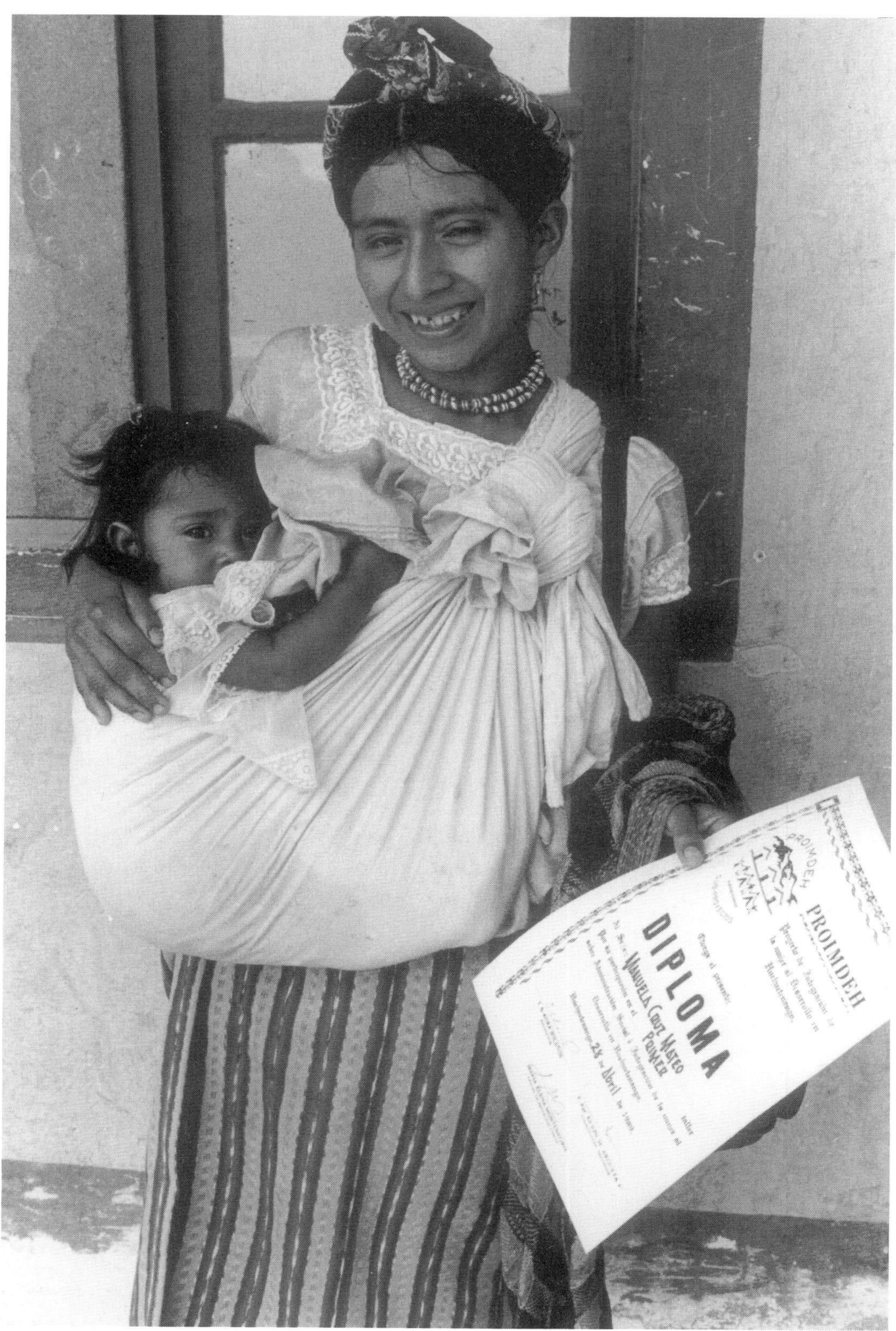

Photo 3

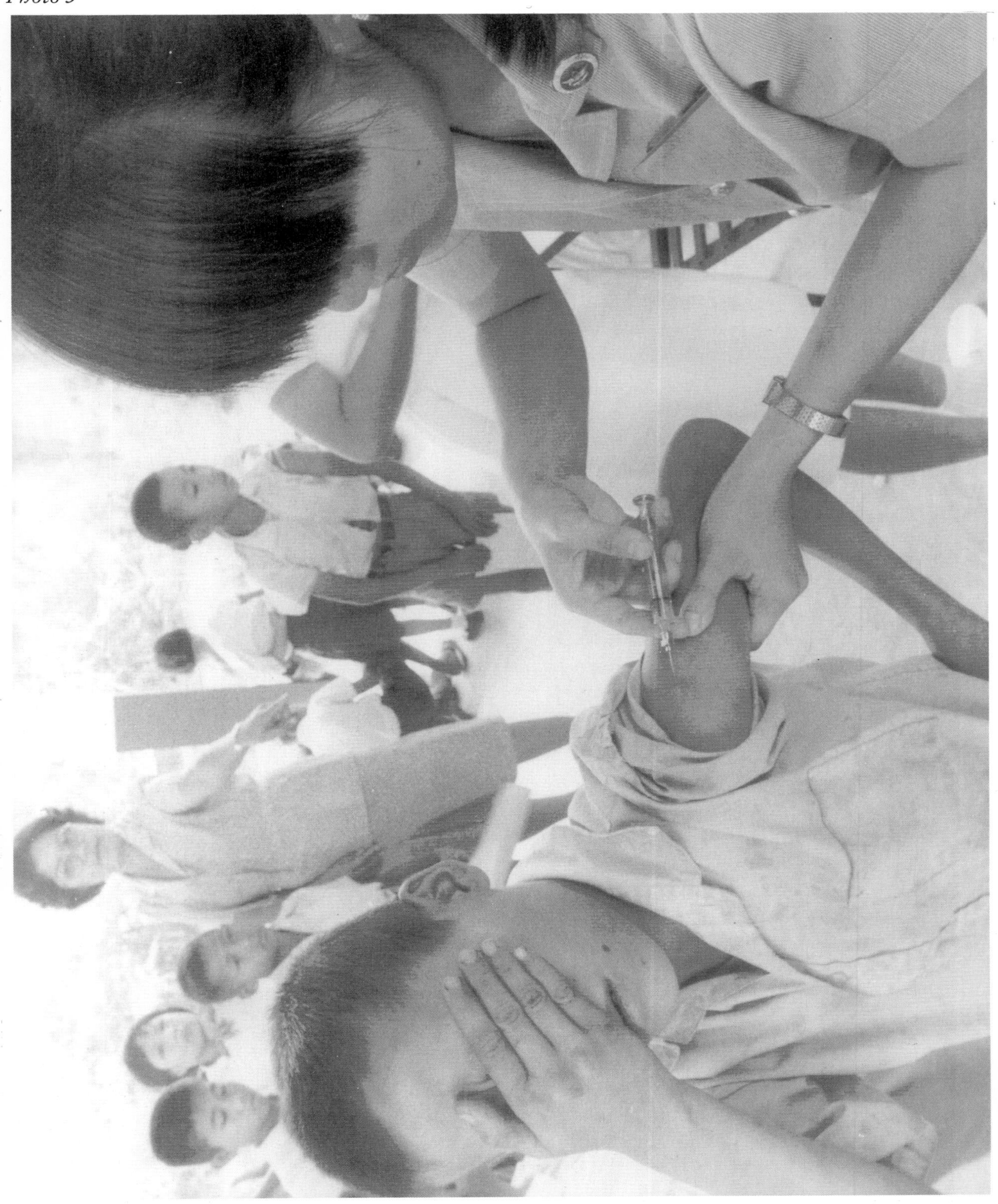

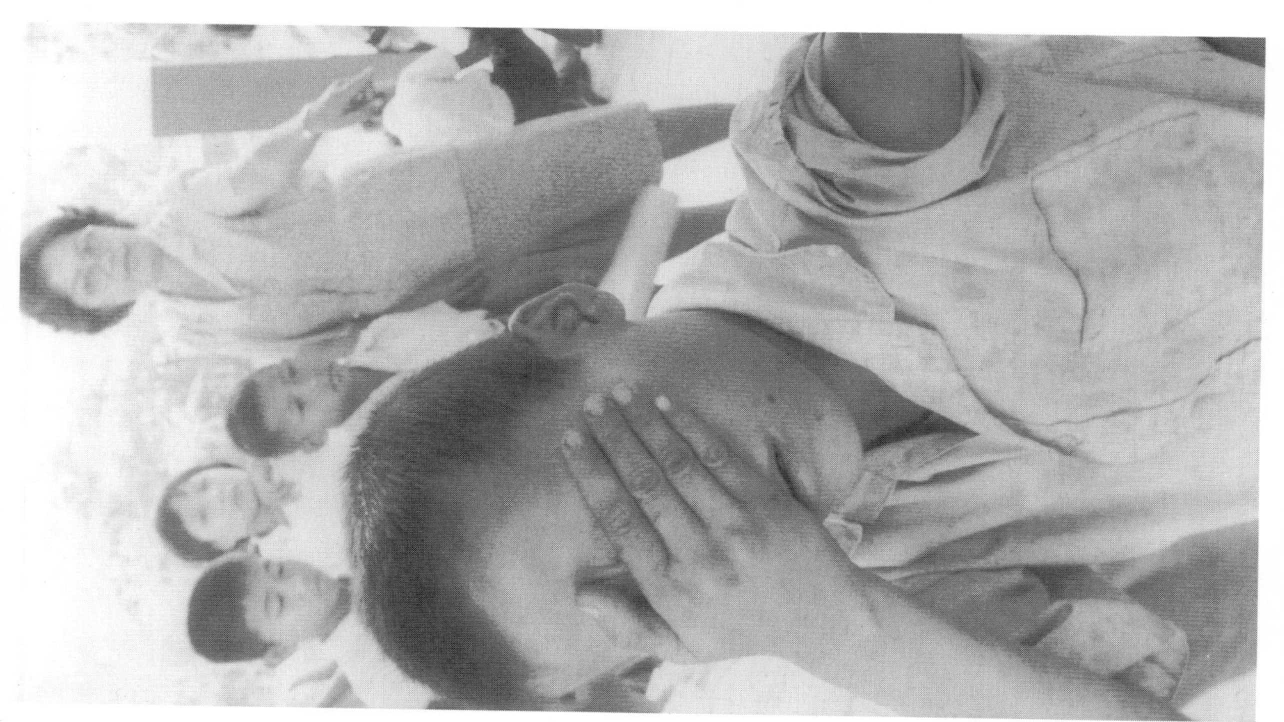

Photo 4

Photo 5

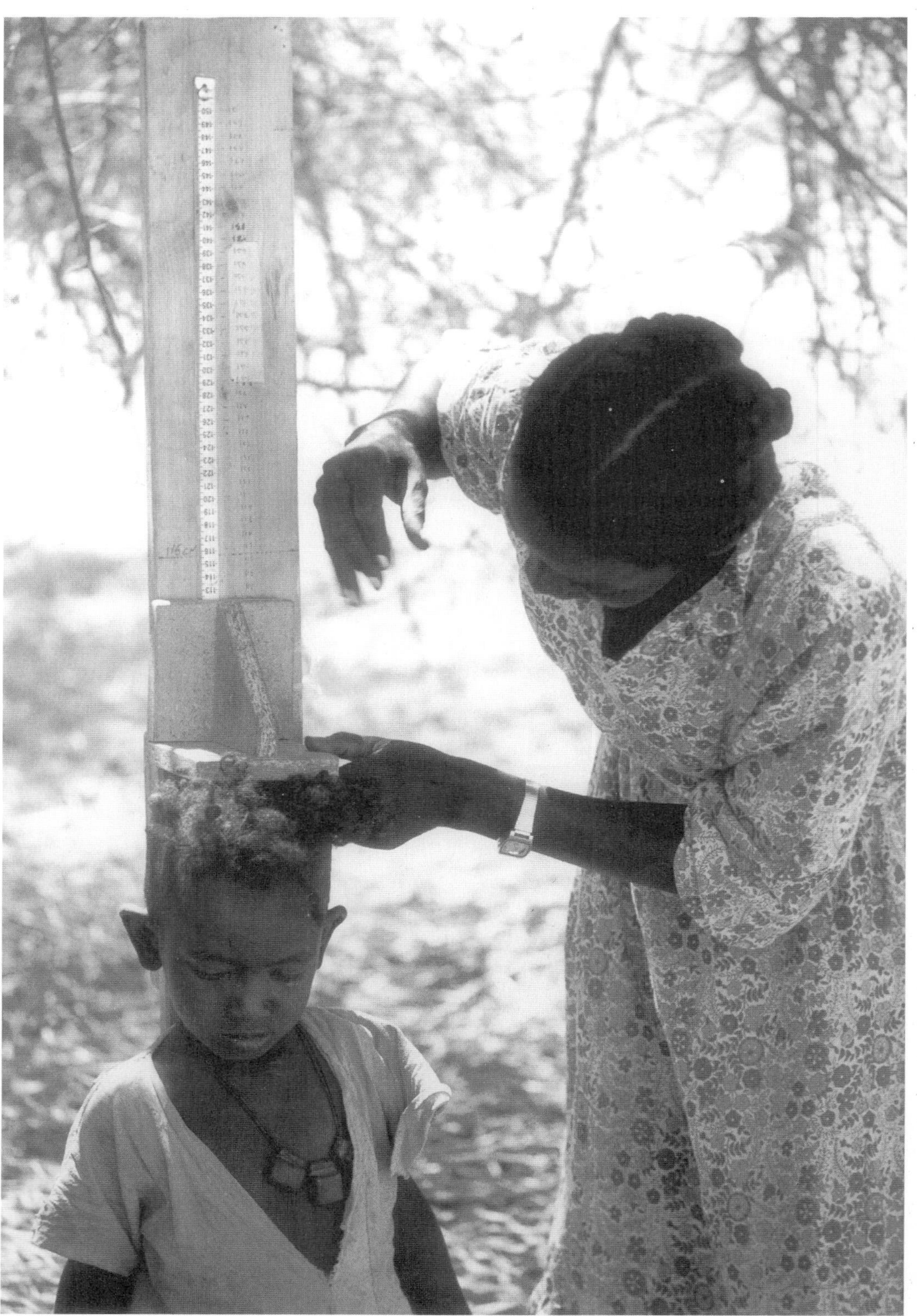

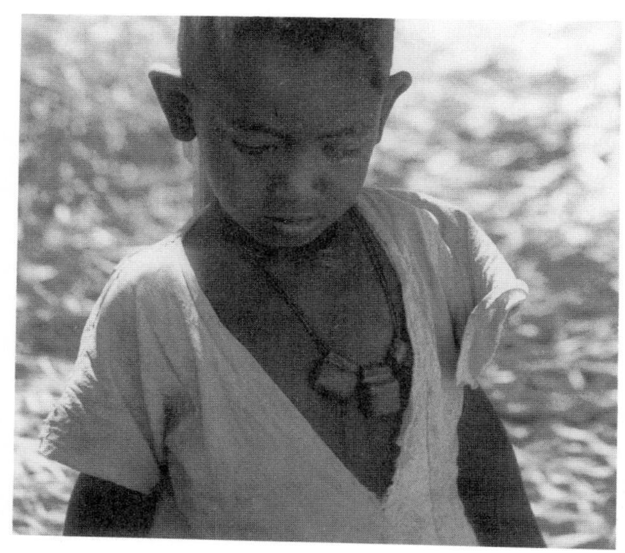

Activity 19

Analysing books

Age level 2: 12–15 years

OBJECTIVES

To sensitise students to gender stereotyping in the text and illustrations of books for young people.

MATERIALS

A **Book analysis** form for each pair (page 122); a collection of fiction books written for the class's age level or younger.

PROCEDURE

Step 1

Pairs of students choose a fiction book from the class, school, or public library. They read the book together, filling in the **Book analysis** form as they go along.

Step 2

Pairs report to the whole class on their findings. The quantifiable results can be compiled into a bar graph.

Step 3

The class then discusses:

- Were there more female or male characters in the stories?
- Did females and males have similar roles in the stories, or were there noticeable differences in the types of things they did?
- Were most of the **main** characters male or females?
- Were there gender differences in the types of concerns, problems or issues that the main characters had to resolve? Were they equally serious?
- Who were more often portrayed as the problem-solvers – females or males?
- Were there differences in the ways that females and males resolved their concerns? If so, what were the differences?
- Did analysing books written for young people teach you anything about gender stereotypes?

VARIATION

The book analysis form can be adapted to examine how other groups are depicted. For example, the column headings on the form can be changed to read:

- Children/Adults/Elderly adults;
- Able-bodied persons/disabled persons;
- Ethnic majority group/Ethnic minority group.

FOLLOW-UP

1 The students attempt to rewrite some of the stories in a non-biased way, or they create a collection of new stories with non-stereotypical characters.

2 With the permission of the school librarian, students insert a short summary of their analysis of each book inside the front cover; other students who read the book can consult this analysis and be alerted to the nature of the images, positive or negative, presented therein.

3 Students write to authors or publishers either to express their appreciation for books that avoid biased images, or to suggest ways of presenting more positive images in future publications.

IN THE CURRICULUM

The activity requires observation and recording, reading comprehension and analytical skills. It is appropriate for an English class, or a lesson on media studies. It could also be used in a humanities class to examine ways in which groups of people within one's country, or people from other countries, have been depicted. If graphs are used to present data on the number of persons from various groups that are represented in the books, mathematical skills can also be incorporated.

worksheet

Book analysis form

Title ______________________ **Author** ______________________

	Girls, women	***Boys, men***
How many are there?		
What do they do most often?		
Who is the main character?		
Describe any special concern, problem or issue that the main character has to resolve.		
How is it resolved?		
Who resolves it?		

Was there gender stereotyping in this book? ______________

What comments or reactions do you have about this book? __

____

____

____

Activity 20

Challenging stereotyping – role plays

OBJECTIVES

To make clear to young people the negative impact that stereotyping can have; to help them develop the skills necessary to confront and challenge bias.

Age level 2: 12–15 years

MATERIALS

One role play scenario (pages 126 and 127) for each group of four.

Note: The scenarios described are suggestions only. They deal with types of stereotypes which may be fairly common in many Western industrialised countries. They should be modified by the teacher to address stereotypes or issues which are more relevant to the class.

PROCEDURE

Step 1

The students form groups of four. Each small group is given one role play scenario.

Step 2

Everyone in the small group reads the card, and then two students volunteer to act out the scene. The other two students act as observers.

Step 3

Once the role play is completed, the small group members discuss it. The observers give feedback about what approaches they thought worked best in challenging the stereotype which was expressed.

Step 4

The small group can then act out a second scenario, with the two observers as actors. Alternatively, it may repeat the first scenario, with the observers playing the roles and confronting the biased person in a different way from the first role play.

Learning to confront bias

Step 5

The whole class then discusses the following questions:

- How were the various role play situations similar? How were they different?
- How did it feel to play the part of the biased person?
- How did it feel to play the part of the person who challenged the prejudice?
- What techniques were used in confronting the stereotype? Asking for clarification or more information about how the biased person is feeling and why? Reasoning? Attempting to persuade the person? Giving examples you know of persons who do not fit that stereotype? Providing factual information which counters the stereotype? Using concepts such as rights and justice? Arguing or threatening?
- What approaches were most effective in changing the biased person's attitude?
- Have you ever had to challenge prejudice in real life? What did you do?
- Have you ever been the object of unfair prejudice in real life? What did you do?

VARIATIONS

1 Students who are acting reverse roles half-way through the role play.

2 Role play scenarios can be derived from real incidents that the class knows of in their school or community. However, this should be done with awareness of the range of perspectives which may exist within the class on the incident in question; it may not be appropriate to use over-sensitive issues in this context.

3 Role plays may be enacted by a pair in front of the whole class if the students are familiar and comfortable with role play techniques.

FOLLOW-UP

1 The class discusses what types of stereotyping commonly go on in their school or community. They consider possible ways to raise the awareness of others about potential problems: by using the role play exercise as the basis for an article on bias in the school or local newspaper, for example, or a dramatisation to be presented at a school assembly.

2 Students use the role play scenarios as the basis for creative writing assignments.

IN THE CURRICULUM

The activity involves taking a variety of perspectives, decision-making, analysis and taking action. It may be used in a drama class, or in English as a way of exploring incidents of conflict and prejudice in literature. It could be used in the context of a humanities lesson on the experience of immigrants, or of other minority groups who have encountered prejudice from members of the dominant culture.

worksheet

Role play scenarios (1)

1 Your teacher has given the class an assignment to work in groups of four to write a report. Theo, whose family comes from a developing country, is in your group. As your group goes off to the library, another student, Marc, whispers to you, 'I wish Theo wasn't in our group. People from his country are all so lazy. They never do anything for themselves. We'll probably have to do his work for him.'

You respond . . .

2 The teacher is planning an all-day trip for the class. She tells the students to ask their parents if any of them would be able to come along for the day to help out. You say that you will ask your grandmother. The teacher says, 'This is going to be a very long trip, and we will be walking for quite a distance. I think it would be too tiring for your grandmother. Maybe your mother or father could come.'

Your grandmother is a very active and fit person. You say to the teacher . . .

3 Some families from a developing country have recently moved to your town, and their children go to your school. While walking in the corridor, one of your friends says to you, 'I don't like having all these poor people going to our school. My father says they all come to our country looking for work and they take jobs away from the people who live here. I think they should all go back to wherever they came from.'

You say . . .

Role play scenarios (2)

4 It is Sonia's first day in your class. Sonia uses a wheelchair to move around. Just before recess time, one of your friends says to you, 'When it's time to go outside, I'm going to go help Sonia put her coat on. She probably can't do it by herself.'

You say . . .

5 Jena is a girl in your class who comes from another country. One day you are eating in the school canteen when one of your friends says to you, 'Look at the weird food that Jena brought for lunch! Doesn't it smell disgusting? How can people in her country eat that stuff?'

You answer . . .

6 You are a boy who has to do a chemistry experiment with one other boy and one girl, Rima. You are talking about how to divide up the work. One of the boys says to you, 'You measure the chemicals and I'll light the burner. Rima can take notes – girls have better handwriting than boys.'

Rima doesn't say anything.

You say . . .

Age level 3:
16–18 years

Activity 21 What kind of news?

OBJECTIVES

To help young people become aware of the different ways in which industrialised and developing countries are portrayed in the media; to encourage them to reflect on how this can perpetuate stereotyping.

MATERIALS

A collection of current newspapers and magazines, large sheets of sugar paper on each of which is written the name of one of the regions (listed below), glue, felt-tip pens, and A4 paper.

PROCEDURE

Step 1

The class is divided into groups of three. Each small group is assigned one of the following regions of the world:

Africa
The Middle East
Western Europe
Central and Eastern Europe
Countries of the Commonwealth of Independent States (former Soviet Union)
South Asia
East Asia, Australia, and countries of the South Pacific
North America
Central America, South America, and the Caribbean

Small groups look through current magazines and newspapers and collect articles about the countries of the region they have been assigned. (They may wish to exclude articles about their own country, or to limit them to the five or ten which they judge to be most significant, or to create a separate category for them.)

Step 2

Students glue their articles onto the large sugar paper, giving each a number.

Examining newspaper articles to see how different regions of the world are represented

On a sheet of A4 paper, they list the number of each article, followed by a few words or a short sentence summarising the topic of the article.

Step 3

The articles and summaries are posted on the wall around the room. The students walk around and look at each group's collection of articles.

Step 4

In a plenary, the class decides on what the dominant themes or topics of the articles from each region were.

Step 5

They then discuss the following questions:

- Were all regions of the world equally represented? What regions had the most news coverage? (How does this change if you exclude articles about your own country?)
- What regions had the least coverage? How do you account for the difference?
- What were the predominant themes or topics of news stories about each of the regions?
- How were developing countries portrayed?
- What proportion of the stories presented positive images of developing countries? Do you think this represents an accurate representation of life in those countries?

- What reactions might readers have to stories about typical life, or about positive changes in developing countries?
- How could exposure to negative news stories over time create or reinforce stereotypes about developing countries?
- What might be some sources of news about developing countries that would give a fuller picture of life there?

<u>Africa</u>

There were seven articles.
There is a definite negative slant to these articles.
They are mostly about violence and crimes.
The articles on current political developments are mostly about militant groups and shootings
There is one article about a plane crash.
Articles on the economy are rare.

What kind of news do we receive about developing countries?

VARIATIONS

1 The same activity can be carried out using stories from international radio or television news broadcasts.

2 Reporting about developing countries which focuses on extreme poverty, famine, natural disasters, ethnic conflicts, etc., fails to give a full picture of life in those countries. Such reporting can create stereotypes because readers seldom have first-hand knowledge of typical events in those countries against which they can balance more sensationalistic stories.

To demonstrate this point to students, have them write about a typical day in their lives, in the style of a television news broadcast. Would such a story ever really be broadcast? Why or why not?

Then have students collect newspaper articles about an event in their own country, such as a flood, crime, an ethnic conflict, a drug problem, or a serious road or rail accident. What kind of image would such articles convey to a person in another part of the world, who had no idea of what normal daily events in the students' country are like?

FOLLOW-UP

1 The class visits a travel agency to collect tourism brochures from developing countries. These can be compared with the collection of newspaper articles. How do they differ? What are the different intentions of the writers of news stories and tourist brochures? How are the audiences different? Why is it that neither of these sources of information gives a balanced picture of a country?

2 The class contacts organisations working in developing countries (such as UNICEF) to request material on successful programmes in those countries. This information can be contrasted with the prevailing themes found in news articles.

IN THE CURRICULUM

The activity requires skills in reading comprehension, critical thinking, categorisation and analysis. It can be used in a media studies lesson; a history or geography class on a particular country or region; or in an English class on styles of writing used in journalism.

Activity 22

Aid agency advertisements

Age level 3: 16–18 years

OBJECTIVES

To sensitise young people to the ways in which aid agency advertising, intended to encourage financial support of developing countries, often acts to perpetuate stereotypes.

MATERIALS

Copies of the six **Sample aid agency advertisements** on pages 134–5 for each pair of students. (The advertisements are based on materials used in actual fundraising campaigns in several industrialised countries.)

PROCEDURE

Step 1

Pairs read their sample aid agency advertisements together. They then list both positive and negative aspects of each one. They should give special consideration to any stereotypes of people in developing countries which might be inferred from these advertisements.

Step 2

As a class, students discuss any erroneous images that might be conveyed by the advertisements. These may include:

- Development problems can be solved simply by donating money (rather than by addressing the underlying political, social and economic causes of poverty).
- Only aid from the industrialised countries can 'save' poorer nations and their children.
- Since solutions to the problems of children in developing countries are so inexpensive, there must be something wrong with people in those countries if they cannot solve the problems themselves.
- All children in developing countries are poor, dirty, uneducated, in ill health, hungry, joyless and unloved.

Step 3

The class votes on which of the six advertisements are the best and worst, from the standpoint of how effective they would be at raising money.

Step 4

Students then vote again on which of the advertisements are the best and the worst, from the standpoint of how well they avoid negative stereotypes of people in developing countries.

Step 5

The class discusses the following questions:

- Why do you think aid agencies run these various types of advertisements?
- What response are they trying to provoke in their audience? Who is their audience?
- What are the characteristics of a 'good' fundraising advertisement?

Note: In discussing the advertisements, it is important that young people understand that the aid agencies do not intentionally set out to create negative stereotypes. Rather, they often use techniques which aim to encourage the public to donate money by appealing to the emotions. The class should also be made aware that the intent of this activity is not to deny the fact that there are children in developing countries who need help, but to show how aid agency advertising can unwittingly promote stereotypes.

VARIATION

Pairs attempt to write their own advertisements which do not perpetuate stereotypes. Is this possible to do? Are there any contradictions inherent in attempting to create advertising which will encourage donation while respecting the dignity of the recipients?

FOLLOW-UP

Young people examine advertising from aid agencies in their country. They could write to the agencies, suggesting changes in their advertising approach, and explaining why such changes are needed.

IN THE CURRICULUM

The activity involves reading comprehension and critical thinking. It can be used as part of a media studies lesson, a writing class, or a history or geography class on a developing country.

worksheet

Sample aid agency advertisements (1)

Little Jeni never celebrates her birthday!

For a young girl who lives on the dangerous streets of city A, every day could be her last.

But you can help. Sponsor little Jeni for just £10 a month. This will provide her with enough to eat, clothing, school fees, and medical care.

She just might live to see her next birthday.

Mira escaped civil war. Now she risks death from starvation.

Would you give £10 to keep her alive?

Your contribution of only £10 will provide a month's worth of food for a hungry refugee child in country B.

Send your donation today. Time is running out for Mira.

Help them help themselves.

AAA agency's irrigation project in country X has transformed drought-stricken land into thriving farms. The villagers of XX now produce almost 75 per cent of their food themselves.
These are hard-working people who want to be 100 per cent self-sufficient. Help them reach their dream.
Support the expansion of the irrigation project. Give to AAA today.

25 pence could save his life.

All over the world, children like Tomi are dying from dehydration. This condition, caused by diarrhoea, is one of the biggest killers of children in the developing world.
But 25 pence will buy a packet of oral rehydration salts – a simple mixture of salt and sugar – which can save his life.
If 25 pence can save Tomi, £25 could save 100 children.
It's that simple.

Sample aid agency advertisements (2)

Think about how you live. In your home you have clean running water every day. You have plenty of electricity for cooking and heating. You have a cupboard full of nutritious food, and money to buy more at the corner shop.

Now think of how millions of people on the other side of the world live. They battle diseases caused by dirty water. They walk for miles to collect scarce wood for cooking fuel. Hunger and malnutrition cut too many young lives tragically short.

Won't you give – just a little – to help someone less fortunate?

Jane Smith was born and raised in country C. Today, she is a project officer there for XYZ agency. Jane talks about her work:

'My first project for XYZ was to work with the people of village CC on plans for a new school building. The old one was overcrowded, and the roof leaked badly when it rained.

Funds from XYZ provided the construction materials. The villagers provided the labour. What a sense of accomplishment when the roof went on!

The number of children who attend school in village CC has now doubled. More girls than ever before are attending. It makes me feel good to know that with an education, more of them will have the chance for the kinds of job opportunities that I have had.

We have a long way to go to improve education in my country. Too many people still believe that a girl's place is in the home, not in school. And too often children are taken out of school to help with farming. This has been especially true lately, since bad weather has caused several years of poor harvests.

But building a new school in village CC has caused many parents there to feel more involved in the education of their children. I hope to be part of many more projects like this one with XYZ.'

Activity 23

Terrorist or freedom fighter?

Age level 3: 16–18 years

OBJECTIVES

To help young people become more aware of the fact that there are differing perspectives on the same event; that news stories are often written from only one perspective and don't explore alternative points of view; and that stories can be written with the intent of provoking a particular emotional reaction in the reader.

MATERIALS

A copy of one of the **Reporter's Worksheets** (pages 139–141) for each pair.

PROCEDURE

Step 1

The teacher reads aloud to the class the two **Sample Newspaper Articles** on page 138.

Step 2

The class is then asked to compare the two articles, and discuss the fact that they describe the same incident.

- How do the two articles differ?
- What was your reaction to the first one?
- What was your reaction to the second one?
- What techniques were used in each of the articles to draw out your reaction?
- What might the intention of the writer of the first article have been?
- What might the intention of the writer of the second article have been?
- Can you tell from listening to the two articles which version is more accurate? What additional information might you need to help you decide?
- Are there any other possible perspectives on this same event?

Step 3

The students form pairs. Each pair is given a copy of one of the **Reporter's Worksheets**. They work together to complete it.

Step 4

Each pair joins with two other pairs to form a group of six. Each of the three pairs in this small group should have a different **Reporter's Worksheet**. The pairs take turns reading their work aloud to the others in the small group, and the group discusses it.

Step 5

The class then meets to discuss what was learned from the activity. The discussion should focus on the variety of perspectives that may exist on a given event, and the ways that language can be used to shape or manipulate emotions and reactions. Students can also consider:

- Can any news reporting be totally objective?
- How can young people obtain the fullest and most accurate information possible about local and global issues?

VARIATIONS

1 The class looks for articles in newspapers that it thinks provide only one perspective on a local or global issue. Students research alternative perspectives, and/or attempt to write an article that presents another point of view.

2 Students look for examples in different newspapers of an event that is reported from two very different viewpoints, and make a scrapbook or display of these.

3 They can also look for examples of articles that they feel represent balanced reporting of as many sides of an issue as possible, and make a scrapbook or display of these.

FOLLOW-UP

The class can write letters to local newspapers, commending them for balanced reporting, or encouraging them to include more diverse perspectives in their news coverage.

IN THE CURRICULUM

The activity involves listening comprehension, critical thinking, taking perspectives, and writing skills. It can be used in an English class to heighten awareness of point of view, or as a way of exploring controversial issues in humanities.

worksheet

Sample newspaper articles

VERSION 1

Vicious rioting took place last night in the Lakeview section of the city. Rock throwing youths confronted police officers, who attempted to calm the disturbance. After enduring an hour of hostilities, including shouted insults and threats to set fires, the police arrested five youths who seemed to be instigating the violence. The five are currently being held in custody while they await questioning. Leaders of the riot claim that the incident was triggered by an event earlier in the week, when a member of one of the local youth gangs was caught fleeing the scene of a suspected burglary, and was arrested. These leaders are demanding a public apology from the chief of police for the treatment of the youthful offender.

VERSION 2

Young people marched in the streets of the Lakeview section of the city last night to protest at the detention and beating of a 13-year-old boy. Youths chanted slogans calling for the release of the boy, and an end to police brutality. Police in riot gear attempted to confine the peaceful protest to a two block section of the city. When a rock was thrown by an unidentified protester, police threw tear gas at the young people, and dispersed them with clubs. Five of the demonstrators are being held without bail by the police. Community leaders say that because of the recent history of tension between the police and the young people, they fear for the safety of the five students who are being held. They report that outrage over the unjust arrest and mistreatment of the 13-year-old boy, who had been running to escape two men who attempted to rob him, has inflamed the residents of the neighbourhood.

Reporter's worksheet 1

Event: A group of armed citizens enters a town that is occupied by soldiers, and drives out the occupiers.

A Write an article about this event that presents the group of armed citizens as terrorists who are disrupting the peace.

What kind of reaction would this article produce in the reader?

What might be the motives of the person who wrote it?

B Write an article about the same event that presents the group of armed citizens as freedom fighters liberating the oppressed townspeople.

What kind of reaction would this article produce in the reader?

What might be the motives of the person who wrote it?

worksheet

worksheet

Reporter's worksheet 2

Event: A group of citizens temporarily halts the construction of a power plant and requests an environmental impact study.

A Write an article that presents the citizens as environmental fanatics who ignore the need for local economic development because they care more about wild animals.

What kind of reaction would this article produce in the reader?

What might be the motives of the person who wrote it?

B Write an article that presents the citizens as concerned about the long-term development of the community, who feel that human progress must maintain harmony with the natural environment.

What kind of reaction would this article produce in the reader?

What might be the motives of the person who wrote it?

Reporter's worksheet 3

Event: A study of literacy rates in a developing country indicates that 60 per cent of girls complete primary education.

A Write an article that expresses outrage over the fact that in the last decade of the 20th century, 40 per cent of the girls still are not receiving basic education.

What kind of reaction would this article produce in the reader?

What might be the motives of the person who wrote it?

B Write an article that shows that a 60 per cent literacy rate among girls represents a vast increase in the past ten years.

What kind of reaction would this article produce in the reader?

What might be the motives of the person who wrote it?

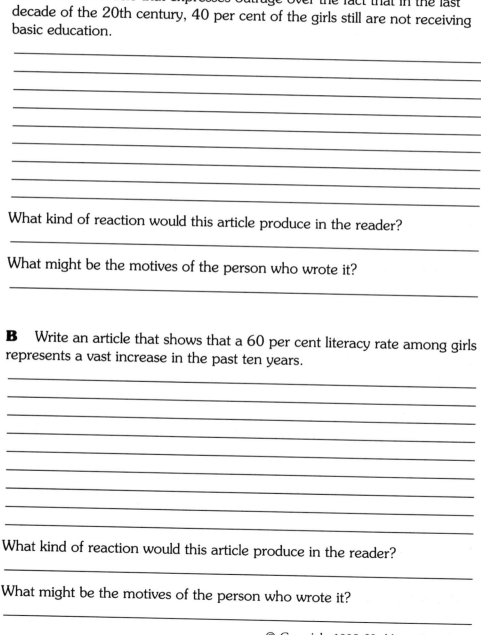

worksheet

Activity 24

The Tourists and the Touyats – a simulation

Age level 3: 16–18 years

OBJECTIVES

To simulate the clash of cultures which can occur when tourists visit developing countries (or *any* countries), bringing stereotypes about the local residents; to help young people become more aware of the potential for conflict and misunderstanding that such a situation creates.

MATERIALS

Paper and coloured pencils for both groups; copies of **Tourists – background information** and **Questions for Tourists** for one half of the class, and **Touyats – background information** and **Questions for Touyats** for the other half (pages 145–8).

PROCEDURE

Before beginning the simulation, an extra adult should be asked to help out, so that one adult can work with each group. If two adults are not available, one young person who is a strong leader should take responsibility for the Tourist group, while the teacher works with the Touyats. The role of the two leaders during the simulation is to remind students of the characteristics of their group, and to help group members to adhere to them. The leaders should familiarise themselves with the background information of *both* the Tourists and the Touyats before starting the simulation.

Step 1

The class is divided into two groups, with an equal number of girls and boys in each group. The groups meet in two separate rooms, for approximately 20 to 30 minutes, to familiarise themselves with their background material and to prepare their roles.

Step 2 (5 minutes)

Tourists and Touyats return to a common room, and take positions at opposite ends of the room. Tourists use their pencils and paper to make paper money; they can also make sample 'photographs' to show to the Touyats. Touyats use their pencils and paper to draw geometric designs which simulate cloth that they are weaving.

Step 3 (3 to 5 minutes)

One Tourist who has been previously selected goes to the Touyats' side of the room and attempts to make friends, show photographs, and buy cloth.

Step 4 (3 to 5 minutes)

The Tourist returns to her side of the room and reports to the other Tourists on what the experience was like. The Touyats discuss among themselves their impressions of the visitor.

Step 5 (3 to 5 minutes)

Two more Tourists go over to the Touyats' side and attempt to make friends, show photographs, and buy cloth.

Step 6 (3 to 5 minutes)

The two Tourists return to their side of the room, and report to the other Tourists what their experience was like. The Touyats discuss among themselves this latest contact with the Tourists.

Step 7 (10 minutes)

The leader of the Tourists reminds them that they will only be in this village for a short time before their bus comes to collect them. The leader urges them to make the most of their time and get to know some of the natives, get as many photographs as possible, and try to buy plenty of handicrafts to take home as souvenirs. The Tourists all go to the Touyats' side of the room and begin interacting simultaneously. The Touyats attempt to maintain their standards of behaviour.

Step 8

The teacher calls a halt to the simulation. The two groups sit in one circle to discuss the activity – Tourists and Touyats should sit with members of their own group. Points for discussion can include the following:

- How are the Tourists feeling right now? Why?
- How are the Touyats feeling right now? Why?
- What do the Tourists think about the Touyats?
- What do the Touyats think about the Tourists?
- For the Tourists: explain what the Touyats did or didn't do that caused problems.
- For the Touyats: explain what the Tourists did or didn't do that caused problems.
- For the Tourists: what could the Touyats have done to make your visit smoother?
- For the Touyats: what could the Tourists have done to make their visit less disruptive?
- For the Tourists: if you came back on a trip, what should you know or do in order to be less upsetting to the Touyats?

- For the Touyats: if more Tourists come in the future, what should you know or do in advance in order to be ready?

VARIATION

A small group prepares the simulation as a role play to be presented to the whole class.

FOLLOW-UP

1 The class reflects on tourism in its own country. What are some of the benefits of tourism for the students' country? What are the benefits for the tourists? What are some of the problems of tourism for the students' country? What are the problems for the tourists?

2 Students interview members of their community who have visited other countries to find out more about their experience of the meeting of different cultures.

IN THE CURRICULUM

The simulation develops perspective-taking and communication skills. It would be appropriate for a drama or English class, or a humanities class in which the interactions of two different cultures – due to trade, immigration or tourism – is being examined.

Tourists – background information

You are about to visit Touyatland! The information below will help you to make this special, once-in-a-lifetime trip an experience you will never forget!

Touyats are simple country people who live in small villages. They are very poor, and have no formal education system. They don't have any modern equipment such as televisions, cameras, or refrigerators, and use only simple hand tools. They don't speak any major world languages, so you will have to communicate with them by using sign language. They are hungry for contact with people from more advanced cultures, and after a while, they will be eager to get to know you. Be patient!

Bring your cameras and don't miss out on the opportunity to take photographs of these exotic people and their picturesque ways. Remember, as their country starts to become more developed, some of these old ways may be lost, so take photos of their quaint lifestyle before it disappears. Touyats may be shy at first around cameras, because they are unfamiliar with modern technology. If you bring sample photos to show them they will understand what being photographed is all about.

The one thing that the Touyats excel at is weaving cloth. They weave cloth with colourful geometric patterns which they use to make clothing, bed covers, and wall hangings. The Touyats are proud of their crafts; be sure to show your admiration of their clothing or weaving in progress.

There can be no more precious souvenir to take home with you than some samples of lovely Touyat cloth, shirts, skirts, or trousers. These can be purchased at bargain prices – the Touyats have a real need for currency from industrialised countries and should be happy to do business with you! Remember, native people love to haggle over prices. Don't be discouraged if your first offer for a piece of cloth or an item of clothing is refused – just keep trying, and offer a little more if you have to.

worksheet

worksheet

Questions for Tourists

Tourists should consider the following questions before visting the Touyats:

1 How can you try to make friends with the Touyats, who don't know your language?
(Use lots of sign language; be patient with them; keep trying.)

2 What are the two most important things to bring back from a visit to the Touyat tribe?
(Lots of photographs; Touyat cloth and items of clothing.)

3 How can you encourage Touyats to let you photograph them?
(Show them a sample photograph so that they will understand what you want; keep trying!)

4 How can you let the Touyats know that you like their clothing if they can't understand your language?
(Again, use lots of sign language: gestures and touching their clothing in an admiring way will show your appreciation.)

5 What should you do if you offer a Touyat some money for their cloth, and they refuse it?
(Remember, primitive people love to haggle and bargain. Keep offering the original amount; offer more only if the Touyat is particularly stubborn about refusing to sell you the cloth.)

> Note for the leader of the Tourists: After reviewing the **Background information** and **Questions**, ask for one volunteer who will make the first contact with the Touyat group, so as not to overwhelm them. Then ask for two additional volunteers to make the next contact. After this, the entire group of Tourists will visit the Touyats' village together. Remind them that they will not be able to use their language with the Touyats.

Touyats – background information

worksheet

You are members of the Touyat nation, an ancient and highly developed civilisation. You spin plant fibres into thread, through a complex process developed by Touyat scientists. This thread is woven into beautiful cloth which is famous worldwide. Touyats are proud of their skills as weavers. Your economy is based on trading this cloth. Touyats do not rely on money to trade with other countries. Rather, you exchange cloth directly for products which have value for you – food, tools, building materials, livestock, etc.

The barter system arises from your belief in the dignity of each individual. You show your respect for others by showing that you value the products they produce. Money is nothing but paper. Exchanging money does not show respect for another's work. Therefore, you trade goods directly. This system not only supplies you with everything you need, but prevents the problems that money brings (such as overpricing and theft).

You are quiet in public or with strangers. You feel that acting in a too familiar way with strangers indicates disrespect. If someone you don't know well tries to talk to you, you lower your eyes and turn your head away. You especially dislike casual conversation while you are working on your weaving – again, this indicates a disrespect for the seriousness of your work.

You are talkative, sociable, and physically affectionate with your family and friends. But physical contact of any kind between strangers is considered very rude. Touching another Touyat's weaving before it is finished is also rude. Weaving is a form of art which must be respected.

Because of your great respect for all people, you feel it is wrong to make representations of the human figure. To try to do so would be an insult to the individual. You do not have pictures of people on your walls or in your books, and your weaving contains only geometric designs.

Touyats are a close-knit group. In times of difficulty, they band together and make decisions as a group, rather than as isolated individuals.

In recent years, Tourists have visited your nation. You treat them with respect, but you do not forget the aspects of your culture that are important, such as the barter system, and the ban on images of the human figure. To show your respect for the Tourists, you have learned to say these words in their language: 'yes', 'no', 'hello', 'goodbye', 'please', 'thank you', 'shirt', 'skirt', 'trousers', 'camera'.

worksheet

Questions for Touyats

Touyats should consider the following questions before a visit from Tourists:

1 What is Touyat culture like?
(Ancient, highly developed, proud, sophisticated, scientific, wealthy, highly respectful of others.)

2 What is your economy like?
(Trade goods, but do not use money – this is considered insulting.)

3 What could you do if a Tourist offered you money?
(Refuse, walk away, consult with other Touyats, possibly even destroy it.)

4 How do you act with other Touyats?
(Warm, friendly, hugging; making important decisions as a group, not as individuals.)

5 How do you act with strangers?
(Respectful, reserved, quiet, don't have casual conversations – this would indicate disrespect; no physical contact.)

6 What could you do if a stranger tried to talk too much to you, or tried to touch you or your weaving?
(Lower your eyes and turn your head away, walk away, consult with other Touyats.)

7 What are your beliefs about making representations of the human figure?
(It is wrong, disrespectful.)

8 What could you do if someone brings a representation of the human figure into your culture?
(Lower your eyes and turn your head away, walk away, consult with other Touyats, take the picture and destroy it.)

9 What words can you say in Tourist languages?
('yes', 'no', 'hello', 'goodbye', 'please', 'thank you', 'shirt', 'skirt', 'trousers', 'camera'.)

> Note for the leader of the Touyats: After reviewing the **Background information** and **Questions**, show the group how to use the paper and coloured pencils to draw intricate geometric designs – these are meant to represent the weavings that they as Touyats will be working on.

Why teach about social justice?

All human beings, no matter where they live, have certain basic needs in common. These include the need for food, shelter, health care, affection, identity, education, and self-expression, to name but a few. Each individual is entitled, simply by the fact of being human, to have these needs met at the appropriate stage of their development.

But in industrialised and developing countries alike, there are too many instances of injustice, when these basic human needs are not met. Poverty is perhaps the most fundamental and widespread injustice, for it limits access to almost every other basic need, such as a reasonable standard of living, proper nutrition, medical treatment, a clean environment and fair employment. Similarly, discrimination interferes with the chances of individuals to develop to their full potential. This is equally true whether such discrimination is based on race, gender, class, religion, language, nationality, or physical ability.

Justice, then, is essential to development, not only of individuals but of communities and countries as well.

The denial of justice is closely linked to conflict issues in both industrialised and developing countries. Injustice, real or perceived, is one of the most common sources of conflict and violence between individuals, groups, and nations. And violent conflict in turn can perpetuate further injustice.

In view of the importance of justice to long-term global development, the growing international consensus on the need for teaching about justice is a promising sign. The 1989 *Convention on the Rights of the Child* states that education shall be directed to, among other things, 'the development of respect for human rights and fundamental freedoms'. The 1990 *World Declaration on Education for All* states that one of the reasons for meeting basic learning needs is to empower the individual 'to further the cause of social justice'.

But learning about social justice involves more than becoming familiar with certain legal texts, and absorbing abstract concepts of rights. It requires that students see the relevance of justice issues to their own lives and immediate environment – home, school or community. It demands that they move beyond reactions of guilt, blame, or resentment and instead make an active commitment to promoting justice and equality on all levels, whether personal, institutional, national or global.

Some key concepts

RIGHTS

Central to the issue of social justice is the concept of human rights. Rights may be defined as those things – both material and non-material – which one is, in fairness, entitled to have or to do. Human rights are sometimes thought of in terms of *freedom from* and *freedom to.*

Freedom from

All people have the right to protection from obvious forms of injustice, such as violence, exploitation, abuse, and torture. They also have a right to have their basic survival needs met, to be free from the more subtle injustices of poverty, hunger, lack of health care, and environmental pollution. It is essential that children are aware that such injustices occur not only in developing countries, but in the wealthier nations as well.

Freedom to

Everyone has the right to participate in those human activities which allow one to develop fully, such as education, the practice of one's religion, culture, and language, the freedom to express opinions, to be part of associations and to have access to information.

RESPONSIBILITIES

With every right come responsibilities. A person who desires the right to health, for example, cannot at the same time mistreat his body with illegal drugs. Perhaps the broadest responsibility borne by each person who wishes to have her rights respected, is the responsibility to uphold and promote others' rights, to ensure that justice is available to *all* members of society.

MAJOR DOCUMENTS

Three documents on justice issues are especially important for teachers and students. The ground-breaking 1948 *Universal Declaration of Human Rights* set forth a list of basic human rights to be observed worldwide. In 1959, the United Nations *Declaration on the Rights of the Child* focused on ten clauses which particularly have to do with the welfare of children. In 1989, the *Convention on the Rights of the Child* went even further in establishing global recognition of children as a group of persons entitled to special rights. Its 54 articles detail rights relating to the survival, development, protection and participation of children. The Convention is legally binding, and has been ratified by over 150 countries.

A number of activities in this chapter refer to the *Convention on the Rights of the Child*. To obtain copies, contact the UNICEF office or National Committee in your country.

Teaching about social justice: Aims and objectives

Knowledge	*Skills*	*Attitudes*
• Knowledge of widely accepted principles of human rights and justice (such as those contained in the *Convention on the Rights of the Child*). • Understanding that personal, institutional and societal behaviours, attitudes and structures can have the effect of either promoting or denying social justice. • Knowledge of current situations in which human rights are not recognised and social justice is not available to all, both locally and globally. • Understanding that along with rights come responsibilities.	• Being able to apply ideals such as freedom, equality and respect for diversity in the classroom and in the learners' daily lives, as well as seeing them in the global context. • Skills of being an effective advocate for the rights of oneself and others (including discussion, negotiation and assertiveness). • Ability to take responsibility for one's own actions.	• Empathy with those who have been denied justice. • Willingness to take constructive and realistic action on the part of others. • Commitment not only to defending one's rights, but to accepting and fulfilling one's responsibilities as well.

Age level 1:
7–11 years

Activity 25

What's fair?

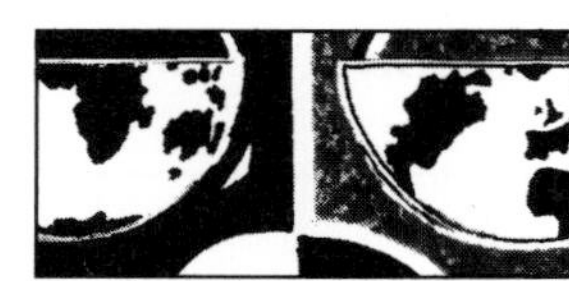

OBJECTIVES

To help students clarify their ideas about what is 'fair' and what is 'unfair', as a way of introducing the ideas of justice and injustice.

MATERIALS

For each pair of students: a set of four **What's fair?** situations (on pages 154 and 155), scissors, large paper with columns headed **Fair**, **Unfair** and **Not Sure**, glue.

PROCEDURE

Step 1

Working in pairs, the students read through their four **What's fair?** situations. They cut the situations into separate strips and sort them into three categories: those in which they think the student is being treated fairly, those in which they think the student is being treated unfairly, and those they are not sure about.

Step 2

When this is done, each pair joins with another pair that had four *different* **What's fair?** situations. As a group of four, they discuss their opinions about each of the situations. When they have reached a consensus as to whether a situation is fair or unfair to the child involved, they glue it onto the large paper under the heading **Fair** or **Unfair**.

Step 3

The whole class then discusses the activity:

- What kinds of situations were described as fair? Why?
- What kinds of situations were described as unfair? Why?
- Were some situations difficult to decide upon? Why?

VARIATIONS

1 The activity can be done using photos instead of the situations.

2 Younger students may be given only one situation per pair. They decide if it is fair or unfair. The whole class then makes one large chart to show how the situations were classified.

FOLLOW-UP

1 Each pair of students selects one of the unfair situations, and uses it as the beginning of a story. They complete the story in such a way that the ending is fair to the student.

2 Students discuss how families, schools, groups, the community, and the nation prevent unfair occurrences from happening. Some possible ways might include having rules or forming laws.

IN THE CURRICULUM

The activity involves reading, analysing, categorising, decision-making. By using situations derived from literature or historical events, it could be linked with English or humanities.

worksheet

'What's fair?' situations (1)

1 Gina wants to play football with a group of boys at break time, but they won't let her play because she is a girl. Is this fair to Gina?

2 Saleema's grandfather gave her some money for her birthday. Saleema wants to use it to buy sweets. Her parents say that she cannot, because that would be bad for her health. Is this fair to Saleema?

3 Ali is ten years old, and likes to go to school. But his family needs him to get a job to earn some money, because there are younger children to feed. So Ali does not get to finish primary school. Is this fair to Ali?

4 Marta comes to school without having done her homework. The teacher makes her stay indoors at break time to do it. Is this fair to Marta?

'What's fair?' situations (2)

5 Lee lives in a country which is at war. It is dangerous to travel. He cannot go to the health clinic to get his immunisation shots. Is this fair to Lee?

6 Chris doesn't like school, and wants to leave. His parents say he can't leave because he is only ten years old. Is this fair to Chris?

7 Rose and Tahira have come to live in a new country, and are learning to speak a new language. Sometimes in school, they speak their home language. The teacher makes them stop, and says that they must learn to speak like everyone else in the school. Is this fair to Rose and Tahira?

8 George, who is white, tells a joke about black people. The teacher tells George that he must stop, that saying cruel things about people of another race is not allowed in this school. Is this fair to George?

Activity 26 The toy contest

OBJECTIVES

To give students a simulated experience of injustice; to help them understand the range of reactions people may have to incidents of injustice.

MATERIALS

Art materials for each group of four as described in the **Procedure** section.

PROCEDURE

Step 1

The students are divided into groups of four. Their task is to use the art materials they will be given to design the best toy they can; if possible, it should be one that really works.

The small groups receive art materials as follows:

Small groups 1 and 2 – A large sheet of sugar paper and four pencils for each small group.

Small groups 3 and 4 – A large sheet of sugar paper, four pencils, two erasers, and one set of coloured pencils for each small group.

Small group 5 – A large sheet of sugar paper, four pencils, two erasers, one set of coloured pencils, four sheets of coloured paper (different colours), two pairs of scissors, glue.

Small group 6 – A large sheet of sugar paper, four pencils, two erasers, one set of coloured pencils, four sheets of coloured paper (different colours), four pairs of scissors, glue, four sheets of coloured card (different colours), craft sticks, toothpicks, a ruler, a hole punch, a length of wire, glitter.

> The materials used may vary according to what the teacher has available; however, it is important that the distribution of materials is unequal, with one small group being particularly favoured over the others. If it is necessary to have more than six small groups, additional groups can be given the same materials as groups 3 and 4.

Step 2

After the students have worked for ten to 15 minutes, the teacher should announce that they have ten minutes remaining to work, and that when all the toys have been designed, a contest will be held to select the best one.

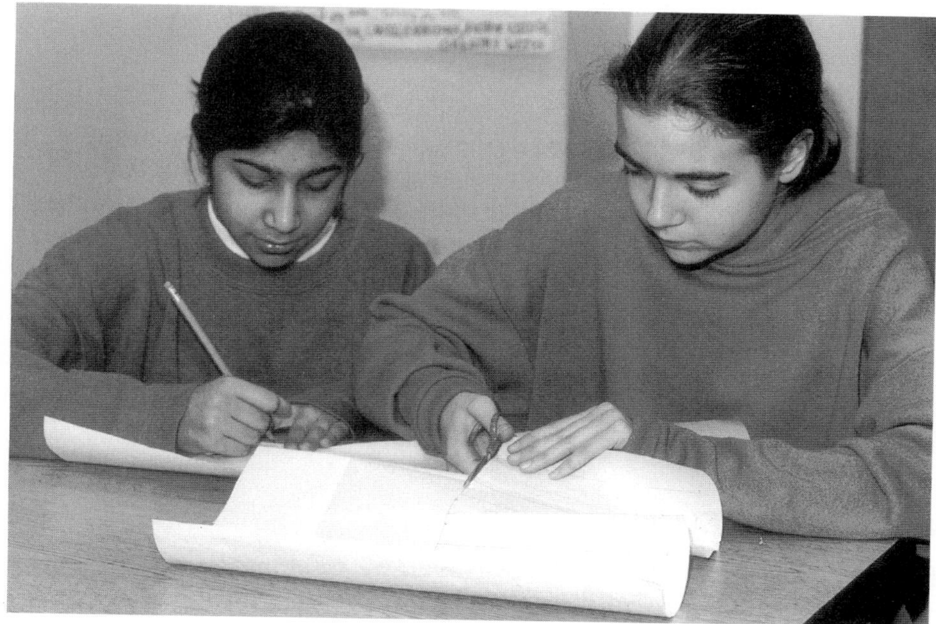

Designing a toy with limited resources

If students object to the unfair distribution of materials, they can be told that the class will discuss this later, and to try to do their best with what they have.

Step 3

At the end of the work period, the small groups come together. One member of each small group shows the toy that the group designed.

Step 4

The teacher then invites discussion of the results. The following points should be raised:

- How did you feel when you realised that the small groups had different materials?
- How did it feel to be in a group that had lots of materials? How would you have felt if you had been in one of the other groups?
- How did it feel to be in a group that had few materials?
- Did any small groups try to do something about the inequality? If so, what? Was this effective?
- What would have been a fair way to distribute the materials?

- Would it be fair to hold a contest and give prizes when the students had different materials to begin with? Why or why not?

If strong feelings have been raised by this activity, it may be necessary actually to redistribute the supplies, and allow each small group an equal opportunity to create their invention.

VARIATION

The task may be varied according to the age and interests of the group so that students must create their ideal house, a school they would like to attend, an invention that would make the world a better place, or a poster promoting world peace, etc., rather than a toy.

FOLLOW-UP

Encourage the students to discuss situations in real life in which people have different resources (money, clothing, shelter, access to health care, food), and yet are judged by the same standards. Is this just?

IN THE CURRICULUM

The activity requires imagination and divergent thinking, group decision-making and problem-solving. It could be incorporated into an art class, or a science lesson on inventions.

Activity 27

The obstacle course

OBJECTIVES

To help students understand the inequality that arises when some people receive privileges which others do not; to enable them to see that not everyone will reach the same goals when opportunities are unequal.

Age level 1: 7–11 years

MATERIALS

Four benches of the same size; one long piece of rope; copies of the **Instructions for teams** cards (on page 161).

PROCEDURE

Step 1

The class is divided into four teams of equal size; the teams should be equal in terms of athletic ability.

Prior to the activity, the teacher should prepare an obstacle course in the gymnasium (or on the playground) as follows: the one long piece of rope should be placed at right angles to the direction in which the students will run, at a location one-third of the way between the starting line and the opposite wall. A bench for each team should be placed two-thirds of the way between the starting line and the opposite wall:

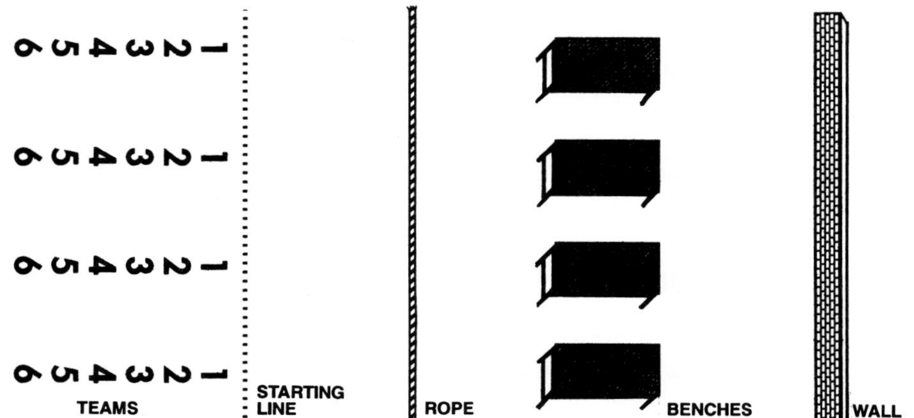

The obstacle course

Step 2

Each team is given one of the **Instructions for teams** cards. Team members read their card together and make sure that they understand how to run the race. They should not look at any of the other teams' instructions, or be told that the cards are different.

Step 3

At a signal from the adult, the students run the obstacle course as a relay race.

Step 4

When all teams have finished, the class as a whole discusses the results:

- Which team finished first? Why?
- Which team finished last? Why?
- Was the race fair?
- How did it feel to be in the team that had the advantage? How did it feel to be in the team that had the disadvantage?
- What could be done to make this race fair?

The class may choose to repeat the race, so that each team has the chance to experience both advantage and disadvantage.

VARIATIONS

The obstacle course can be made longer, or different types of obstacles used, depending upon what equipment is available. **Instructions for teams** cards can be rewritten accordingly. Regardless of what types of objects are used, the teacher should ensure that each team has different instructions, with one team being placed at an advantage, and one team placed at a particular disadvantage.

FOLLOW-UP

Students discuss or write about real life situations in which people must compete despite the fact that some have received advantages or disadvantages (obstacles) which place them on an unequal footing. These may be due to race, gender, physical ability, language, social class, etc. They may occur in the school, in the larger community, or on a national or global level.

IN THE CURRICULUM

The activity uses skills in following directions, comparing and analysing, anticipating outcomes and drawing analogies. It is suitable for a physical education lesson.

The obstacle course: Instructions for teams

worksheet

Team 1

In turn:
Jump over the rope.
Jump over the bench.
Touch the wall.
Jump over the bench.
Jump over the rope.
Touch the next person in line.

Team 2

In turn:
Jump over the rope.
Run around the bench once.
Touch the wall.
Run around the bench once.
Jump over the rope.
Touch the next person in line.

Team 3

In turn:
Jump over the rope.
Run around the bench twice.
Touch the opposite wall.
Run around the bench twice.
Jump over the rope.
Touch the next person in line.

Team 4

In turn:
Lift up the rope and crawl under it.
Run around the bench three times.
Touch the wall.
Run around the bench three times.
Lift up the rope and crawl under it.
Touch the next person in line.

Activity 28

A journey to a new planet

Age level 1: 7–11 years

OBJECTIVES

To help students differentiate between things that they want, and things that they need; to introduce the idea that people's basic needs are considered rights.

MATERIALS

A set of 20 **Wants and needs cards** (pages 164–5) for each pair of students, pencils.

PROCEDURE

Step 1

The students form pairs, and each pair is given a set of **Wants and needs cards**, cut into individual cards.

Step 2

The students are told that they have been chosen to go and live on a new planet. Since they will be setting up a new society there, Mission Control wants them to have all the things they need and want in order to live and grow. Mission Control has made a list of 16 things it thinks the students should take with them. The students are allowed to bring four more that they choose. They draw these four items onto the four blank **Wants and needs cards**.

Step 3

Announce to the group that because space is limited on the spaceship, students can take only 14 items, instead of all 20. They must decide on six items to eliminate. They can draw an X through these, place them in an envelope, or give them back to the teacher.

Step 4

Inform the students that Mission Control has found that there is still less available space than they had realized. Students will only be able to take eight items with them, instead of 14. Have them eliminate six more items, leaving only the eight that they consider most essential for their survival.

Step 5

Discuss the following questions with the entire class:

- Which items were most commonly eliminated in the first round? Why?
- Was the second round of eliminations more difficult than the first? Why?
- Did you and your partner have any disagreements over the items to eliminate? Which ones, and why?
- What is the difference between wants and needs? Which items on the list were wants, and which ones were needs?
- What are some of the things you want in real life? What are some of the things you need?
- Do you have everything you want? Do you have everything you need? Why or why not?
- Do wants and needs differ for different people? Why or why not?
- Do all people in your country have everything that they need? What about people in other countries?

Explain to the group that people's most basic needs – to survive, develop, be safe, and participate in their communities – are often referred to as *rights*. Rights can be thought of as those things that it is fair and just for all people to have, or to be able to do.

VARIATION

With younger children, the number of cards can be reduced.

FOLLOW-UP

1 Ask students to come up with their own definition of rights.

2 Have them make a list of rights that they think are basic for people of their age, using the **Wants and needs cards** as a starting-point. Encourage students to think about non-material needs – such as the right to express their opinions – as well as material needs. Would their list be similar to or different from a list drawn up by a class in another country?

3 Have students compare their own lists of rights with the articles of the *Convention on the Rights of the Child.*

IN THE CURRICULUM

The activity involves imagining, anticipating consequences, prioritising and negotiation skills. It can be used as part of an English or science class.

worksheet

Wants and needs cards (1)

Healthy food	A personal stereo
Books that will teach you what you need to know	Toys
Nice clothes	Medical supplies
The opportunity to practise your own religion	Sweets
A computer of your own	Clean water

Wants and needs cards (2)

worksheet

Videos and a VCR 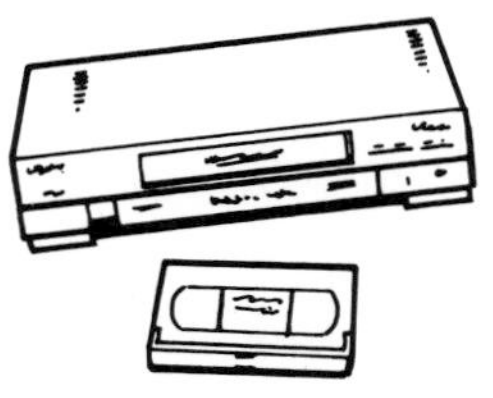	Someone who will love and care for you 
Friends 	Materials you need to build shelter 
Money 	The chance to say what you think is important and be listened to 

Age level 2:
12–15 years

Activity 29

Rights and responsibilities

OBJECTIVES

To help students see the link between rights and responsibilities in their immediate environment.

MATERIALS

Blank index cards (or slips of paper) of two different colours; pencils.

PROCEDURE

Step 1

The students form groups of four. Each small group is given a number of blank index cards or slips of paper (all of one colour). The students write down all the rights they think they have, one right per card.

If students have difficulty in deciding what their rights are, the teacher may suggest some of the rights covered in the *Convention on the Rights of the Child*.

Step 2

The teacher then explains that with every right come certain responsibilities:

- Adults who have the right to vote, for example, have the responsibility to use their vote to express their opinions in elections.
- Persons who have the right to drive a car also have the responsibility to do so safely and obey traffic laws.
- Students who feel they have the right to be listened to also have the responsibility to listen to adults and other students.

Once the students grasp the idea of responsibilities being linked to rights, the teacher distributes cards or slips of paper of the contrasting colour. The students write down one responsibility to go with each right that they have thought of.

Step 3

Each group of four mixes up its set of rights and responsibilities cards, and exchanges the entire set with those of another small group. Students then work together to match the rights and responsibilities on this new set of cards. When they feel they have completed the task, they ask the other small group to check their work.

Step 4

As a class, the students discuss the activity:

- Did any small groups list rights you hadn't thought of?
- Was it easy or difficult to think of what responsibilities go with different rights?
- Do you think most of the rules in schools, home or the community exist to protect students' rights, or to ensure that they fulfil their responsibilities (or is there a balance between the two)?

VARIATION

Students list the rights they think they *should* have, and then list the responsibilities that those rights would entail. Are there any rights they feel they should have which are denied to them? Why might this be so?

FOLLOW-UP

1 Students consider times when they feel rights and responsibilities have come into conflict; they write a story about this, or illustrate it as a comic strip.

2 Students discuss rights that adults have in their community or nation, and responsibilities that go along with those rights.

3 The class examines the *Convention on the Rights of the Child*, and thinks of responsibilities that relate to each of the articles.

IN THE CURRICULUM

The activity requires seeing relationships, making associations and anticipating consequences. It could be used in a humanities class.

Activity 30 The vocabulary quiz

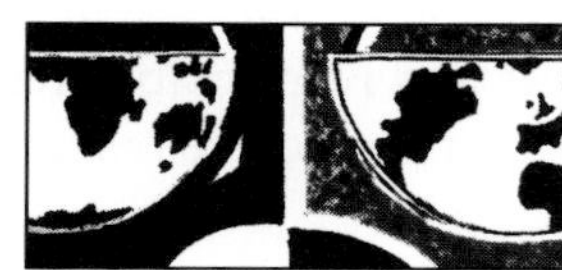

Age level 2: 12–15 years

OBJECTIVES

To enable students to understand that injustice – in this case, unfairly distributed educational resources – can place certain groups at a disadvantage in attempting to succeed in society; to explore possible responses to injustice.

MATERIALS

A **Vocabulary Words** list for each student (page 172; these words are taken from articles 28 and 29 of the *Convention on the Rights of the Child*; any other words may be substituted, according to the level of the class); one sheet of paper, a pencil, and a dictionary for each student.

PROCEDURE

Step 1

Students use chalk or tape to mark a rectangle on the floor of the room equal to one-eighth of its area. (This can be quickly done by measuring off a rectangle whose length is one-half the width of the room, and whose width is one-quarter the length of the room.)

Step 2 (Optional)

Students move one-eighth of the total number of desks and chairs into the area which is one-eighth of the floorspace, and leave the rest in the larger area.

Step 3

The students then distribute the vocabulary lists, paper, pencils, and dictionaries so that one-eighth of them are in the smaller space, and the rest are in the larger space.

Step 4

The class then divides into two groups, with one-eighth of the students in one group and seven-eighths of the students in the other. The *smaller* group of students is told to take seats in the *larger* area of the room. The *larger* group takes seats in the *smaller* area of the room.

In a class of 32 students, for example:

4 students would have:
- 7/8 of the floorspace
- 7/8 of the desks and chairs
- 28 vocabulary lists
- 28 dictionaries
- 28 sheets of paper
- 28 pencils

. . . while 28 students would have:
- 1/8 of the floorspace
- 1/8 of the desks and chairs
- 4 vocabulary lists
- 4 dictionaries
- 4 sheets of paper
- 4 pencils.

Step 5

The students are told that they will now take a vocabulary quiz. They must look up the words on their lists in the dictionaries, and write the definitions on a *separate* piece of paper. Each student must turn in her *own* word list.

Students are told that if they score 80 per cent or better on the quiz, they will be given a privilege, such as being allowed to have extra break time, go to the library to read, etc. Those who score under 80 per cent will be required to stay indoors at break to continue working on the quiz.

The students can then be given ten to 20 minutes, depending on their skill level, to complete the quiz.

While they are working, the teacher can give attention to the smaller group, while giving as little as possible to the larger group. Any objections should be ignored or dismissed by saying something such as 'Do the best you can with the materials you have', or 'This is how it's going to be for this lesson'.

Students from the larger group should be forbidden to leave their assigned area, or take materials from the smaller group.

Step 6

When time is up, the teacher collects the students' papers and quickly checks them. In all likelihood, all of the students in the smaller group will have passed, while few, if any, in the larger group will have correctly completed 80 per cent of the definitions. The teacher announces which students will receive the privileges, and which will have to stay indoors during recess.

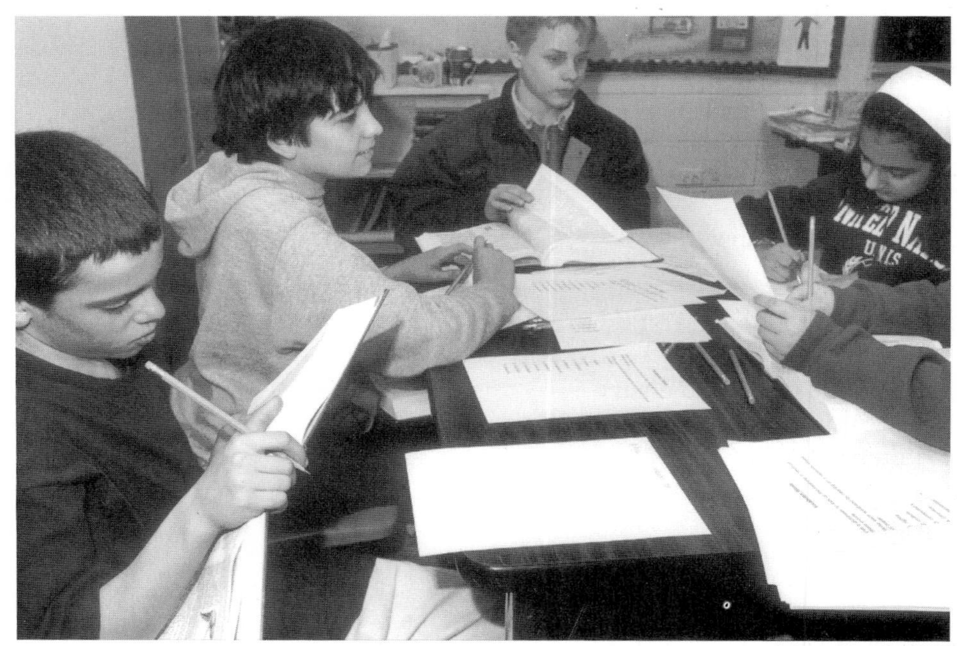

When educational resources are unfairly distributed . . .

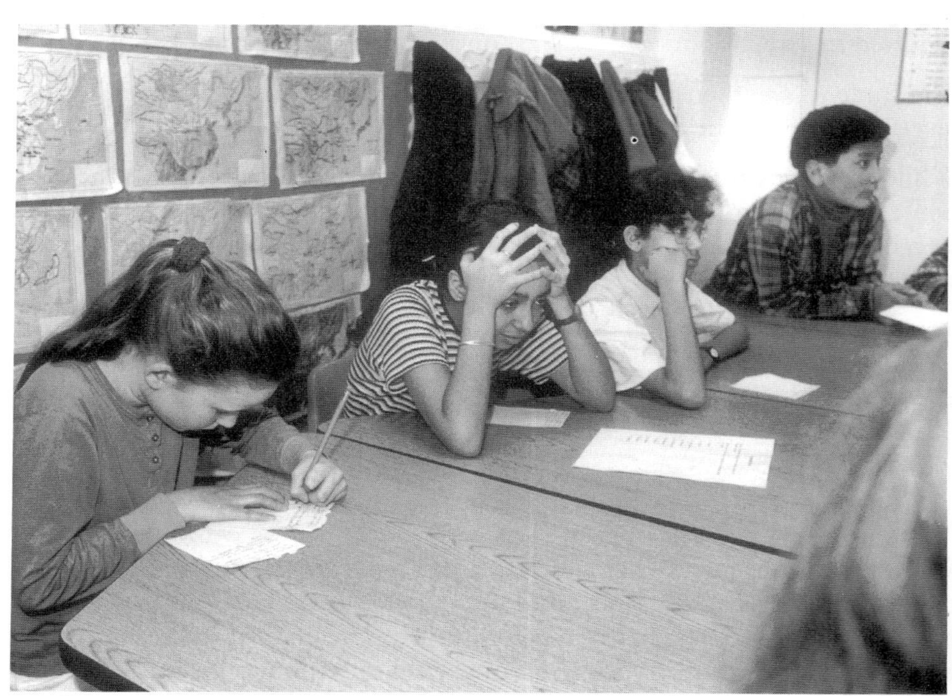

. . . does everyone have an equal chance to succeed?

Step 7

At this point, the students will have strong feelings about the activity that they will want to express. The teacher should explain that this has been a simulation, and that neither group will be receiving a privilege or a punishment. The following questions can then be discussed:

- How did the larger group feel during the activity? Why?
- What strategies did the larger group use to attempt to complete the quiz?
- How did the smaller group feel during the activity? Why?
- Did anyone in the smaller group attempt to do anything about the unjust situation? Why or why not?
- Did anyone in the larger group attempt to do anything about the unjust situation? Why or why not?
- How would the distribution of resources have interfered with school success for the larger group, both in the short-term and in the longer term?
- How would the distribution of resources have placed the smaller group at an advantage, both in the short-term and in the longer term?

At some point in the discussion, the teacher may wish to let the students know that this simulation is based loosely on statistics on South Africa under apartheid laws in the mid-1980s. At that time, whites made up 15 per cent of the population. The per capita school expenditure for black South African schoolchildren was approximately one-eighth the amount spent on white students.

VARIATION

Any subject matter can be substituted for the vocabulary quiz, as long as it involves the use of resources which can be unfairly distributed.

FOLLOW-UP

1 Students can use this activity as a basis for researching the effects of apartheid on black South Africans.

2 They may also wish to explore how funds for education are allocated on a local or national level in their own country. Is the allocation equal? If not, what groups are potentially disadvantaged by the present system? What might the long term impacts of this be?

IN THE CURRICULUM

The activity requires skills in mathematics, decision-making and anticipation of consequences. While it might logically be used in a humanities class on the treatment of minority groups, it could also be incorporated into a mathematics lesson.

worksheet

Vocabulary words

Use a dictionary to look up the meaning of each of these words. Write each word and its meaning on a separate sheet of paper.

1 rights
2 culture
3 compulsory
4 illiteracy
5 fundamental
6 tolerance
7 construe
8 accessible
9 discipline
10 potential

Activity 31

Linking rights

OBJECTIVES

To introduce students to the *Convention on the Rights of the Child*; to help them see the links between various justice issues, and how they affect the lives of real children; to encourage thinking about the consequences of rights denials; to introduce the idea that rights denials can occur in any part of the world.

Age level 2: 12–15 years

MATERIALS

For Step 1

Eight cards summarising selected articles from the *Convention on the Rights of the Child* (pages 176–7). Eight **Children from around the World** cards, each describing a violation of the corresponding right from the Convention (pages 178–9).

For Step 2

Eight extra copies of each card with an article from the Convention on it.

PROCEDURE

Step 1

The students form pairs. Each pair receives either a) a card on which is written a summary of an article from the *Convention on the Rights of the Child*, or b) a **Children from around the World** card, with a child's story illustrating a violation of one of those rights. (If the class size is under 32, some students may be asked to work on their own.)

Step 2

The pairs move around the room together, reading each others' cards. When they match an article from the Convention with its corresponding story, they form a group of four.

Step 3

Once groups of four are formed, the pair holding the card with the article from the Convention sits down. They are given eight additional copies of the article from the Convention that they are holding.

Step 4

The other two people, who represent the child, walk around to each seated pair in the room, and discuss with them whether there is any sort of link between the child's story and the other articles of the Convention. (See the example in the box below.)

Each time a link between a child's story and another article of the Convention is established, the seated pair gives a copy of that article to the pair representing the child.

Step 5

Once all possible links have been established, the class discusses the types of links that were found.

AN EXAMPLE OF LINKS BETWEEN RIGHTS

In this activity, one child's story reads:

Because my family lived so far from the health centre when I was a young child, I was never vaccinated. Now I am eight years old, and I have polio.

This story illustrates article 24 of the Convention, the child's right to the highest possible standard of health, and to access to health and medical services.

In negotiating with other class members, links between this story and the following articles might be found:

Article 28, the right to education: because if the child does not receive adequate health care, his or her ability to take full advantage of educational opportunities may be impaired.

Article 32, the right to be protected from economic exploitation: because if a child has to work at an early age, he or she may be unable to get to a clinic for treatment, and may be exposed to situations which threaten the child's health.

VARIATIONS

1 Use other rights from the *Convention on the Rights of the Child*. Students could write their own **Children from around the World** cards.

2 The students write stories which demonstrate ways in which children's rights have been upheld, rather than denied, and carry out the activity using these.

FOLLOW-UP

1 Students discuss ways in which these basic rights have been upheld or denied in their own lives.

2 They use newspaper and magazine articles to find local and global examples of violations of children's rights, as well as steps that are being taken to protect them.

IN THE CURRICULUM

The activity involves reading and thinking analytically, seeing relationships, understanding consequences and developing empathy and concern for others. It could be used in a history or geography class, or in an interdisciplinary study of human rights. It could also be used as a basis for a creative writing assignment; students could be asked to extend further their ideas about the effects on the imaginary students of a particular rights denial, and develop them into a story.

Selected articles from the Convention on the Rights of the Child (1)

Article 24
Children have the right to the highest possible standard of health, and access to health and medical services.

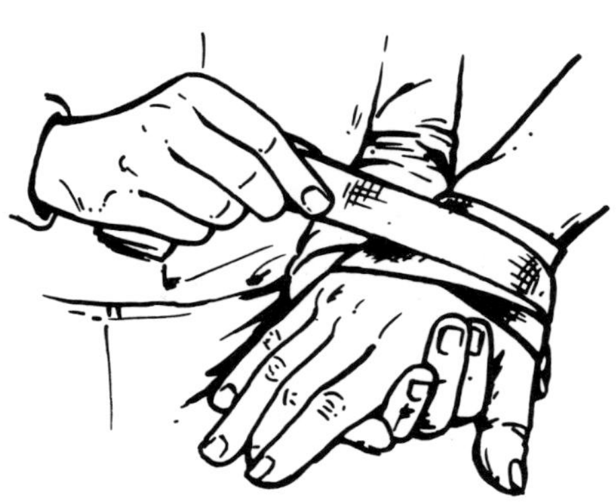

Article 30
Children have the right, if members of a minority group, to practise their own culture, religion, and language.

Article 27
Children have the right to a standard of living adequate for their physical, mental, spiritual, moral and social development.

Article 28
Children have the right to education.

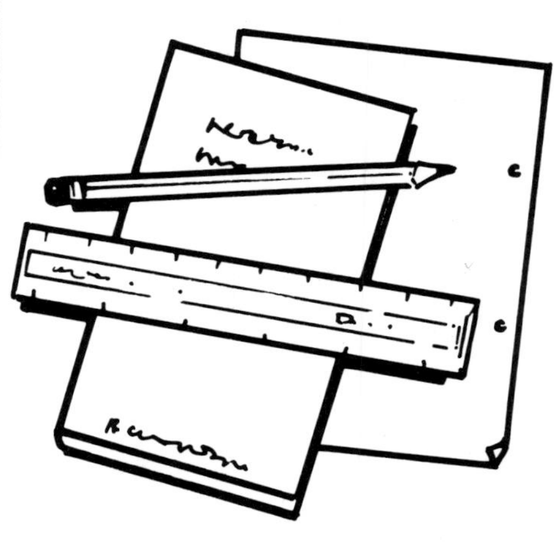

Selected articles from the
Convention on the Rights of the Child (2)

Article 31
Children have the right to rest, leisure, play, and participation in cultural and artistic activities.

Article 33
Children have the right to protection from the use of drugs, and from being involved in their production or distribution.

Article 32
Children have the right to be protected from economic exploitation, from having to participate in work that threatens their health, education, or development.

Article 38
Children have the right, if under the age of 15, to protection from taking part in armed conflict.

worksheet

worksheet

Children from around the World cards (1)

Because my family lived so far from the health centre when I was a young child, I was never vaccinated. Now I am eight years old and I have polio.

My brothers go to the local school, but I am the only daughter, and my family needs me to help out with work in our home. So I cannot go to school. I am seven years old.

I am 11 years old, and I go to school every day. When I get home, I help in my parents' shop until the evening. Then I eat dinner, and wash the dishes, and look after my younger brother and sister while my parents finish their work in the shop. After the younger children go to sleep, I try to do my homework, but usually I am too tired and I just fall asleep.

I am six years old and my family doesn't have much money. We live in two small rooms; we have to carry our water from a well a kilometre away. The houses in our village don't have indoor toilets, so we use a pit in the ground at the end of our street.

Children from around the World cards (2)

worksheet

I am 13 years old, and my country has been fighting over a boundary with another country for three years. A captain from the army came to my home to tell me that because I am so big and strong, I should join the army and fight for my country.

I am ten years old, and I speak the language that my parents and grandparents and all my family have always spoken. In the local school, none of the teachers speaks my language, and they don't allow me to speak it either – they say we must all learn how to speak *their* language.

I am 12 years old and I started to work at a farm picking fruit in the summer when I was nine years old. Now the owner of the farm wants me to work there every day, all year long. The money I would earn would help my family buy a little extra food.

I am 15 years old and I live in a big city. A man on my street told me I could make a lot of money if I would help him sell a drug called crack. He let me try some, and now I buy it from him all the time.

Activity 32

Rules for justice

Age level 2: 12–15 years

OBJECTIVES

To help students think specifically about injustices that could occur in their school, and to consider changes that will lead to greater equality.

MATERIALS

Paper, pencils and copies of one of the cards from the **Think of a rule . . .** sheet (page 182) for each group.

PROCEDURE

Step 1

Students form groups of four. They are told that they will be drawing up a list of rules for an ideal school, one in which everyone is treated fairly and equally.

Each small group is given *one* of the cards from the **Think of a rule . . .** sheet, and asked to devise some rules that will ensure that the statement on their card will be true.

Students should be urged to think creatively, and not to limit themselves to ideas that they judge to be practical at this stage. They can be encouraged to think not only of rules or practices that *prohibit* certain types of behaviour, but ones which *encourage* certain behaviours as well.

Step 2

Once the lists are completed, they are read aloud to the class, and suggestions from other students may be added.

Step 3

As a class, students then classify the rules as follows:

- ones they think they could carry out themselves, and would be willing to adopt as class rules;
- ones they think could be carried out with the cooperation of other people (either students or adults in the school or community);
- ones they think could not be carried out, or are not good rules to have.

Step 4

Students return to their small groups, and select one of the rules which would require the cooperation of others in order to be effective. Together they devise a plan for how they would go about informing others of the need for this rule, and encouraging their participation. Plans might involve letter-writing, presentations at assemblies, articles in the school or local newspaper, or meeting with significant individuals or groups. The teacher should be prepared to enable the students actually to carry out these plans.

When people are bullying other people in the playground, they should have to do something to help other people in the school. They could help younger children in their classes, or they ~~should~~ could do some cleaning.

Rules for justice

VARIATIONS

1 Students examine existing school rules and discuss how they promote fairness and equality. Are there any rules whose effect is to create injustice or inequality?

2 After making the list of ideal rules, students make a list of the responsibilities they would have in relation to each rule.

FOLLOW-UP

A teacher reads summaries of the articles of the *Convention on the Rights of the Child* (available from UNICEF) to the class. Which items on the students' list of rules are similar to articles of the Convention?

IN THE CURRICULUM

The activity requires discussion, negotiation, classification, anticipation of consequences and planning skills. It could be used in a humanities class as a way of introducing the function of laws or the *Convention on the Rights of the Child*.

worksheet

Think of a rule . . .

Think of a rule that will allow all students to feel safe and protected from all kinds of dangers.

Think of a rule that will allow all students to feel that they are respected and valued.

Think of a rule that will allow all students to have an equal chance to take part in everything that goes on in the school.

Think of a rule that will allow all students to have the same amount of the resources and materials that they need (supplies, clothing, food, etc.), and ensure that these materials will be of the same quality.

Think of a rule that will allow all students to have an equal chance to learn and to succeed.

Activity 33 Perspectives on justice

OBJECTIVES

To help young people understand that there may be differing perspectives on justice issues; to explore the relationship between rights and responsibilities with regard to two particular issues: freedom of speech and child labour.

MATERIALS

Copies of the **Perspective A** and **Perspective B** sheets (pages 185–6) for *one* of the rights issues; blank paper and pencils.

PROCEDURE

Step 1

The teacher chooses *one* of the rights issues to focus on, either freedom of speech or child labour.

Step 2

Students divide into groups of four to six. Within these small groups, two or three members are given the **Perspective A** sheet. They meet together to prepare as many arguments as they can in support of the statement on their sheet.

The other two or three group members are given the **Perspective B** sheet. They also meet to prepare their position, justifying the statement on their sheet.

Step 3

After these sub-groups have prepared their positions, they come back together to meet as the original group of four to six students. The As spend five to ten minutes presenting their point of view to the Bs, who should listen carefully and take notes. The Bs then present their point of view while the As listen. The presentations can be followed by five to ten minutes in which members of either sub-group ask each other questions.

Step 4

The teacher then announces that the As and Bs are to change roles (they should *not* be informed of this part of the activity in advance). They are given a few minutes to rethink their arguments.

Step 5

Then the As present what was formerly the Bs' perspective, followed by the Bs presenting what was formerly the As' perspective.

Step 6

When both sides have finished, they work together to attempt to write a consensus statement on the issue debated.

Step 7

The consensus statements are read aloud to the whole class and discussed. Questions to consider might include:

- What difficulties were encountered in trying to write the consensus statement? Is it possible to reach a consensus on this issue?
- Did reversing roles make it easier or more difficult to write the consensus statement? Why?
- What instances do you know of in your community, nation, or the world in which the freedom of speech issue (or child labour) is the subject of controversy?
- How do responsibilities and rights interact? Do some responsibilities by their nature impose limits on certain rights?

VARIATION

The format of this activity can be used to explore other justice issues on which there might be opposing perspectives: for example, the right to freedom of association versus the responsibility to restrict the actions of organisations which might violate the rights of others.

FOLLOW-UP

Students collect stories from newspapers, radio or television which describe situations in which perspectives on rights are in conflict, or in which rights and responsibilities are in conflict.

IN THE CURRICULUM

The activity involves the skills of preparing and presenting positions, listening, critical thinking, taking alternative perspectives, negotiation and consensus-building. It can be used in a humanities or English class.

Perspectives on freedom of speech

PERSPECTIVE A: FREEDOM OF SPEECH

In a just society, freedom of speech is one of the most basic human rights, and should not be limited.

Consider such points as:

- the negative effects of censorship;
- the political implications of limited free speech and dissent;
- the conditions in other countries where free speech is limited;
- the importance of free speech to democratic societies;
- any other relevant issues.

PERSPECTIVE B: FREEDOM OF SPEECH

In a just society, sometimes it is necessary to limit freedom of speech in order to protect the rights of others.

Consider such points as:

- the effect on minority groups of racist speech;
- the way that speech can be used to encourage violence;
- conditions in other countries where free speech is unrestricted and results in rights violations;
- the need to promote responsibilities as well as rights;
- any other relevant issues.

worksheet

Perspectives on child labour

PERSPECTIVE A: CHILD LABOUR

In order to protect the right of children to play, learn and develop into healthy adults, laws against child labour must be strictly enforced.

Consider such points as:

- the loss of education that occurs when children are forced to work;
- the fact that children often labour under unhealthy conditions;
- the way that child labour is often exploited because children are not organised to protest unjust treatment;
- any other relevant issues.

PERSPECTIVE B: CHILD LABOUR

In order to help families that struggle to survive in difficult economic conditions, and to help children grow up to take a useful role in society, children should be allowed to work to help support their families.

Consider such points as:

- the fact that in some societies where jobs are scarce, children may be one of the only sources of income for a family;
- the fact that in many societies, children have traditionally worked alongside adults;
- the point of view that keeping children from doing productive labour isolates them unnecessarily from the adult world;
- the fact that working can be an educational experience for children;
- any other relevant issues.

Activity 34

'The world is just'

Age level 3: 16–18 years

OBJECTIVES

To help students realise that there may be a range of perspectives on any situation involving justice and injustice, and that certain groups may benefit from injustices done to others.

MATERIALS

One copy of the **'The world is just'** cartoon (page 189) for each group of four students; blank sheets of paper and pencils for each small group.

PROCEDURE

Step 1

Students form groups of four, and are given a copy of the **'The world is just'** cartoon. They take five to ten minutes to look it over, and to write a short statement saying what they think the message of the cartoon is.

Step 2

The students then work together to write a conversation between the three fish that clarifies and explains the message of the cartoon. Or, rather than write a conversation between the fish, they can write a conversation between individuals or groups in society that they feel are represented by the fish.

Step 3

As a class, students explain what they felt the message of the cartoon was, and read aloud their conversation.

Step 4

The class then discusses the following questions:

- Did everyone agree on the meaning of the cartoon, or were there different interpretations?
- Do you know of any situations involving people in your community that have something in common with the one depicted by the cartoon? In your country? In the wider world?

- What are the conditions that have led to these types of injustices?
- What factors might bring about change in these unjust situations?

People in this city who have a lot of money think everything is fine and don't understand why poor people are complaining. But people who are poor have lots of reasons to think things are unfair.

Points of view on justice

VARIATIONS

1 Students present their interpretations of the cartoon in the form of a role play or drama.

2 They extend the cartoon into a comic strip, and show events leading to a situation of greater justice and equality.

FOLLOW-UP

Students look for newspaper, radio or television accounts of current situations in which injustice is occurring, and is viewed differently by different groups; or accounts which indicate that certain groups are benefiting directly or indirectly from an injustice being imposed on another group.

IN THE CURRICULUM

The activity develops skills of analysis, evaluation, negotiation, consensus-building, and applying information to new contexts. It would be appropriate in a humanities class on human rights or the experience of minority groups. It could also be used in the context of an English lesson.

'The world is just'

worksheet

(Hicks and Steiner, *Making Global Connections*, 1990, Oliver & Boyd, Edinburgh.)

Activity 35

How much is justice worth?

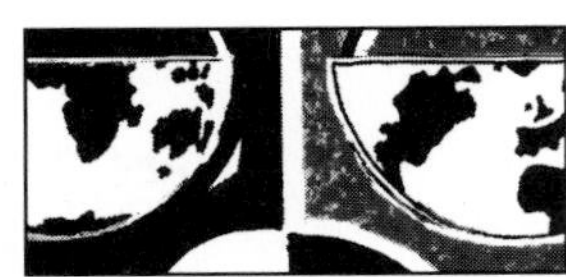

Age level 3: 16–18 years

OBJECTIVES

To encourage young people to consider whether certain rights should take priority over others; to help them reflect on the ways in which different rights are linked.

MATERIALS

Copies of the **Projects requesting funding** sheets (pages 192–5) for each group of four; blank paper and pencils; copies of the *Convention on the Rights of the Child* (available from UNICEF) should also be at hand for reference.

PROCEDURE

Step 1

Participants form groups of four. They are told that they are the newly-appointed members of the Justice Commission for an imaginary country. This country has recently signed the *Convention on the Rights of the Child*. As Commission members, their job is to read the eight different funding requests from organisations that are working on children's rights issues. They are given the **Projects requesting funding** sheets.

Step 2

In small groups, students decide which projects they feel should receive funding. They discard descriptions of any projects they feel should not be funded.

Step 3

Students are then told that the Prime Minister has allocated one million units of currency to funding for these projects. The students are to decide how much money to give to each project. In making funding decisions, they must consider both the short- and long-term impact of each project.

Step 4

Small groups report back to the whole class on the ways they have allocated funds. Alternatively, groups may prepare large charts showing their funding decisions, post these on the classroom walls, and have an exhibition session in which other students view the plans, while one group member remains with the chart to answer questions.

Step 5

The whole class then discusses the following questions:

- Which children's rights were considered the highest priorities? Why?
- Which rights were given the least priority? Why?
- Did any small groups decide that all or some of these projects should receive equal priority? Why?
- Did any small groups decide that certain rights were closely linked with others? Which ones? How were they linked?
- Can you think of any other rights projects that should have been on this list?
- In your own country, which of the rights issues addressed by the imaginary projects do you consider to be most critical? Least critical? Why? Do you think the views of your current government on rights and justice issues agree with your own? Why or why not? Which projects do you think would be most likely to receive funding? Why?
- Would children's rights priorities be different in different countries? Why or why not?

VARIATION

Pairs are each assigned a different article from the *Convention on the Rights of the Child*, and asked to outline some ways to put its goals into practice. These are reproduced and distributed to the entire class, which then carries out the funding activity as above, using these outlines as possible projects.

FOLLOW-UP

Young people investigate whether or not their country has ratified the *Convention on the Rights of the Child*. If not, they can contact an appropriate member of the government to ask why the Convention has not been signed, and to express their opinion on this issue.

If their country has ratified the Convention, they can research what measures are being put into place to see that its provisions are implemented.

IN THE CURRICULUM

The activity requires anticipating consequences, prioritising, negotiation, decision-making and consensus-building. It can be used in a humanities class on rights issues, or in an economics class.

worksheet

Projects requesting funding (1)

1 THE FREEDOM OF EXPRESSION PROJECT

Helping students to express their opinions, and giving them access to information about justice issues, is the best way to ensure that they will be able to participate in democratic decision-making as adults. This project will work with schools to ensure that students' opinions are heard on issues of importance to them. It will:

- produce a free magazine for students informing them about rights issues;
- fund regular television programmes for students on social justice;
- set up legal counselling for students on issues relevant to them;
- establish a hotline to the Justice Commission so that students may directly express their views and receive information.

2 THE CHILD LABOUR PROJECT

Many children in our country are forced to work at hazardous jobs from an early age. This project is essential to protect children from abuses, and ensure that they grow up in a situation which will allow them to develop all their capabilities. It will:

- work with the government to establish a minimum working age and regulate conditions of employment;
- provide support services to families who need their children's income;
- establish a confidential reporting system for children and young people who are being forced to work at an early age;
- provide parent education on this subject;
- pay special attention to the situation of minority children, who are more likely to be involved in child labour.

Projects requesting funding (2)

worksheet

---

3 THE STANDARD OF LIVING PROJECT

A decent standard of living is essential to the healthy development of children, and their future ability to contribute positively to society. This project will raise the standard of living in our country so that children can develop adequately. It will promote:

- construction of affordable housing with sanitary facilities;
- distribution of food to the hungry;
- setting up of agricultural programmes to enable families to meet their basic nutritional needs;
- organisation of food cooperatives to make basic food items more affordable.

---

4 THE PROTECTION FROM ABUSE AND NEGLECT PROJECT

All forms of abuse and neglect prey on the most defenceless members of society, the children, who may grow up physically, mentally, and emotionally handicapped as a result. This project aims to eliminate physical and mental abuse and neglect of children and young people; this includes drug abuse, sexual and other forms of exploitation. It will:

- set up programmes in schools and youth groups on coping with abuse and neglect, resisting drug use, and dealing with sexual abuse and exploitation;
- establish drop-in centres where young people may receive advice and counselling;
- set up education and counselling for parents on issues of abuse and neglect, and train social workers, police, and health care workers.

worksheet

Projects requesting funding (3)

5 THE EDUCATION FOR ALL PROJECT

A basic level of education is essential to participation in a democracy, maintenance of good health, and economic well-being. High levels of literacy and school attendance are essential if the citizens of this country are to prosper in a global society. This project will:

- build primary schools in every community;
- lobby the government to make primary education compulsory;
- provide financial support to secondary schools and work to enable more children to attend;
- set up financial assistance programmes to increase university attendance.

6 THE NON-DISCRIMINATION PROJECT

Concern for the rights of children and young people is meaningless if those rights are only bestowed on certain privileged groups. This project will:

- set up a monitoring board in each county to ensure that all children and young people are being treated equally, and having their basic needs met;
- investigate all charges of discrimination, especially those brought by young people themselves;
- pay special attention to the needs of minorities, girls, and the disabled.

Projects requesting funding (4)

7 THE AIMS OF EDUCATION PROJECT

While many issues may seem more urgent in the short term, changes in education are needed now in order to lay the foundation for a stable and prosperous future. This project will work on producing constructive change in the educational system. It will:

- produce curriculum materials on human rights and social justice issues, understanding of students' own culture and the cultures of others, peaceful conflict resolution, and environmental education;
- educate teachers on these issues;
- advise the Ministry of Education and inform the parents on how young people can be helped to develop the skills and attitudes needed for life in a diverse and interdependent society.

8 THE HEALTH SERVICES PROJECT

Unless children can be assured of survival and healthy development, they will never be able to take full advantage of their other basic human rights. This project will:

- establish health care centres in every community;
- provide care for pregnant women;
- offer education on children's health and nutrition, breast-feeding, and hygiene;
- ensure that all children receive basic health care, including immunisations;
- monitor the availability of clean water and levels of environmental pollution.

Why teach about conflict and conflict resolution?

Ask a group of students to brainstorm the ideas and feelings they associate with the word 'conflict'. Regardless of their age or nationality, the responses tend to centre around images of violence: bombs, killing, guns, war, enemies, fighting, hitting, screaming, anger, hatred.

For many adults, the associations are similar. Teachers who consider approaching issues of conflict with their students often think first of teaching about war and armed conflict.

Local and global news media focus heavily on reports of violent events. Even in media whose supposed aim is to entertain, violent images are just as prevalent. It is not surprising, then, that for many people, 'conflict' is synonymous with 'violence'. There is an urgent need for children and young people to understand that not all conflicts result in violence. It is *not* part of human nature to be violent. Violence is a *learned* response to conflict – and if violence can be learned, other responses are possible and can be learned as well.

Education can help students take a broader view of conflict, exploring not only situations of violence but the conflicts which inevitably occur between people over ideas, values, positions, and perspectives on a range of issues. These are the types of conflict that, when not dealt with constructively, often explode into violence.

It is unlikely that any educational initiatives can eliminate all such conflict, for conflict is a fact of life. But schools can help young people learn that they have choices in the ways they respond to conflict. Students can develop negotiation and problem-solving skills that will allow them to approach conflict not as a crisis, but as an opportunity for creative change. They can first learn to apply these to the conflicts that are part of their daily lives – conflicts with friends, family, and even teachers! They can then reflect on how those approaches to problem-solving might be applied to conflicts over ethnic and religious differences, resources, borders or varying political ideologies in their community, nation, or the wider world.

One effect of such education is corrective. Many children who have grown up in situations of actual or anticipated conflict struggle with anxiety, fear, feelings of hopelessness about the future, and a sense of powerlessness in the face of forces which seem beyond their control. For these children, learning conflict resolution skills can be part of a healing process, providing practical ways of coping and a sense of empowerment.

At the same time, education about conflict and its resolution is preventative. If the knowledge, skills, and attitudes of peace-making can be learned, students have both the opportunity and the responsibility to take action that will bring a culture of peace to a conflict-ridden world.

Some key concepts

EDUCATION ABOUT PEACE

This tends to treat the topic as a subject area, and focuses on issues such as disarmament, international institutions, the nuclear question, and development, as well as case studies of war and peace, and the work of famous peacemakers.

EDUCATION FOR PEACE

This may explore the above content areas, but also addresses the skills and attitudes necessary for peace and cooperation to occur. These may include self-understanding and self-esteem, community building, communication, conflict management, the practice of non-violence, exploring diversity, and ways of taking action. Its aim is to change behaviours, ways of thinking, values, and ultimately the institutions which perpetuate conflict and violence.

NEGATIVE PEACE

This refers to the absence of war and the reduction of violent conflict.

POSITIVE PEACE

This encompasses the absence of war, but goes further to include the reduction of factors that harm the quality of life and thus promote a climate of conflict. Positive peace is not possible without economic and social justice, the elimination of poverty and discrimination, and ecological balance.

STRUCTURAL VIOLENCE

This refers not to overt physical violence, but to the more insidious violence of poverty, racism, sexism, and human rights violations.

Whenever institutions or social systems put some people in positions of power while depriving others of their fundamental human rights, structural violence can be said to exist.

Teaching about conflict and conflict resolution: Aims and objectives

Knowledge	*Skills*	*Attitudes*
• Knowledge of the various types of conflict (e.g. over values, needs, resources), common causes of conflict and potential outcomes. • Understanding that conflict can have many possible solutions, of which violence is only one. • Knowing about the many conflict resolution techniques which exist (e.g. mediation, arbitration, negotiation, etc.). • Understanding that peace has many manifestations, and includes peace within oneself, the absence of those structures which cause conflict (e.g. injustice, inequality, poverty and deprivation), as well as the absence of armed conflict.	• Skills of resolving conflicts peacefully, e.g. generating alternatives, ranking, compromising, decision-making, communicating effectively, working with others cooperatively. • Ability to see how these skills can be applied in one's own personal life and on a global scale.	• Commitment to peace (in all its manifestations). • Willingness to take action on behalf of peace. • Awareness that conflict can provide opportunities for creative growth and positive change.

Activity 36 Discoveries

Age level 1:
7–11 years

OBJECTIVES

To help students appreciate their own positive qualities and strengths, as well as those of their peers; to encourage an environment in which each student feels positively about herself as a way of laying the foundation for later work in conflict resolution.

MATERIALS

A copy of the **Discoveries** sheet (page 201) for each student.

PROCEDURE

Step 1

Each student receives a copy of the **Discoveries** sheet. The students move around the room and try to find a classmate who can answer one of the

Making discoveries about classmates

questions. That student's name is recorded on the sheet, along with any information about the particular skill or achievement. Each student's name may be used only once, to encourage students to speak to as many others as possible. Students may also use their own names, but only once. The activity continues until each student has found answers to as many questions as possible.

Step 2

After 15 to 20 minutes, the class comes together. It discusses the following questions:

- What new things did you learn?
- Did anything you discovered about your peers surprise you?
- Did you find you had anything in common with other students?

If time permits, the teacher can call out the name of each student in the class, one at a time, and ask for a volunteer to tell something new that she found out about that person.

VARIATION

Students work in pairs to complete the sheet.

FOLLOW-UP

1 Some of the questions can be further investigated and the information compiled into a graph showing, for example, what languages are spoken by students in the class.

2 Individual questions may be used as the basis for writing assignments, and turned into class books on, for example **People we care about**.

IN THE CURRICULUM

The activity involves communication skills such as questioning, listening and recording. It can be used in an English lesson, or at the beginning of a humanities topic exploring the local community and the people who live there. It is also usefully done at the beginning of the school year as a way of helping students get to know each other better.

Discoveries

worksheet

Find someone who:

1 has a favourite story or book ______________________

What is it? ______________________

2 has an interesting or unusual hobby ______________________

What is it? ______________________

3 can name something she or he especially likes to do in school

____

What is it? ______________________

4 has learned how to do something new recently ______________________

What is it? ______________________

5 did something she or he is proud of recently ______________________

What was it? ______________________

6 helped someone recently ______________________

How? ______________________

7 knows what kind of work she or he wants to do as a grown-up

____

What is it? ______________________

8 knows some words in a language different from the one we speak in school ______________________

Which language? ______________________

9 knows someone that she or he cares a lot about ______________________

Who is it, and why? ______________________

10 has ever helped someone stop fighting ______________________

How? ______________________

Activity 37 Active listening

Age level 1: 7–11 years

OBJECTIVES

To develop in students the listening skills, and ability to understand another person's point of view, that are essential in resolving conflicts.

MATERIALS

Active Listening Is . . . sheet on page 204 (optional).

PROCEDURE

Step 1

Active listening can be introduced through two brief role plays. Two students are asked to volunteer for the first role play. One plays the role of a student with some important news to tell – having just received an invitation to a party, having been selected for a part in the school play, or any other event appropriate to the students' age and situation.

The first student tells this news to the second student. The second student's reaction is to *not listen*. He may demonstrate *not listening* in a number of ways: by turning away from the speaker, not looking at the speaker, interrupting, changing the topic, busying himself with something else, or saying things that show a lack of interest. The role play need only last one to two minutes. (The teacher may play one of the roles if necessary.)

Step 2

After watching the role play, the students make a list of the behaviours that showed *not listening*, either as a whole class or in small groups.

Step 3

The role play is then repeated with two new volunteers. This time, the listener is to demonstrate genuine interest.

Step 4

The class is then asked to list the behaviours that indicated *listening*. They may include facing the speaker, looking at the speaker, saying encouraging things such as 'Tell me more', staying on the topic, asking questions, or reflecting what the speaker has said.

Step 5

The teacher then explains that these behaviours are called 'active listening'. The sheet **Active listening is . . .** may be handed out at this point, or the students may use their own list to prepare an **Active listening is . . .** chart.

Step 6

The students form pairs to practise active listening; they decide who will be the speaker and who will be the listener. A topic is chosen, such as 'A time I felt proud of myself', 'Something I would like to be able to do when I grow older', 'Something about the world that I would like to change', etc. The topic can vary with the age and interests of the students.

Step 7

The listener practises as many of the guidelines for active listening as possible while the speaker talks on the topic for two to three minutes.

Step 8

They then switch roles within the pair, so that each student has the experience of being actively listened to.

Step 9

Finally, the class comes together to discuss these questions:

- How did it feel to listen actively to your partner?
- Was it different from the way you usually listen?
- How did it feel to be actively listened to?
- Did active listening help you to better understand your partner?

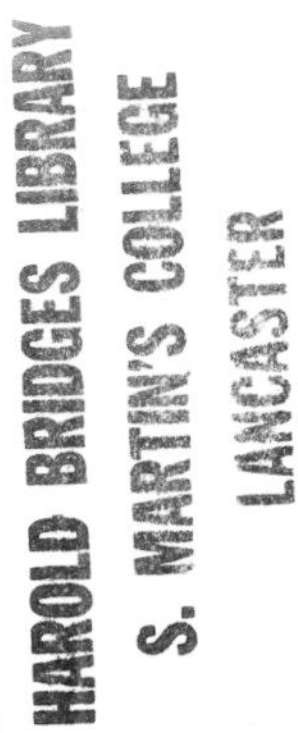

VARIATION

Steps 6 to 8 may be done in groups of three. One student can be the speaker, one the listener, and one the observer. The observer should have a copy of the sheet **Active listening is . . .**, and notice which behaviours the listener uses. When the speaker is finished, the observer lets the speaker know, in a positive way, what aspects of active listening she saw being used.

FOLLOW-UP

This skill takes time to develop, and is best practised at regular intervals.

IN THE CURRICULUM

The activity develops skills in observation, listening, speaking, memory and understanding another's point of view. While it can logically be used in an English lesson, active listening can be practised in other curriculum areas simply by varying the topic to be discussed.

worksheet

Active listening is . . .

PAYING ATTENTION

1 Turn your body toward the person who is talking.

2 Look at the person who is talking.

3 Listen in a quiet place, so that you can really hear.

FOLLOWING

1 Say things like:

'Can you say more about that?', or

'Really?', or

'Is that so?'

2 Ask questions, but not too many!

REFLECTING

1 Every now and then, repeat what the speaker has said in your own words.

2 Try to say in your own words what the speaker might be thinking: 'So you think that if you study hard, you could be a doctor when you grow up'.

3 Try to say in your own words what the speaker might be feeling: 'It sounds like you're really happy about the way you solved this problem'.

Activity 38 *Defining peace and conflict*

Age level 1: 7–11 years

OBJECTIVES

To encourage students to come up with their own definitions of peace and conflict; and to help students see that conflict can take many forms that are less obvious than physical violence.

MATERIALS

A set of **Peace and conflict pictures** (pages 207–11) for each group of three students.

PROCEDURE

Step 1

The word **Conflict** is written on the blackboard; the students are asked to brainstorm as many different words or phrases as they can that come to mind when they see this word. These are written on the board without comment or discussion at this stage.

Step 2

After all responses have been exhausted, the word **Peace** is written on the board. The class repeats the brainstorm of associated words or images.

Step 3

The class discusses the results of the two brainstorms.

Step 4

In groups of three, the students receive the **Peace and conflict pictures**, one complete set per small group. They discuss what is happening in each picture, and sort them into categories: **Pictures that show peace**, **Pictures that show conflict**, and if necessary, a category for **Other**, **Both**, or **Not sure**.

Step 5

Finally, the class comes together to discuss how they classified each picture and why. If they repeated the brainstorm on the words 'conflict' and 'peace', would their responses be different after classifying the pictures? If so, how?

VARIATIONS

1 Steps 1 and 2 can be done by drawing pictures of conflict and peace, rather than brainstorming.

2 Steps 1 to 3 may be carried out on one day, and the remainder of the activity on another.

3 Younger groups of students need not use all of the pictures.

FOLLOW-UP

Students start a collection of pictures from magazines and newspapers that show either peace or conflict; these can be used to create a bulletin board. Students' own drawings of peace and conflict situations that they are familiar with can also be included.

IN THE CURRICULUM

The activity requires skills of working cooperatively in a group and analysing images. It can be used in an English, humanities, or art class.

Peace and Conflict pictures (1)

worksheet

worksheet

Peace and Conflict pictures (2)

Peace and Conflict pictures (3)

worksheet

Peace and Conflict pictures (4)

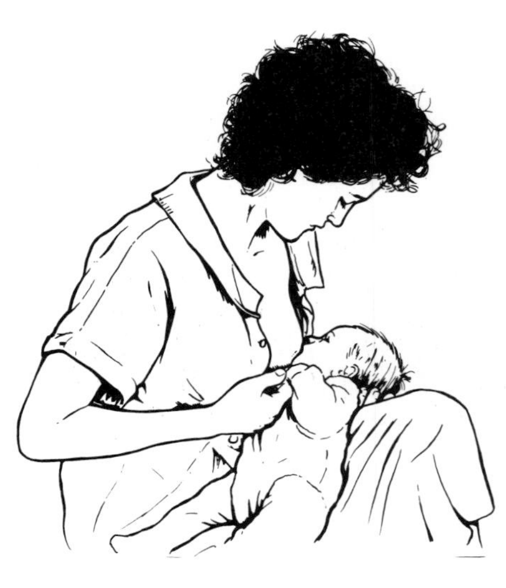

Peace and Conflict pictures (5)

worksheet

Activity 39 Faces

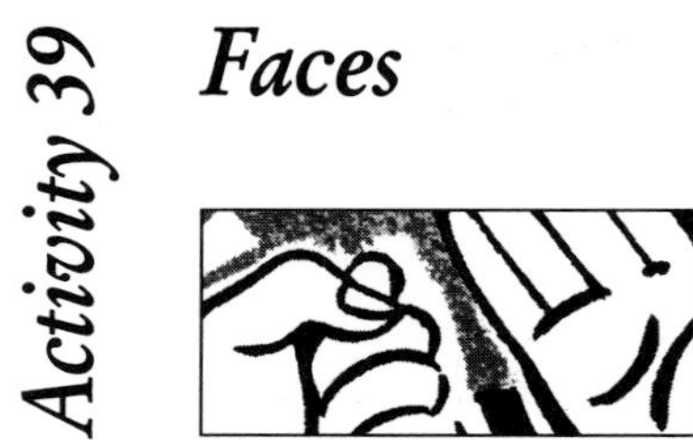

OBJECTIVES

To help students evaluate alternative solutions to conflict, and to see that sometimes solutions are possible that will satisfy both parties in a conflict.

MATERIALS

Age level 1: 7–11 years

Paper and pencils.

PROCEDURE

Step 1

Two students are asked to briefly role play this situation in front of the class, *without* coming to a solution:

> **It is recess time, and the class is going to the playground. There is one soccer ball in the playground. Two students run to get it; they get there at the same time, and both grab it. The first one says, 'It's mine! I got here first!' The second says, 'I had it first, and now you're trying to take it from me! Give it back!' They struggle with the ball.**

Step 2

As a class, the rest of the students brainstorm possible solutions to this conflict. These can be listed on chart paper. They should attempt to think of as many options as possible, without evaluating or judging them.

Step 3

Together, the students classify the solutions into three groups:

- solutions in which each person gets what she wants or needs; for example, one person uses it for 10 minutes, and then the other uses it for 10 minutes;
- solutions in which only one person gets what she wants or needs; for example, one person hurts the other and runs away with the ball;

- solutions in which neither person gets what she wants or needs; for example, the teacher takes the ball away and tells them both to find something else to do.

Each solution can be cut out and stuck or written directly onto the following chart:

The two smiling faces represent solutions in which each person gets what she wants or needs. The one smiling and one sad face represent solutions in which only one person gets what she wants or needs. The two sad faces represent solutions in which neither person gets what she wants or needs.

Step 4

As a class, students then discuss the types of solutions. Which ones seem to be the best? The activity can be repeated with different conflict situations: personal, local, and global. Students should consider:

- Are solutions in which both parties get their needs met always possible?
- Are they always preferable?
- Can violence ever result in a solution in which both parties get their needs met?

VARIATION

Older students can evaluate possible solutions by using a similar chart, but substituting a plus symbol (+) for the smiling face, and a minus symbol (-) for the sad face.

FOLLOW-UP

Students look for examples of conflict situations in the news. How often are the solutions ones in which both parties get their needs met? How do you account for this?

IN THE CURRICULUM

The activity develops skills in generating alternatives, evaluating, classifying and making decisions. It can be used in English or humanities, to consider solutions to conflicts in stories or in history.

Activity 40 *Six-step problem-solving*

OBJECTIVES

To introduce students to a structured way of resolving interpersonal conflicts that is applicable to a variety of situations.

MATERIALS

Copies of the **Six-step problem-solving** sheet (page 217).

PROCEDURE

Step 1

Two volunteers are chosen to role play a conflict, either from the list below, or one that the students suggest.

POSSIBLE ROLE PLAY SITUATIONS

- A student is trying to study at home; his sister wants to listen to the radio and has it turned up loudly.
- One student ridicules another who comes from a different country, by speaking with an exaggerated accent.
- A student has let her best friend borrow a book that was a special gift; when the friend returns the book, it is dirty and two pages are torn.
- A student wants to do volunteer work for an organisation that helps the poor, but her parents will not permit it.

The two volunteers proceed with the role play for a minute or two without reaching a solution.

Age level 2: 12–15 years

Step 2

The teacher then introduces the **Six-step problem-solving** process using the sheet on page 217 as a handout.

Step 3

Once the students understand the process, the role play is repeated, with a third student helping the two students in conflict resolve their problem.

Step 4

The students form groups of four to practise **Six-step problem-solving** with a different role play situation. Two students act out the conflict, while the other two attempt to help them work through the process.

Step 5

Finally, the class comes together to discuss these questions:

- What conflicts did you role play and what solutions did you arrive at?
- Was the **Six-step problem-solving** process helpful in finding a solution? Why or why not?

VARIATION

The students use the problem-solving process in role plays of conflicts that they read about in books, newspapers, or see on television. The activity can be used with younger students by creating role play situations appropriate for their age group.

FOLLOW-UP

Once students have become familiar with the process through role playing, it can be applied to actual conflicts that occur in the class. When a third person helps two parties resolve a conflict through the use of the six steps described in this exercise, the process is sometimes referred to as *mediation*. Students may wish to set up a space for mediation in their classroom or school, so that students in conflict can come to work out a solution with the help of a mediator.

IN THE CURRICULUM

The activity develops skills in generating alternatives, anticipating consequences and decision-making. It may be applied to conflicts in students' literature as part of an English lesson; it may also be used in a humanities class to consider alternatives in historical conflicts.

Six-step problem-solving

worksheet

1 IDENTIFY NEEDS

'What is it that you need (or want)?'

Each person in the conflict should answer this question, without blaming or accusing the other person.

2 DEFINE THE PROBLEM

'What do you think the problem is here?'

The whole class can help to come up with a response that includes both persons' needs, but does not blame. The persons in the conflict must agree to the definition.

3 BRAINSTORM LOTS OF SOLUTIONS

'Who can think of a way that we might solve this problem?'

Anyone in the class may offer a response. These should all be written down, without comment, judgement, or evaluation. The aim of this step is to come up with as many solutions as possible.

4 EVALUATE THE SOLUTIONS

'Would you be happy with this solution?'

Each party in the conflict goes through the list of alternatives and says which ones would or would not be acceptable to her/him.

5 DECIDE ON THE BEST SOLUTION

'Do you both agree to this solution? Is the problem solved?'

Make sure both parties agree, and acknowledge their efforts in working out the solution.

6 CHECK TO SEE HOW THE SOLUTION IS WORKING

'Let's talk to each other again soon to make sure the problem is really solved.'

A plan should be made of how to evaluate the solution. The evaluation may take place in a few minutes, or an hour, or the next day or week, depending on the nature of the conflict and the age of the people involved.

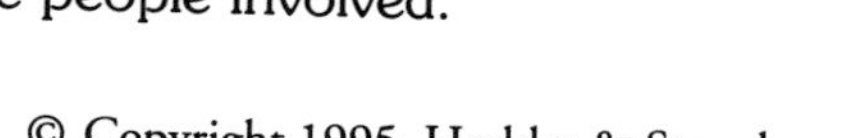

Activity 41 Classifying conflict

Age level 2:
12–15 years

OBJECTIVES

To deepen students' understanding of the causes of conflict.

MATERIALS

Small pieces of blank card or paper; sets of **Peace and conflict pictures** from **Activity 38, Defining peace and conflict** on pages 207–11 (optional).

PROCEDURE

Step 1

Students form groups of four, and are given a stack of blank cards or small pieces of paper. They are asked to write down at least five conflicts each; these can be conflicts that they have been involved in or ones that they know of. They can be conflicts that have occurred in school, in a youth group, at home, in the community, in their own country, or between countries.

Alternatively, the **Peace and conflict pictures** from **Activity 38, Defining peace and conflict**, can be used as a collection of different types of conflict.

Step 2

Once the small group has written down these situations, students read them aloud to each other and try to put together conflicts that seem to have something in common. The students try to come up with a name or category for each cluster of conflicts.

Step 3

The class then comes together to discuss the categories it devised, giving an example of each one.

Step 4

The words **things**, **feelings**, and **ideas** are written on the chalkboard. The teacher explains that these are categories which can be used to classify conflicts. The terms can be explained as follows:

Conflicts over things – these occur when two or more persons or parties want the same object, material, or resource, and there is not enough to go around.

Conflicts over feelings – these have to do with people's needs for friendship, love, self-respect, power, status, attention or admiration. Every person has some of these needs; sometimes groups of people or countries have these needs as well. Conflict can arise when feelings are hurt, denied, or not taken into consideration.

Conflicts over ideas – these have to do with the beliefs and values that a person, a group of people, or even a country feels are most important and fundamental. They often come from religious beliefs, cultural traditions, and political systems. They may also be highly personal.

Step 5

Students can look again at the conflicts they wrote about, and, in small groups, classify them according to whether they are conflicts over things, feelings, or ideas. Some conflicts have different elements, and will seem to fit into two, or even all three categories. Some may not appear to fit into any of them.

Step 6

The class comes together to discuss the activity:

- How did this way of classifying conflicts compare to the one that the students themselves devised?
- Which system would be most useful in helping them find a solution to a conflict? Why?

VARIATION

The students explore other ways of classifying conflicts, such as the following:

- easy to resolve/difficult to resolve;
- violent/non-violent;
- important/not important;
- between people/within groups/between groups/between nations.

FOLLOW-UP

The students look for newspaper articles about local, national, or international conflicts and classify them according to whether they are about things, feelings, or ideas. Are there any patterns among these conflicts? Do most international conflicts seem to be about one or two of these categories in particular? What about interpersonal or intergroup conflicts?

IN THE CURRICULUM

The activity develops skills in classification and decision-making by consensus. If used to analyse conflicts in literature, the activity could be used in an English class. Current or historical conflicts could be analysed in a humanities lesson. In mathematics, the students' findings about the frequency of different types of conflict could be represented graphically.

Activity 42

Conflict stories

OBJECTIVES

To encourage students to refine their notions of peace and conflict; to help them understand that not all conflict involves physical violence; to introduce the concepts of negative peace, positive peace, and structural violence.

Age level 2: 12–15 years

MATERIALS

A copy of one of the **Conflict stories** (pages 224–7) for each group of three.

PROCEDURE

Step 1

In groups of three, students read over one of the **Conflict stories** and devise a realistic ending.

Step 2

Students discuss the following questions for each story:

- Were there elements of peace in this story?
- Was the peace in this story based on the absence of violence or conflict?
- Was the peace in this story based on social, economic, and political justice?
- Were there elements of conflict in this story?
- Was there conflict of a physically violent nature?
- Was there conflict that did not involve physical violence?
- Was anyone being harmed by cultural or institutional attitudes, values, or ways of operating?

Step 3

Each group of three meets with another small group, describes its **Conflict story** and the ending they devised, and discusses the elements of peace and conflict that were present in each story.

(Conflict:) All girls have to take home economics but Teresa wants to take carpentry. Since home economics are required and it's at the same time as carpentry, Teresa can't take carpentry.

(Violence:) On her way home Teresa's friend trys to console her but Teresa just shouts at her.

(Peace:) Teresa's friend suggests that a group of girls write a letter to the head of the school, to say that they feel the home economics requirement is not fair.

(Coflict continues:) We think that the school made home economics and carpentry at the same time so that girls had to do home economics and not carpentry. Because they thought that a girl's place was at home cooking, cleaning and taking care of kids. And not with a career.

Student's reaction to a conflict story

Step 4

Students are then introduced to the terms 'negative peace', 'positive peace', and 'structural violence' (see **Key concepts**, page 197). They discuss whether these three states were reflected in the stories, and how.

Do they feel that negative peace or positive peace currently exists in their school, community, country? Has anyone ever felt her/himself to be the object of structural violence? How do issues of injustice or prejudice lead to conflict?

VARIATIONS

1 Students write two possible endings for each story, one that is peaceful, and one that is violent. Which ending is more likely to happen? Which is preferable?

2 Students create a time line based on their **Conflict story**. They may try to extend the time line beyond the ending they devised, to see if they can anticipate what the possible outcomes of situations involving structural violence might be, as well as the outcomes of different approaches to resolving conflict.

3 After completing this activity, students come up with their own definitions of peace and conflict.

FOLLOW-UP

Students discuss instances of structural violence in their school, community, or country. What kinds of action could they appropriately take to address structural violence?

IN THE CURRICULUM

The activity involves reading for meaning and making inferences. It can be used in the context of an English or literature lesson, or in a history or economics class.

worksheet

Conflict stories (1)

Rena is a 70-year-old woman who used to work as a school cleaner. She wants to work, and could use the money, but she had to stop because the school district does not allow people of her age to continue working.

She lives alone in an inner city neighbourhood. Because there is so much crime in her area, she is afraid to go out by herself. She would like to live in a safer part of the city, but she cannot afford a more expensive apartment.

She enjoys having visits in her apartment from friends, her children, and her grandchildren. But she wishes that she could get out more and be with other people as well.

She would like to go to meetings at the senior citizen centre in another part of the city, but there is no bus service to that area. So Rena decides to . . .

Conflict stories (2)

worksheet

Teresa is a 16-year-old secondary school student. She wants to learn carpentry, and signs up for a course at school. When she talks to the school counsellor, she is told that the carpentry course is scheduled at the same time as the home economics course, and home economics is required for girls. When she insists she wants to take carpentry, she is told that it will not be possible this year, and that she should wait until next year. She leaves school feeling angry.

On the way home, Teresa's best friend wants to walk with her, and asks her why she is looking so unhappy. Teresa shouts at her to go away and leave her alone; that she doesn't feel like talking. Her friend simply keeps walking with her. Finally Teresa starts to cry, and explains what the problem is. Her friend suggests that . . .

Conflict stories (3)

worksheet

Paul is 14 years old and uses a wheelchair to get around his school. The building is all on one level and the doorways were built to be wide enough so that people with a range of physical disabilities would still be able to attend the school. Paul has many friends in his class; he often goes to visit them after school, or invites them to visit him at his home.

One day Paul's literature class takes a trip to a local theatre to see a drama performance. When they arrive at the theatre, they discover that there is a steep flight of steps leading to the entrance, and no ramp. The theatre manager says that he is sorry, and that if Paul's teacher had phoned ahead, he would have told her that the theatre is not one that handicapped people can easily go to. Two of Paul's friends decide to . . .

Conflict stories (4)

worksheet

Victor is a black student in a secondary school with students of many different races and nationalities. Many students in this school do not get along well with people of different cultures. The school has no programme to help students understand its different people and their ways of life.

One day as Victor is walking down the hall, two white students call him a racist name. Victor goes to the headteacher to report the incident. The headteacher says he is sorry about the name-calling, but since no one actually got into a fight, he feels it is best to ignore it for now. He tells Victor that if he has any other problems with these two students, to come and talk to him about it.

Victor leaves the office feeling angry that the headteacher doesn't care enough to do anything. He tells two friends about it at lunch time. The two friends decide to . . .

Activity 43

Conflict in the media

Age level 2: 12–15 years

OBJECTIVES

To sensitise students to the pervasiveness of conflict in the media, particularly conflict which is resolved violently; to encourage them to question stereotypes which are conveyed through the media; to enable them to consider alternatives to violence.

MATERIALS

Copies of **Conflict in the media – a worksheet** (page 230).

PROCEDURE

Step 1

Each student is given a copy of **Conflict in the media – a worksheet**. They are to select a television programme to watch at home which contains some sort of conflict, and answer the questions on the sheet. (A letter of explanation may need to be sent home to parents before beginning this activity.)

Step 2

Once each student has completed a sheet, the class discusses any patterns that they noted. The results of the survey may by clearer if presented in the form of a graph. Questions to consider might include:

- What types of conflicts were most common? (Refer to categories suggested in **Activity 41, Classifying conflict**, if necessary.)
- Were there more males or females involved in conflicts? What types of conflicts were males most commonly involved in? What types of conflicts were females most commonly involved in?
- Were persons of various racial/ethnic groups shown being involved in conflicts? Of what type? If any patterns emerge with regard to gender or ethnicity, why do you think this occurs in media presentations of conflict?
- What percentage of the conflicts shown had violent solutions?
- Why do think violence is so frequently shown on television?

VARIATION

If access to television is not widespread in the class, other media such as students' magazines or comics may be used. Ideally, portrayals of conflict in two different types of media should be compared.

FOLLOW-UP

Students may wish to write letters expressing their views on media violence to children's television producers or publishers of comics.

IN THE CURRICULUM

The activity develops skills in observation and recording, collating and presenting data, critical thinking, clarification of values, writing and taking action to effect change. It can be used in an English or media studies lesson. It can also be incorporated into a mathematics period, as analysing and graphing the data is necessary.

worksheet

Conflict in the media – a worksheet

Name of television programme/comic/magazine ____________

Date of programme __________ Channel/station ____________

Who had the conflict? ____________

What was the conflict about? ____________

What did the first party want/need? ____________

____

What did the second party want/need? ____________

____

How did they try to solve their conflict? ____________

____

Did the first party get what she or he wanted/needed? ____________

Did the second party get what she or he wanted/needed? ____________

How did you feel about the way they resolved their conflict? ____________

____

Was it realistic? Why or why not? ____________

____

What are some other ways they might have resolved their conflict?

____

If there was violence, were any special techniques used to highlight the violence? (music, lighting, different ways of filming) What effects did these have? ____________

____

How did you feel about this programme/comic/magazine? ____________

____

Activity 44

Considering positions

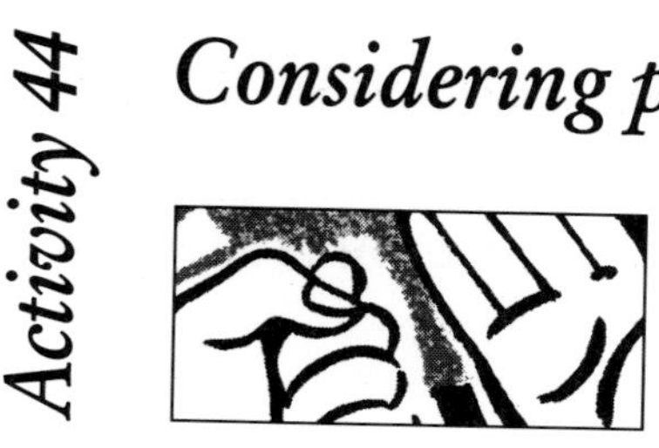

Age level 3:
16–18 years

OBJECTIVES

To encourage young people to reflect on whether violence is ever justified; to encourage listening to other perspectives, and an understanding of what causes attitudes to change.

MATERIALS

An index card and a pencil for each participant.

PROCEDURE

Step 1

Each student is given an index card and pencil. The following statement is read aloud to the class:

'The use of violence is justified in order to bring about peace.'

Ask the students to consider the statement in silence for a minute. Five possible positions on the statement are written on a blackboard:

- strongly agree
- agree
- neutral/not sure
- disagree
- strongly disagree

Students choose one of these positions, which most closely represents their reaction to the statement, and write it on their card. Students should be told that at any point during the activity, they may cross out their original position and write in a new one if their point of view on the statement changes.

Step 2

Each person then finds another who is holding an index card with the same position written on it, and discusses his position with that person for two or three minutes.

Step 3

When the teacher calls time, each person moves on to someone who is holding a card one position removed from her own. They again discuss their points of view on the statement for two to three minutes.

Step 4

They then move on to someone whose card is two or three positions removed from their own, and discuss the statement again.

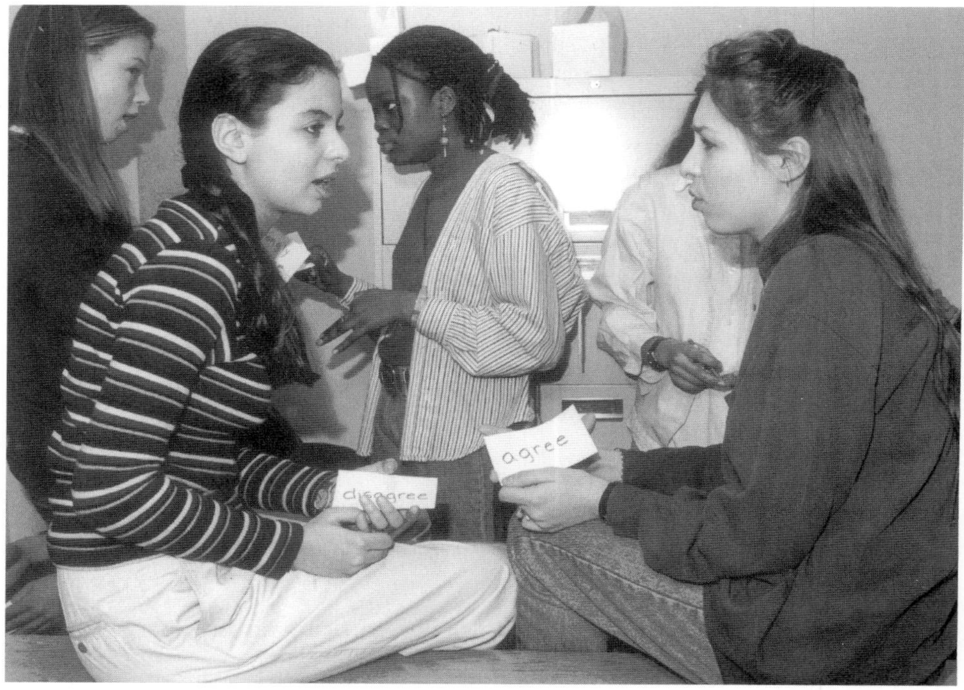

Considering another's position on a controversial issue

Step 5

Students return to the first person they talked to, and discuss whether they have changed their original position on the statement.

Step 6

The whole class comes together to discuss both the statement, and the process of the activity:

- Did any students find their position changing during the course of the activity?
- What factors influenced a change in position?
- What factors caused resistance to listening to others, or to change?
- What did they learn from others?

VARIATION

The activity can be repeated with any controversial statement as a way of encouraging sharing of perspectives. Other statements relevant to issues of peace and conflict include:

> **'The world would be a better place if all conflict could be eliminated.'**
>
> **'It is only human nature to be violent.'**
>
> **'In the interests of peace, ethnic-identity movements should be limited.'**
>
> **'There should be an international ban on all war toys.'**

FOLLOW-UP

The activity could be used to introduce an exploration of ways in which attitude change occurs, especially ways in which popular media create or influence attitudes on current events and conditions.

IN THE CURRICULUM

The activity involves clarifying one's own position, active listening and considering other points of view. It can be used with a variety of controversial statements in different subject areas such as history, economics, or religious education.

Activity 45

Local conflicts – a survey

Age level 3: 16–18 years

OBJECTIVES

To increase young people's awareness of conflict in their community; to assess reasonable possibilities for taking action to improve a conflict situation.

MATERIALS

A selection of local newspapers, a local map, copies of the sheet **A local conflict** (page 237) for each pair.

PROCEDURE

Step 1

Over a period of one to two weeks, students collect articles from local newspapers that describe any form of conflict. These might include crimes, vandalism, debates on how local funds are to be spent, discussions in planning boards of proposed development projects, racial or ethnic conflicts, demonstrations for particular causes, local environmental issues, etc. Conflicts which occur at a specific location can be marked with pins on a map of the community.

> **If conflict in the community tends to occur largely in one particular neighbourhood, it may be best to eliminate mapping, since this may tend to reinforce prevailing stereotypes about certain localities or groups of people.**

Step 2

Once a collection of articles has been established, pairs work together to select one conflict. They complete the questions on the sheet **A local conflict**. (This may require writing to one or both of the parties in the conflict to get additional information.)

Step 3

When all the pairs have completed the sheet, they present the results to the class. As each situation is presented, the alternative solutions are discussed, and other possibilities added.

Step 4

The class then votes on whether this conflict is one that they, as young people, could take some form of constructive action on. Two lists can be made on the chalkboard as this is done: **Conflicts we can do something about** and **Conflicts we can't do anything about**. What patterns exist in the types of conflicts to be found on each list?

Step 5

Finally, the class can decide on one conflict that they can reasonably have an impact on, and devise a realistic action project to be carried out. The teacher should help the young people clarify whether the project they carry out is addressing the cause of the conflict, or the effects of the conflict.

Projects that address the causes of conflict might include writing letters to local authorities, conducting surveys to gather more information, circulating petitions, designing a presentation for younger students about a local ethnic or cultural group, planning a playground for an unused area, etc.

Projects that address the effects of conflict might include picking up litter, cleaning up graffiti, raising funds to help an individual or a cause, forming a 'buddy system' to escort younger students to and from school, etc.

The actual nature of projects will vary greatly depending on local conditions.

VARIATION

Rather than use newspapers, the survey can be conducted by taking the class on a walk in the local area, and having students record evidence of conflict. If this is done, it is essential to first ensure that the local area is safe enough for the class to do this sort of work; it is also advisable to notify parents of the nature of the project.

FOLLOW-UP

1 It is useful to keep a record of the action project, possibly in the form of a book, photos, or a video, depending on the resources available. It may also be appropriate for the class to communicate its action project to the wider community in the form of a presentation to other classes in the school, an article in the local newspaper, a display at a community festival, a poster on a bulletin board in the town, etc.

2 Students may invite community members who are involved in some way in peacemaking or dealing with conflict to visit them and speak about their work.

IN THE CURRICULUM

The activity builds skills in reading, analysing, mapping, anticipating consequences, decision-making, planning and taking action. It could be included in a humanities unit focusing on the local community. The mapping aspect could be done within a geography lesson.

A local conflict

worksheet

What is the conflict you looked at? ______________________________

Who are the parties in the conflict? ______________________________

What does party A want or need? ______________________________

What does party B want or need? ______________________________

What do you think the causes of this conflict are? ________________

Does this conflict benefit party A in any way? __________________

Does it harm party A? ______________________________________

Does this conflict benefit party B in any way? __________________

Does it harm party B? ______________________________________

Does this conflict benefit or harm anyone else in the community? __

____

What are some things that could be done to resolve this conflict? ___

____

____

What do you think is the best way to resolve this conflict? _________

____

____

Is there anything that you could do to improve this situation? If not, why not? ____

____

____

____

Activity 46

The Seville Statement

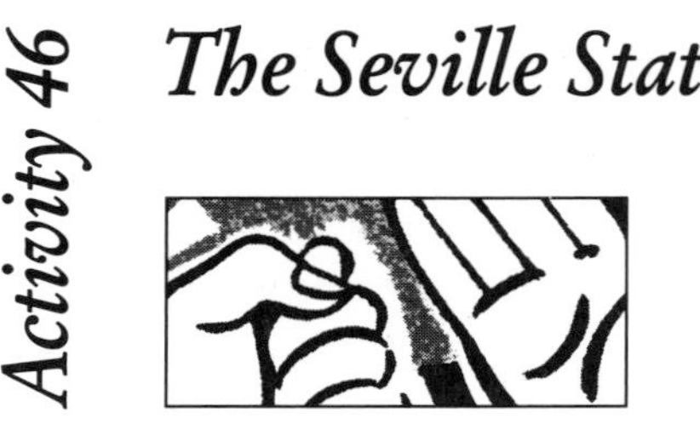

Age level 3: 16–18 years

OBJECTIVES

To help young people examine assumptions about violence and human nature; to practise peer teaching and consensus-building.

MATERIALS

Copies of the four excerpts from **The Seville Statement on Violence** for each group of four (pages 240–1; the complete text of the *Seville Statement* is also reproduced following this activity, for teachers who wish to refer to it); 20 blank cards or slips of paper for each small group.

PROCEDURE

Step 1

Young people form groups of four, and each person in the small group is given a *different* excerpt from **The Seville Statement on Violence**. It can be explained that the *Seville Statement* is a statement on violence and human nature. It was written by a group of twenty scholars – biologists, psychologists, neurophysiologists, anthropologists, geneticists – from 12 different countries.

Step 2

Everyone who has Excerpt 1 then joins together to form a new group. Everyone with Except 2 forms another group, and so on. In these groups, participants carefully read their excerpt, making sure that they fully understand it; dictionaries or encyclopedias may be consulted if necessary.

Step 3

Students then return to their original groups of four. They take turns explaining to the members of the original group in their own words what their portion of the Statement says. They are responsible for answering questions from the small group and for making sure everyone fully understands that excerpt.

Step 4

Each student takes five blank cards or slips of paper. In silence, they write five different reactions they had to the *Seville Statement*, each one on a different piece of paper. A reaction may be simply a word ('sceptical'), a phrase ('Interesting – I'd like to know more'), a question ('Why don't more people know about this paper?'), or a more involved thought requiring a sentence or two ('If violence is not biological, then it should be possible to do something about it. Schools should find a way to address social violence.').

Step 5

All the reactions are collected by one person in the small group, and dealt out at random as if they are playing cards. Students look at their cards. They place any cards that they themselves wrote, or any with which they disagree, face down in the centre of the table. They can pick up any of the discarded reactions to add to those they are holding. The aim is to end up holding three reaction cards that they themselves did not write, but with which they can agree.

Step 6

Once this is done, they report to each other in the small group on the three reactions they are holding, and why they have chosen them.

Step 7

Finally, the class comes together to discuss any further thoughts on the *Seville Statement* and its implications.

VARIATION

During Step 6, students attempt to write a composite reaction to the *Seville Statement* that all four can agree on.

FOLLOW-UP

Students may wish to interview others in school, in a youth group, parents, or community members to see how widespread is the notion that violence is simply part of human nature. What may be appropriate ways of changing this attitude?

IN THE CURRICULUM

The activity develops skills in reading comprehension, paraphrasing, making summaries, presenting information clearly, examining other perspectives and building consensus. It can be used in a biology class on inherited traits, or in a psychology class.

worksheet

The Seville Statement on Violence (1)

EXCERPT 1

It is scientifically incorrect to say that we have inherited a tendency to make war from our animal ancestors. Although fighting occurs widely throughout animal species, only a few cases of destructive intra-species fighting between organised groups have ever been reported . . . and none of these involve the use of tools designed to be weapons. Normal predatory feeding upon other species cannot be equated with intra-species violence. Warfare is a peculiarly human phenomenon and does not occur in other animals.

SUMMARY 1

It is untrue to say that we have inherited the tendency to make war from the animals we evolved from. Very few species fight among themselves, and none use weapons. Only humans make war.

EXCERPT 2

It is scientifically incorrect to say that war or any other violent behaviour is genetically programmed into our human nature. While genes are involved at all levels of nervous system function, they provide a developmental potential that can be actualised only in conjunction with the ecological and social environment. While individuals vary in their predispositions to be affected by their experience, it is the interaction between their genetic endowment and conditions of nurturance that determines their personalities. Except for rare pathologies, the genes do not produce individuals necessarily predisposed to violence. Neither do they determine the opposite. While genes are co-involved in establishing our behavioural capacities, they do not by themselves specify the outcome.

SUMMARY 2

It is untrue to say that human genes produce violent behaviour. Genes do not cause people to be either violent or peaceful. They provide the potential for behaviour; but how a person actually acts is shaped by their environment and the way that they are raised.

The Seville Statement on Violence (2)

EXCERPT 3

It is scientifically incorrect to say that humans have a 'violent brain'. While we do have the neural apparatus to act violently, it is not automatically activated by internal or external stimuli. Like higher primates and unlike other animals, our higher neural processes filter such stimuli before they can be acted upon. How we act is shaped by how we have been conditioned and socialised. There is nothing in our neurophysiology that compels us to react violently.

SUMMARY 3

It is not true to say that there is something in the human brain that causes people to act violently. We have the potential to act violently, but whether we do or not depends on how we have been brought up, and what kind of society we live in.

EXCERPT 4

It is scientifically incorrect to say that war is caused by 'instinct' or any single motivation . . . Modern war involves institutional use of personal characteristics such as obedience, suggestibility, and idealism; social skills such as language; and rational considerations such as cost-calculation, planning, and information processing. The technology of modern war has exaggerated traits associated with violence both in the training of actual combatants and in the preparation of support for war in the general population. As a result of this exaggeration, such traits are often mistaken to be the causes rather than the consequences of the process.

SUMMARY 4

War is not caused by some instinct. The violent behaviours of people in war situations are something they have learned through training; they are not in-born. Such behaviours are a result of war, not the cause.

worksheet

The Seville Statement on Violence

EDITOR'S NOTE: *The Seville Statement on Violence* was drafted by an international committee of 20 scholars at the 6th International Colloquium on Brain and Aggression held at the University of Seville, Spain, in May 1986, with support from the Spanish Commission for UNESCO. The Statement's purpose is to dispel the widespread belief that human beings are inevitably disposed to war as a result of innate, biologically determined aggressive traits.

UNESCO adopted the *Seville Statement* at its 25th General Conference Session in Paris, October 17–November 16, 1989. The Statement has been formally endorsed by scientific organisations and published in journals around the world. UNESCO is preparing a brochure to be used in teaching young people about the Statement.

In August 1987 the Council of Representatives of the American Psychological Association voted to endorse the *Seville Statement*. The Board of Scientific Affairs emphasised that this is not a scientific statement on the issue of specific inherited behavioural traits. It is, rather, a social statement designed to eliminate unfounded stereotypic thinking on the inevitability of war.

Believing that it is our responsibility to address from our particular disciplines the most dangerous and destructive activities of our species, violence and war; recognising that science is a human cultural product which cannot be definitive or all-encompassing; and gratefully acknowledging the support of the authorities of Seville and representatives of Spanish UNESCO; we, the undersigned scholars from around the world and from relevant sciences, have met and arrived at the following Statement on Violence. In it, we challenge a number of alleged biological findings that have been used, even by some in our disciplines, to justify violence and war. Because the alleged findings have contributed to an atmosphere of pessimism in our time, we submit that the open, considered rejection of these mis-statements can contribute significantly to the International Year of Peace.

Misuse of scientific theories and data to justify violence and war is not new but has been made since the advent of modern science. For example, the theory of evolution has been used to justify not only war, but also genocide, colonialism and suppression of the weak.

We state our position in the form of five propositions. We are aware that there are many other issues about violence and war that could be fruitfully addressed from the standpoint of our disciplines, but we restrict ourselves here to what we consider a most important first step.

It is scientifically incorrect to say that we have inherited a tendency to make war from our animal ancestors. Although fighting occurs widely throughout animal species, only a few cases of destructive intra-species fighting between organised groups have ever been reported among naturally living species, and none of these involve the use of tools designed to be weapons. Normal predatory feeding upon other species cannot be equated with intra-species violence. Warfare is a peculiarly human phenomenon and does not occur in other animals.

The fact that warfare has changed so radically over time indicates that it is a product of culture. Its biological connection is primarily through language which makes possible the coordination of groups, the transmission of technology, and the use of tools. War is biologically possible, but it is not inevitable, as evidenced by its variation in occurrence and nature over time and space. There are cultures which have not engaged in war for centuries, and there are cultures which have engaged in war frequently at some times and not at others.

It is scientifically incorrect to say that war or any other violent behaviour is genetically programmed into our human nature. While genes are involved at all levels of nervous system function, they provide a developmental potential that can be actualised only in conjunction with the ecological and social environment. While individuals vary in their predispositions to be affected by their experience, it is the interaction between their genetic endowment and conditions of nurturance that determines their personalities. Except for rare pathologies, the genes do not produce individuals necessarily predisposed to violence. Neither do they determine the opposite. While genes are co-involved in establishing our behavioural capacities, they do not by themselves specify the outcome.

It is scientifically incorrect to say that in the course of human evolution there has been a selection for aggressive behaviour more than for other kinds of behaviour. In all well-studied species, status within the group is achieved by the ability to cooperate and to fulfil social functions relevant to

the structure of that group. 'Dominance' involves social bondings and affiliations; it is not simply a matter of the possession and use of superior physical power, although it does involve aggressive behaviours. Where genetic selection for aggressive behaviour has been artificially instituted in animals, it has rapidly succeeded in producing hyper-aggressive individuals; this indicates that aggression was not maximally selected under natural conditions. When such experimentally-created hyper-aggressive animals are present in a social group, they either disrupt its social structure or are driven out. Violence is neither in our evolutionary legacy nor in our genes.

It is scientifically incorrect to say that humans have a 'violent brain'. While we do have the neural apparatus to act violently, it is not automatically activated by internal or external stimuli. Like higher primates and unlike other animals, our higher neural processes filter such stimuli before they can be acted upon. How we act is shaped by how we have been conditioned and socialised. There is nothing in our neurophysiology that compels us to react violently.

It is scientifically incorrect to say that war is caused by 'instinct' or any single motivation. The emergence of modern warfare has been a journey from the primacy of emotional and motivational factors, sometimes called 'instincts', to the primacy of cognitive factors. Modern war involves institutional use of personal characteristics such as obedience, suggestibility, and idealism; social skills such as language; and rational considerations such as cost-calculation, planning, and information processing. The technology of modern war has exaggerated traits associated with violence both in the training of actual combatants and in the preparation of support for war in the general population. As a result of this exaggeration, such traits are often mistaken to be the causes rather than the consequences of the process.

We conclude that biology does not condemn humanity to war, and that humanity can be freed from the bondage of biological pessimism and empowered with confidence to undertake the transformative tasks needed in this International Year of Peace and in the years to come. Although these tasks are mainly institutional and collective, they also rest upon the consciousness of individual participants for whom pessimism and optimism are crucial factors. Just as 'wars begin in the minds of men', peace also begins in our minds. The same species who invented war is capable of inventing peace. The responsibility lies with each of us.

Seville, May 16, 1986

SIGNATORIES

David Adams, Psychology, Wesleyan University, Middletown, Connecticut, USA.
S A Barnett, Ethology, The Australian National University, Canberra, Australia.
N P Bechtereva, Neurophysiology, Institute for Experimental Medicine of Academy of Medical Science of USSR, Leningrad, USSR.
Bonnie Frank Carter, Psychology, Albert Einstein Medical Center, Philadelphia, Pennsylvania, USA.
José M Rodríguez Delgado, Neurophysiology, Centro de Estudios Neurobiológicos, Madrid, Spain.
José Luis Díaz, Ethology, Instituto Mexicano de Psiquiatría, Mexico DF, Mexico.
Andrzej Eliasz, Individual Differences Psychology, Polish Academy of Sciences, Warsaw, Poland.
Santiago Genovés, Biological Anthropology, Instituto de Estudios Antropológicos, Mexico DF, Mexico.
Benson E Ginsburg, Behaviour Genetics, University of Connecticut, Storrs, Connecticut, USA.
Jo Groebel, Social Psychology, Erziehungswissenschaftliche Hochschule, Landau, Federal Republic of Germany.
Samir-Kumar Ghosh, Sociology, Indian Institute of Human Sciences, Calcutta, India.
Robert Hinde, Animal Behaviour, Cambridge University, United Kingdom.
Richard E Leakey, Physical Anthropology, National Museums of Kenya, Nairobi, Kenya.
Taha M Malasi, Psychiatry, Kuwait University, Kuwait.
J Martin Ramírez, Psychobiology, Universidad de Sevilla, Spain.
Federico Mayor Zaragoza, Biochemistry, Universidad Autónoma, Madrid, Spain.
Diana L Mendoza, Ethology, Universidad de Sevilla, Spain.
Ashis Nandy, Political Psychology, Centre for the Study of Developing Societies, Delhi, India.
John Paul Scott, Animal Behaviour, Bowling Green State University, Bowling Green, Ohio, USA.
Riitta Wahlström, Psychology, University of Jyväskylä, Finland.

Activity 47

Thoughts on peace

OBJECTIVES

To expose young people to ideas on peace from thinkers around the world; to help them see the commonalities in the ways people from many cultures view peace; to encourage them to reflect on their own definition of peace.

Age level 3: 16–18 years

MATERIALS

A set of quotes from the **Thoughts on peace** sheets (pages 248–9) cut into individual sections for each group of four; sugar paper, glue, felt pens.

PROCEDURE

Step 1

In groups of four, the students read over the quotes. They then decide on a way to arrange them on a large sheet of sugar paper that will show something about how the various perspectives on peace relate to each other. They may choose to cluster them, make a linear sequence, a pattern or a flow diagram using lines and arrows to connect the different quotes.

Step 2

When the small group has decided on a final arrangement, they stick the slips of paper down with glue, adding diagrams or comments if they wish.

Step 3

With the various quotes in mind, each small group comes up with its own definition of peace.

Step 4

Small groups walk around the room and view each others' charts. One person from each group should remain with the chart to explain or answer questions. As a class, they discuss insights gained from this activity.

VARIATION

Small groups may wish to add quotes that they have come across, or additional thoughts. They may add further sheets to their display if they need more space for this.

FOLLOW-UP

As a follow-up to the activity, young people interpret quotes which had particular significance for them through other media. Various statements would lend themselves to expression through drawing, painting, or collage. Others might be the subject of a role play or short story. These projects could be presented to the class, school, or community.

IN THE CURRICULUM

The activity develops skills in reading comprehension, interpreting inferences and seeing relationships. It can be used in a literature class after reading material relevant to the theme of peace and conflict. It can be used in a history class after studying a war or other conflict. The follow-up activity could also involve art, music, drama, and creative writing.

Thoughts on peace (1)

worksheet

'If there is right in the soul,
There will be beauty in the person;
If there is beauty in the person,
There will be harmony in the home;
If there is harmony in the home,
There will be order in the nation;
If there is order in the nation,
There will be peace in the world.'

Lao Tzu, China

'Every gun that is made, every warship launched, every rocket fired, signifies in the final sense a theft from those who hunger and are not fed, those who are cold and are not clothed.'

Dwight Eisenhower, USA

'If you want peace, prepare for peace.'

motto of University for Peace, Costa Rica

'There is no way to peace. Peace is the way.'

Mahatma Gandhi, India

'Since wars began in the minds of men, it is in the minds of men that the defences of peace must be constructed.'

Preamble to the Constitution of UNESCO

'Violence damages its own perpetrators as much as it harms its victims.'

Bishop C B Daly, Belfast, Northern Ireland

'Non-violence is the weapon of the strong.'

Mahatma Gandhi, India

'Without justice, peace is nothing but a nice-sounding word.'

Dom Helder Camara, Brazil

Thoughts on peace (2)

'The unleashed power of the atom has changed everything except our ways of thinking.'
Albert Einstein, USA

'You will never understand violence or non-violence until you understand the violence to the spirit that happens from watching your children die of malnutrition.'
Food First

'I object to violence because when it appears to do good, the good is only temporary – the evil it does is permanent.'
Mahatma Gandhi, India

'I wondered why somebody didn't do something, for peace . . . Then I realised that I am somebody.'
Anonymous

'Peace *is* development, development *is* peace.'
Johan Galtung, Norway

'Never doubt that a small group of thoughtful committed citizens can change the world. Indeed – it's the only thing that ever has.'
Margaret Mead, USA

'Who is the greatest of heroes? He who converts his enemy into his friend.'
Avot D'Rabbi Nathan 23, Israel

'If we are to reach real peace in this world . . . we shall have to begin with the children.'
Mahatma Gandhi, India

Why teach about change and the future?

Most educational systems have as one of their aims the preparation of students for the future. Indeed, it is only the existence of the future that gives education any sort of purpose. Yet most school curricula are heavily focused on the past, and give students little opportunity to reflect on where they are going, and what they might ultimately be doing with the knowledge they are accumulating.

Talk to a school-age child about what the future will be like, and you are apt to be subjected to a barrage of images – space travel, robots, weapons of destruction, and intergalactic battle. Their impressions of the future are shaped largely by television, films, video and computer games.

> **'... most of learning, especially learning in school, is concerned with the past, and ... students are taught to drive into the future through a rear-view mirror.'**
>
> **S. Nicholson, *The Future of Politics*, 1982**

Rarely are young people given the opportunity to reflect thoughtfully in an educational setting about what kind of world they would really like to live in. But when such an opportunity is provided, students often amaze their teachers with their serious attitudes of concern and caring about the future. Today's young people will spend most of their lives in the 21st century, and it should come as no surprise that they care deeply about what their future holds in store for them.

The future can be treated as a dimension to be considered across all subject areas, as a cross-curricular theme. Education about the future can help to make students more aware of how actions taken in the past have affected the present, and of the fact that actions taken in the present will shape the future. It can help students understand that the future is not fixed and predetermined, but subject to change. There are a variety of alternative futures which may occur, and it is our behaviour today which decides which of these alternatives will become reality. For the purpose of learning about the future is not to make a game of predicting what might happen in a given number of years; students need to learn about alternative futures because of the urgent need for all members of society to make well-informed choices in the present.

It is a fact that change is happening at a faster pace today than in previous centuries. Education about the future must be linked to an exploration of the process of change and an understanding of how change occurs. The rapid changes that are occurring locally, nationally, and globally produce feelings in many students of being overwhelmed or helpless, or lacking in the ability to control the forces that affect their lives. While students need to accept that some alternatives for change and action may not be open to them, exploring realistic possibilities can be empowering, and a healthy antidote to despair. Students need to leave their schools with a belief in their own capacity to affect the change process, and a willingness to do so.

Some key concepts

ALTERNATIVE FUTURES

A number of different futures are possible. The future is not a single, predetermined entity. It can be useful to categorise these alternatives into **possible**, **probable**, and **preferable** futures.

CHOICE AND EMPOWERMENT

All people have the responsibility to make conscious and informed choices about the future. Every choice made in the present has an impact that extends over time, helping to create change and bring about a certain kind of future. Human beings are not at the mercy of the forces of change; human beings *are* the forces of change.

REACTION AND PRO-ACTION

One can face the future by waiting for problems or crises to take shape and then *reacting* to them. It is important to understand that even a person who chooses to do nothing in the face of a local, national, or global problem has made a choice which has social, political, and economic consequences.

One can also face the future by being *pro-active* – by considering current events and trends, anticipating possible outcomes, and taking action either to avert greater problems or promote more just, sustainable, and peaceful alternatives.

Teaching about change and the future: Aims and objectives

Knowledge	*Skills*	*Attitudes*
• Knowledge of major development issues and trends, past and present. • Knowledge of the main factors which cause change. • Understanding the difference between short- and long-term change, and between desirable and undesirable change. • Understanding of one's own personal options for creating change.	• Ability to think hypothetically. • Being able to envisage a variety of alternatives and their outcomes. • Ability to analyse and evaluate alternatives. • Ability to translate knowledge and skills into concrete action at local, regional and global levels.	• Belief in one's own ability to create positive change. • Outlook of hopefulness, of not seeing oneself as, or allowing oneself to become, the victim of larger global issues and problems. • A readiness to take practical action which is appropriate to the learner's own situation.

Activity 48

Simple changes

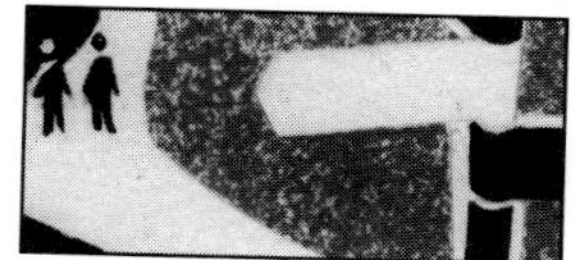

Age level 1: 7–11 years

OBJECTIVES

To encourage students to see the process of change as a series of steps, and to help them reflect on the factors that bring about different types of change.

MATERIALS

A copy of one of the sets of **Simple changes** cards (pages 255–7), cut into individual cards, for each pair of students; glue, paper and pencils.

PROCEDURE

Step 1

Students form pairs. Each pair receives *one* set of **Simple changes** cards (six cards, including one blank card).

Step 2

Students work together to put their cards in a logical sequence that shows how a change takes place. The blank card is to be the last card in the sequence. Students can decide on a final step in the sequence, which they draw themselves on this blank card.

When students have completed the sequencing, they stick their cards onto paper with glue.

Step 3

Students join with another pair that had the same set of cards, and compare both the sequence and the final step.

Step 4

As a class, the students discuss the following questions:

- How were the three sets of cards different? (The teacher may wish to point out that the first set deals with a change in nature, the second with a change in an individual, and the third with a community change.)
- For each set of cards, what were the forces that brought about change?

VARIATIONS

1 Younger students may simply put five cards in sequence, leaving off the blank card with the final step.

2 Students make up new sequencing cards appropriate to their classmates' ages and interests.

FOLLOW-UP

Students collect a series of newspaper articles about a change that is occurring in their community, nation, or the wider world. They make a set of sequencing cards that illustrate the change.

IN THE CURRICULUM

The activity develops skills in interpreting visual images, sequencing, and anticipating consequences. It could be used in an English, humanities, or science class.

Simple changes cards (1)

worksheet

worksheet

Simple changes cards (2)

Simple changes cards (3)

worksheet

Activity 49

Alternative futures cartoons

Age level 1: 7–11 years

OBJECTIVES

To introduce students to the idea that the future is not fixed, but that there are alternative futures; to encourage them to anticipate the consequences of actions.

MATERIALS

A copy of one **Alternative futures** cartoon (pages 260–3) for each pair of students, pencils.

PROCEDURE

Step 1

Students form pairs. Each pair receives one of the **Alternative futures** cartoons. They read the first two frames, and then complete the cartoon by drawing pictures, and writing captions if necessary, in the next four frames.

Step 2

Pairs of students then join together to form groups of four. This should be done by having each pair with Cartoon 1 join with a pair that has Cartoon 2. The first frames of Cartoon 1 and 2 are identical, but the second frames are different. Thus, the outcomes drawn by the students are likely to be different.

Similarly, each pair with Cartoon 3 should join with a pair that has Cartoon 4. These two cartoons also begin in the same way, but the second frames show various alternatives, which will affect the outcome.

Pairs explain their cartoon endings to each other.

Step 3

Students post their completed cartoons around the room, and walk around looking at each others' work.

Step 4

The class comes together to discuss the results of the activity. The following questions can be raised:

- What was your first reaction when you saw the cartoon that the other pair had completed?
- Did pairs whose cartoons had the same first frame also have the same ending? Why or why not?
- What are some other possible events that could have changed the outcome of the cartoon?
- In real life situations, is a particular outcome the only one possible, or are there usually a number of possible outcomes?

VARIATION

Students use the events in story books as the basis for the cartoons.

FOLLOW-UP

Students collect stories of current events, problems or conflicts from radio or television broadcasts. They discuss some of the possible outcomes of these events, and try to predict what will happen next. They reflect on the factors at work that might change the course of events.

IN THE CURRICULUM

The activity requires skills in sequencing and anticipating consequences. It could be used in an English or humanities class, depending on the topic of the cartoon.

worksheet

Alternative futures (1)

Paul, you should go back to your own country. We don't want you here!

You can't talk to me like that!

Alternative futures (2)

worksheet

Paul, you should go back to your own country. We don't want you here!

Paul is my friend. I don't want you to say those things to him.

worksheet

Alternative futures (3)

Our baby needs to go to the clinic to get her shots.

The clinic is too far away. Our baby is not sick. She doesn't need shots.

Alternative futures (4)

worksheet

Our baby needs to go to the clinic to get her shots.

She might cry, but the shots will keep her from getting sick later.

CLINIC

Activity 50

Interviews about change

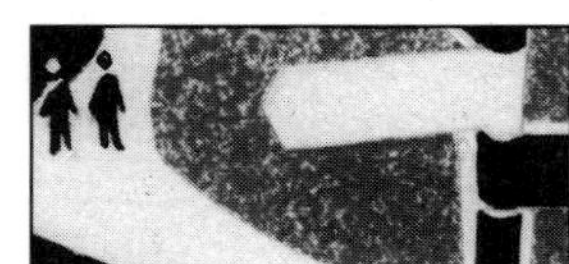

Age level 1: 7–11 years

OBJECTIVES

To help students gain an understanding of the forces that have brought about positive change on a local or national level; to increase their awareness of change as a process which takes place over time.

MATERIALS

Paper and pencils; tape recorders (optional).

PROCEDURE

Step 1

Pairs of students invite an adult member of their family, school, neighbourhood or community to participate in an interview on **Change in our community/country**. The adults being interviewed are asked to think of a community (or national) issue or problem which has changed for the better in their lifetime (for example, a new clinic built to respond to health care needs, a new school built to relieve overcrowding, environmental pollution which was cleaned up, or a conflict between two groups that was resolved).

Step 2

Prior to the interview, students plan the questions they might ask, such as:

- What is a situation that has changed for the better in your lifetime?
- What was it like before any changes took place?
- How did the change begin?
- What happened next?
- How do you feel about this change now?
- Are there things about this situation that you would still like to see changed?
- What might make those changes happen?

Step 3

Students carry out the interview, taking notes. If possible, recording the interview with a tape recorder is helpful.

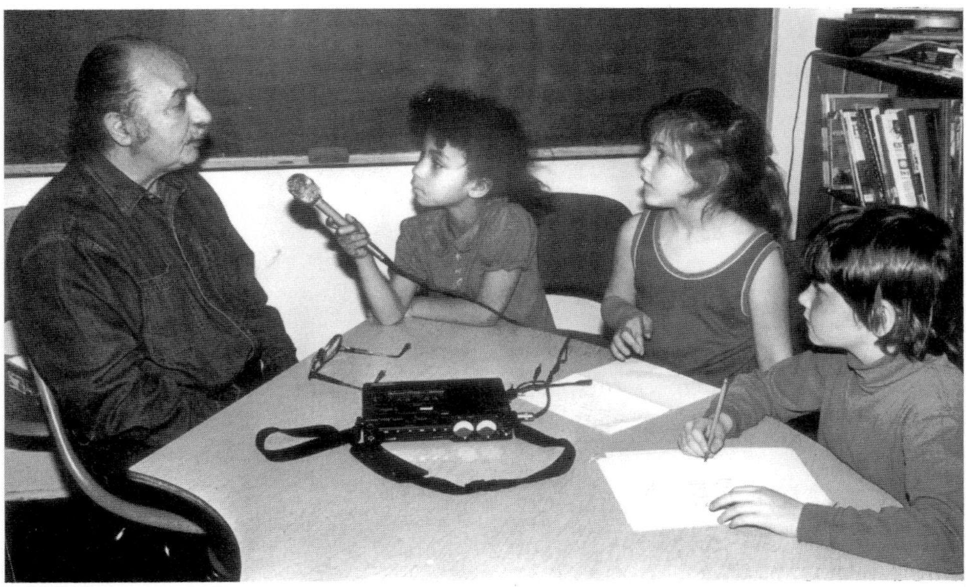

'Tell us about a change that has happened in your lifetime'

Step 4

The students report to the class on what they learned. Summaries of the interviews may be compiled into a class book on 'Change in our world'.

VARIATION

The interviews may be done by older students as homework.

FOLLOW-UP

Students can listen to radio or television news broadcasts for stories of changes that are occurring in their community or country. Summaries of these can be compiled on a large chart.

IN THE CURRICULUM

The activity develops questioning, listening, and recording skills. It can be used in a humanities class, as part of a unit on local or national history.

Age level 2:
12–15 years

Activity 51

Personal time lines

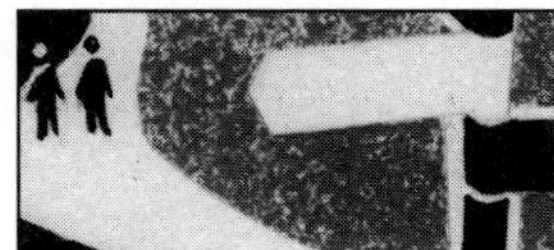

OBJECTIVES

To enable students to see the past, present, and future as a continuum; to introduce the idea of alternative futures.

MATERIALS

Paper and a pencil for each student.

PROCEDURE

Step 1

Working individually, students draw a horizontal line that stops half-way across their sheet of paper. They are told that the point farthest to the left represents their birth, and that the point farthest to the right represents the present. Between these two points, they are to plot along the line the major events of their lives to date.

If necessary, the teacher may suggest what some of these might be – birthdays, moving to a new class in school, births of siblings, moving house, trips, illnesses, starting a new hobby or interest, etc. A sample time line could be drawn on the blackboard (see page 268).

Step 2

From the point representing the present, students are then asked to draw two arms or branches (the time line will now look like the letter Y on its side). Each branch represents a different possible future.

The upper branch indicates events that might happen in the student's *ideal* future. The lower branch indicates events that students think are likely to be part of their *probable* future.

Step 3

Each student joins another and explains her time line. They discuss their alternative futures, any differences between the ideal and the probable future, and why those differences exist.

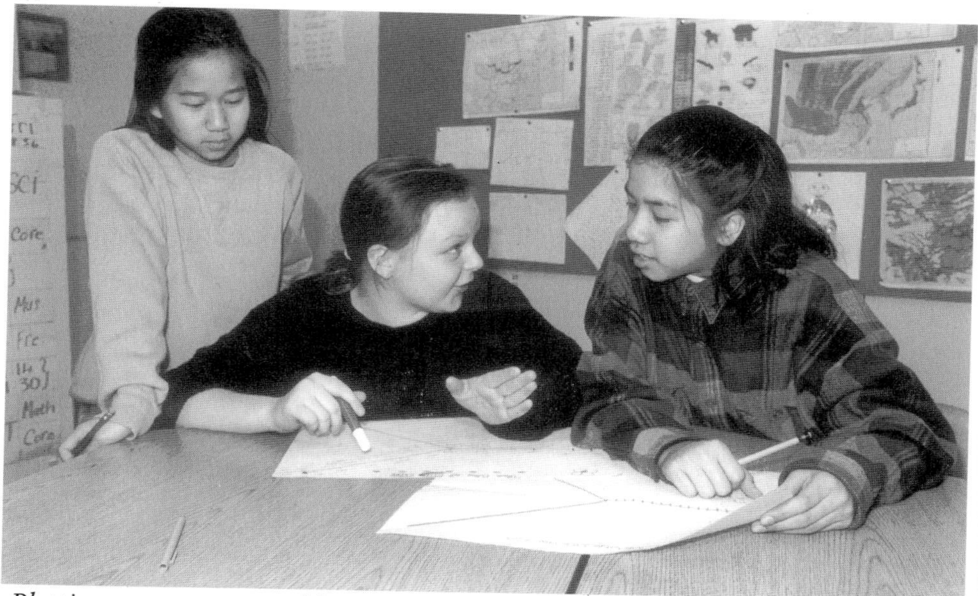

Plotting past, present and future on a personal time line

Step 4

As a class, the students discuss the following questions:

- Did anyone include events (past, present, or future) that were of a global or national nature, rather than only personal?
- Did anyone feel that their ideal future was likely to occur? Why or why not?
- What actions would need to be taken in the present in order for the ideal future to become a reality?
- Which of these actions could practically be taken?

VARIATIONS

1 If younger students find the idea of a time line difficult to grasp, they can begin by plotting the events from a familiar story that the teacher has read to the class along a time line.

Then they can try making a simple personal time line which extends into adulthood, but without the two branches.

2 Older students review their personal time lines, and choose one event which they consider the most significant or important. They imagine how their lives would have been different if this event had not taken place. They then draw new time lines, including projections into the future, which show how their lives would have changed.

3 Or, they pick a significant technological development, and consider how

their lives would be different if, for example, cars had not been invented. (Or computers, television, airplanes, vaccinations.)

4 Older students may also wish to choose a well-known local or national event – perhaps the building of a new road or playground, construction of new shops or a school, the election of a particular official – and project how their lives would have been different if this event had not occurred.

FOLLOW-UP

Students consider the types of actions that might be taken in order to bring about their ideal or preferred future. Students attempt to write a contract with themselves to do one of those things. The contracts can be posted on a bulletin board.

IN THE CURRICULUM

The activity develops skills in sequencing and anticipating consequences. It could be used in a humanities or English class.

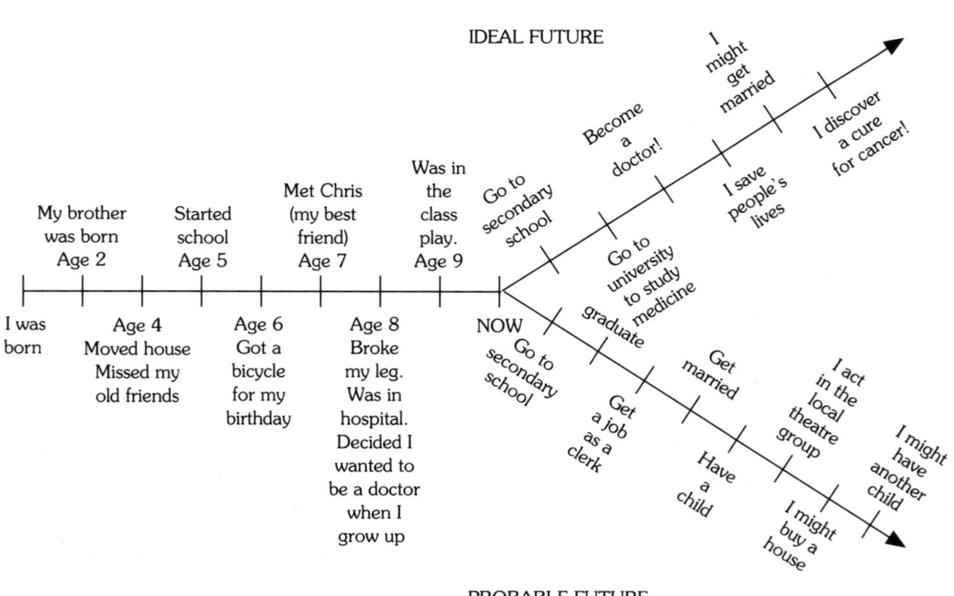

Ideal and probable futures

Activity 52 Steps to change

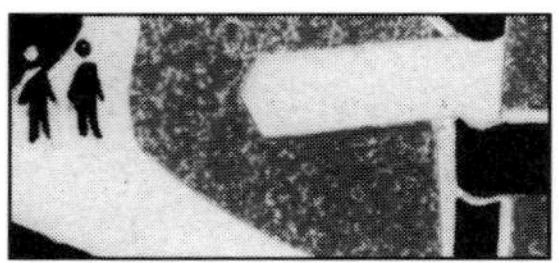

Age level 2: 12–15 years

OBJECTIVES

To help students see that change can come about in a sequence of carefully planned steps; to familiarise them with development issues around the world in which local efforts have brought about change.

MATERIALS

A copy of one of the **Steps to change** sheets (pages 271–3) for each group of three to four students; these should be cut into sections to form eight individual sequencing cards, which are placed in an envelope. Paper and glue are also required. (The teacher should keep a master copy of each of the **Steps to change** sheets for reference, as this shows the steps listed in their correct sequence.)

PROCEDURE

Step 1

The students form groups of three or four. Each small group is given an envelope containing eight sequencing cards from *one* of the **Steps to change** sheets.

The students are told that the envelopes contain cards telling the story of a problem in a developing country and the steps its people took to bring about a positive change. The card with the number 1 on it sets the scene in this country, describing the problem. The card with the number 8 on it tells what the situation was like after the change took place.

Step 2

The students read the other cards and decide what order to place them in so that the story of the change is told in a logical sequence. When this is done, and each person in the small group agrees on the sequence of the story, they may write the numbers 2, 3, 4, etc. on the cards, and glue them to a piece of paper.

Step 3

When everyone has finished, small groups which had the same story can meet together to compare their results. The stories are then read aloud to the whole class.

Step 4

The class discusses the following questions:

- What were the factors that brought about change? (Government action? Action by non-governmental organisations? The work of one committed individual? Local organising by the people involved? Other factors?)
- Do you think the changes made will have a short-term or a long-term impact on the people? Why?
- Can you think of other similar situations in which people would benefit from the types of actions taken in the stories?

VARIATION

Students look only at the first and last sequencing cards, and brainstorm ways in which they think the change might have come about. They follow the brainstorm with the sequencing activity, and compare the results.

FOLLOW-UP

1 Students write to UNICEF field offices to find out more about the projects described.

2 They research local changes which have had a positive impact, create stories about them, and design sequencing activities for each other, or for other classes.

IN THE CURRICULUM

The activity develops skills in critical thinking, sequencing, and imagination. It can be used in a humanities class during a study of a developing country. It could also be used in an English class to help students understand the logical sequencing of events in a piece of writing.

Steps to change in Ceara (North-east Brazil)

1 In 1986, two thirds of the people in the state of Ceara lived below the poverty line. 28 per cent of the children were malnourished, and many of them died before they were a year old.

In 1986, a newly elected government conducted a survey on the health conditions of children in Ceara, and found that action had to be taken to change these conditions.

The government decided it had to work first on getting health care information to the people who needed it most.

The government asked television, radio, businesses, and churches to spread information about health care issues, such as nutrition, immunisation, and preventing diseases.

The response of the Catholic Church was especially strong. It provided thousands of volunteers to bring health care messages to the poorest areas.

When more people had information about health, the government trained thousands of low-income women in basic health practices.

The women who were most skilled were given additional training as community health workers. They were placed around the state, and each was responsible for the needs of 100 families.

8 In Ceara today, malnutrition and the infant death rate have been reduced by one-third. The immunisation rate is up by 40 per cent.

worksheet

Steps to change in Lebanon

1 In 1989, after years of war in Lebanon, children of different religious and cultural groups had practically no contact with each other. They lived in different neighbourhoods and went to different schools.

Because young people of different religions and cultures were full of fear and suspicion toward each other, UNICEF officials in Lebanon decided to try to bring them together by setting up a summer 'Peace Camp'.

First, young people who had experience in summer recreation camps or in scouts were trained to become monitors. They learned how to help children get to know each other, learn from each other, and become friends.

When the monitors were trained, a Peace Camp for children from different religious and cultural groups was opened in July 1989.

Children were brought to the Peace Camp in buses. UNICEF arranged for them to pass the many security checkpoints.

Once they arrived at the Peace Camp, some children were frightened of being with others who were different from themselves. But after living, working, and playing together, many became close friends.

Because of the success of the Peace Camp, other organisations decided to open similar camps.

---

8 By 1990, tens of thousands of young people had attended Peace Camps in Lebanon, overcoming their fears and prejudices about different groups. Now the UNICEF office in Lebanon is preparing an Education for Peace curriculum for schools.

Steps to change in Honiara (Solomon Islands)

1 Several years ago, people living in the capital city of Honiara found that their wages were too low to be able to afford the freshly grown food which was brought in from the countryside. Child malnutrition began to rise, as did diseases related to poor nutrition in adults.

Dr Helen Paton, the Town Council Medical Officer, became concerned about the increase in malnutrition.

With some nurses and other concerned local people, Dr Paton started a gardening club, to help city dwellers grow their own food.

The new gardening club got support from the Town Council, which gave it some land on a hillside near the centre of town.

With this extra land, the club could take in more members. It began advertising, using radio, posters, a special magazine, and a song contest.

The advertising campaign encouraged many women to join the club. UNICEF was asked to provide support for classes in nutrition, gardening, crop rotation, and composting.

Some women who have been gardening club members for several years, and have taken the nutrition and gardening classes, have now begun to return to their villages in the country, taking with them improved ways of growing food.

8 Malnutrition in Honiara is beginning to decrease, and parents can now feed their children nutritious food that they have grown themselves.

worksheet

Activity 53

Jobs and the future

OBJECTIVES

To encourage students to think about how technology has changed, and will continue to change our lives.

MATERIALS

The Help Wanted sections of local newspapers; copies of the sheets titled **Jobs today** and **Jobs in the future?** (pages 276 and 277).

PROCEDURE

Step 1

Working in pairs, students look through the Help Wanted section of a newspaper. They circle jobs which they think would not have existed a hundred years ago.

Step 2

Together they fill in the sheet titled **Jobs today**, noting the name of the job circled and the reason it exists now, but did not in the past.

Step 3

The whole class discusses the reasons why jobs have changed over time. Technology may figure prominently among these reasons. Students should reflect on changing economic and social needs as well.

Step 4

Pairs join together to form groups of four. Together they fill in the **Jobs in the future?** sheet.

Step 5

The whole class then comes together to discuss the results of the activity. Questions might include:

- What types of jobs do you think will be eliminated in the future?
- What types of jobs will still be needed in the future?
- Can you think of a job that will be needed in the future that does not exist today?

- What kinds of changing social or economic conditions might cause a need for a new type of job?
- What are some of the benefits that might be a result of these new jobs?
- What are some of the problems that could arise from these new jobs?
- How might these potential problems be solved?

VARIATION

Students research jobs which existed in the past, but no longer exist today. Why are these jobs obsolete?

FOLLOW-UP

1 Students write a newspaper advertisement for a job that might exist in the future. What skills and qualifications would be required for such a job? How would applicants acquire these skills?

2 Students could invite representatives of the business community and employment agencies to speak to the class about what types of jobs they feel will be most needed in the short-term future (the next ten to 15 years).

IN THE CURRICULUM

The activity involves skills in reading, evaluating, critical thinking, divergent thinking, and anticipating consequences. It would be appropriate in a history or economics class, or in a unit on career awareness.

worksheet

Jobs today

This job didn't exist a hundred years ago:	***The reason this job exists today is . . .***

Jobs in the future?

	Do you think this job will be needed 30 years from now?	***Why or why not?***
Doctor		
Farmer		
Police Officer		
Computer Programmer		
Teacher		

worksheet

Activity 54 A history of the future

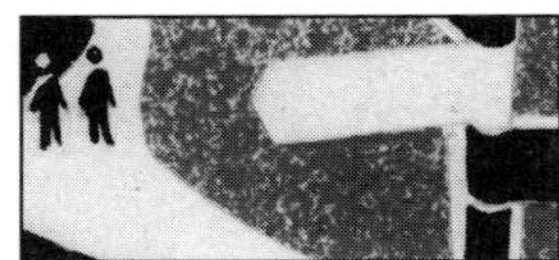

Age level 2: 12–15 years

OBJECTIVES

To encourage students to apply what they know about the factors that bring about change to a current global issue.

MATERIALS

A4 paper and pencils, large sheets of paper or poster board, plus paste or glue.

PROCEDURE

Step 1

Students form groups of four. They are told to imagine that they are living 50 years in the future. At this future time, the world has just achieved a major accomplishment: a clean environment for every individual is now a reality.

The small groups have the task of creating a photo history showing the actions that occurred to reach this milestone. They do this with drawings and captions that show the sequence of steps taken over the last 50 years to create this change. The drawings are pasted on to the large paper or poster board.

Step 2

When each small group has completed its project, they display their results around the room, and students circulate to view them all.

Step 3

They then discuss the following questions:

- Was there one cause of the change, or many causes?
- What were the most important factors which led to this change: individual action, work of non-governmental organisations, community action, government intervention, corporate actions?
- What would the main obstacles have been to this change? Why?
- Did students think that 50 years was a reasonable amount of time to allow for such a massive change? Why or why not?

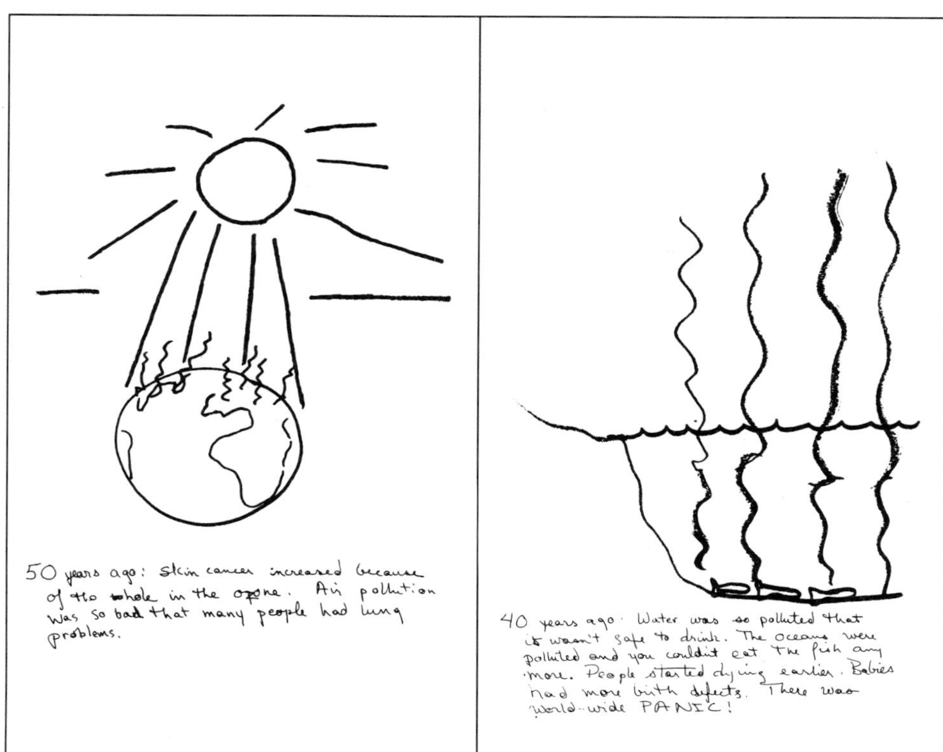

50 years ago: Skin cancer increased because of the whole in the ozone. Air pollution was so bad that many people had lung problems.
40 years ago: Water was so polluted that it wasn't safe to drink. The oceans were polluted and you couldn't eat the fish any more. People started dying earlier. Babies had more birth defects. There was world-wide PANIC!

Environmental clean-up – a history of the future in nine illustrations

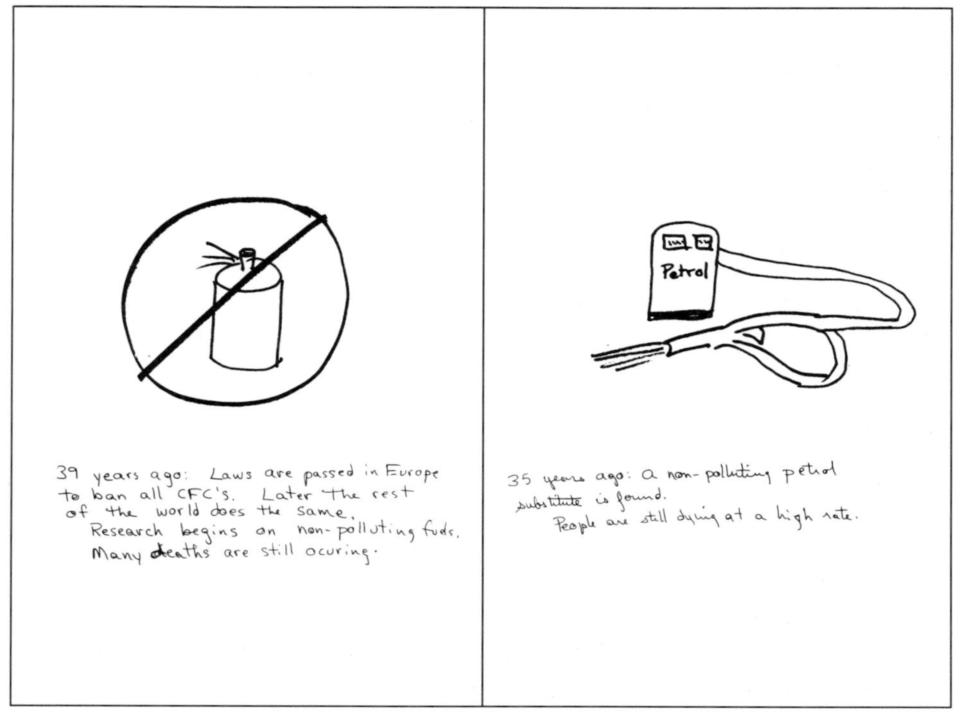

39 years ago: Laws are passed in Europe to ban all CFC's. Later the rest of the world does the same. Research begins on non-polluting fuels. Many deaths are still ocuring.
Petrol
35 years ago: a non-polluting petrol substitute is found. People are still dying at a high rate.

30 years ago the first evidence that the ozone layer is coming back is found.

There are non-polluting cars on the market.

25 years ago: Laws force the industries which have poluted the rivers and oceans to clean up the water and pay heavy fines.

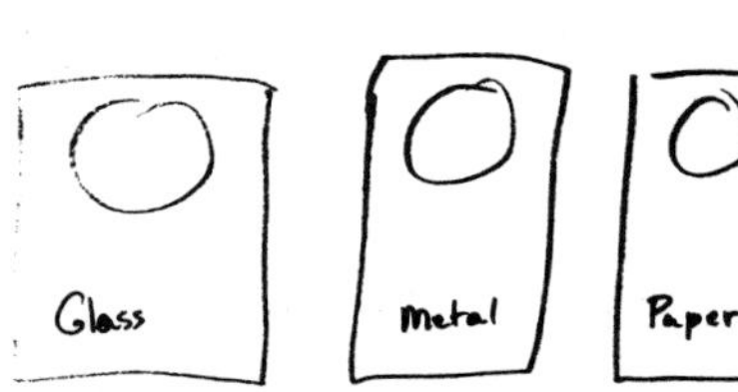

15 years ago: People are living longer. Cancers and birth defects are decreasing.

Laws are passed to make everyone recycle. People who don't recycle pay fines or go to jail.

5 years ago. The ozone hole is almost closed up.

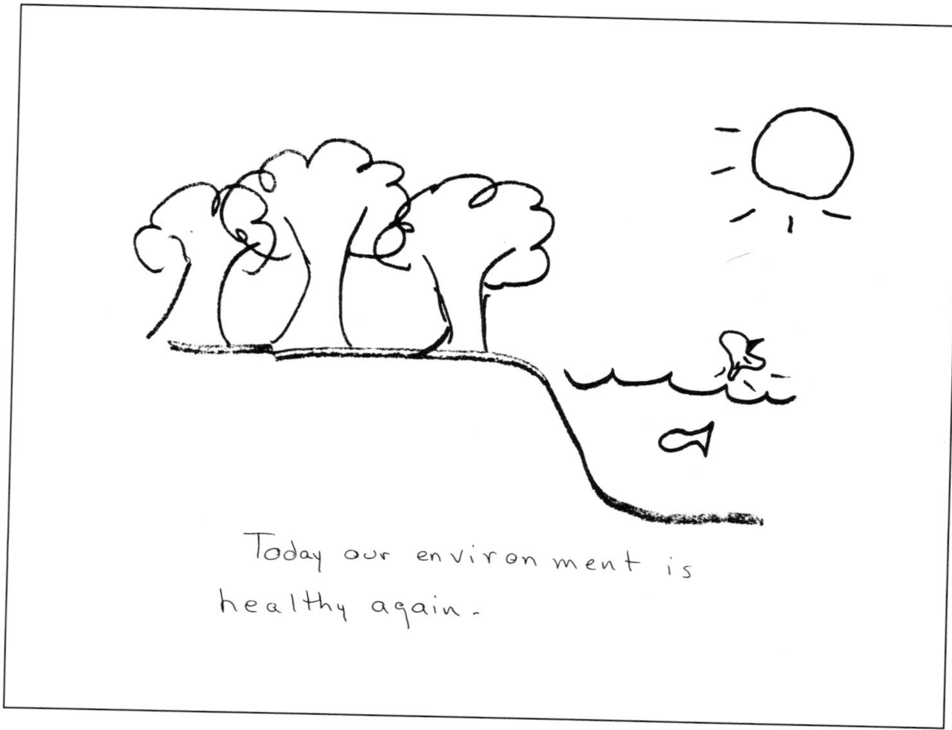
Today our environment is
healthy again.

VARIATIONS

1 Students write their history as if it was to be included in a school textbook.

2 The activity can be applied to other issues. For example, small groups could write a history of how a (current) regional conflict was ended, how racial prejudice was eliminated, or how world hunger was eradicated.

FOLLOW-UP

Students contact a non-governmental organisation working in the area of environmental protection (or another issue chosen by the class), to find out more about its efforts to bring about change.

IN THE CURRICULUM

The activity develops skills in creative and divergent thinking, analysis, understanding of consequences and sequencing. It could be used in a history class, or in an English class in conjunction with the study of a piece of literature which deals with futuristic or Utopian themes.

Age level 3:
16–18 years

Activity 55

Future scenarios

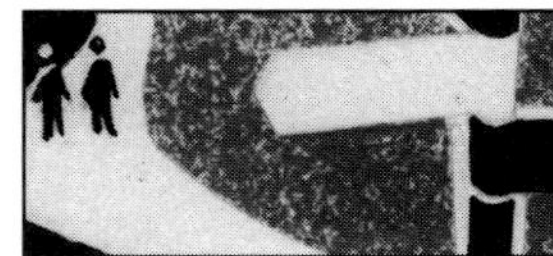

OBJECTIVES

To acquaint young people with a variety of possible perspectives on current issues, change and the future; to explore the consequences of these various perspectives.

MATERIALS

Copies of the **Future scenarios** sheet (page 285); paper and pencils.

PROCEDURE

Step 1

The class picks *one* current global issue or problem as a focus for the activity. Possible issues might include:

- ethnic nationalism;
- global warming;
- hunger;
- increasing drug use worldwide;
- homelessness;
- increased migration of peoples;
- urban crime;
- racism.

The teacher explains that the class will be examining this issue through the perspective of five different future scenarios. Each of these five scenarios shows a different way in which the issue might evolve.

Step 2

Students form groups of four or five. Each small group receives a copy of *one* of the **Future scenarios**.

Within their small group, students are asked to reflect on the chosen issue and collaborate to write a three- to five-minute documentary-style news broadcast on it, according to the **Future scenario** they have been given.

Step 3

One member of each small group is then chosen to read her group's broadcast aloud, in the style of a television news report.

Step 4

The class discusses the following questions:

- What was your reaction to hearing all these different alternative futures?
- Did certain alternative futures seem less likely than others? Why?
- Did certain alternatives seem more likely than others? Why?
- Do you think that in reality this issue's future is reflected by only one of these scenarios, or will it be made up of aspects of several scenarios?
- Did hearing the alternatives cause you to feel like taking some kind of action? If so, was this more true for any particular alternative? What would that action be?
- In writing and listening to the scenarios, did anyone assume that the issue chosen had only to do with developing countries? Is this issue a reality in industrialised countries?

VARIATIONS

1 A variety of local, national, or global issues can be used.

2 A simpler version of the activity may be carried out by having students select one issue, and write a news report that is either pessimistic (emphasising the dangers and problems that will arise from this situation), or optimistic (emphasising opportunities for creative and constructive solutions to the current situation).

Is most news reporting about the future optimistic or pessimistic? What might be the reason for this? What do you think the effects of consistently optimistic news reporting might be on the listener? What do you think the long-term effects of consistently pessimistic news reporting might be?

FOLLOW-UP

Young people listen to radio or television news programmes, or read newspaper articles having to do with the future, and attempt to determine if the reporter/author is basing the story on the assumptions of one of the five future scenarios. Is one type of scenario more common than the others? Which one? Why might this be so?

What might be the effect on the listener of news about current issues which is consistently reported from only one of these various perspectives?

IN THE CURRICULUM

The activity develops skill in becoming aware of different points of view, critical thinking, comparing and evaluating. It could be done in a humanities class on world issues. It could also be used in an English class to examine how points of view are expressed in writing, or on detecting underlying assumptions.

Note: The five scenarios described on page 285 are adapted from those described by James Robertson in *The Sane Alternative* (1983).

Future scenarios

worksheet

1 THE 'BUSINESS AS USUAL' SCENARIO

The future will be basically the same as the present is. Local, national, and global problems will be dealt with in much the same way as they are today, and attitudes toward these problems will be similar to what they are today.

2 THE 'DISASTER' SCENARIO

Present problems, such as hunger, pollution, poverty, and war, will increase. At some point there will be a worldwide disaster or breakdown of human and natural systems.

3 THE 'AUTHORITARIAN' SCENARIO

Disaster will be prevented by powerful and more controlling governments. Strong government action will enforce order and distribute resources.

4 THE 'HYPER-EXPANSIONIST' SCENARIO

Present problems will be solved by the development of new, powerful technologies. Expanding scientific and technological research and development is the only way to deal with critical world issues.

5 THE 'HUMANE ECOLOGICAL' SCENARIO

Global problems can be solved by a shift in attitude, toward ecological awareness, justice in human relationships, and an understanding of the need for a partnership between humanity and nature to promote a climate of peace. The role of central authorities is minimised.

Activity 56 Lawmakers of the future

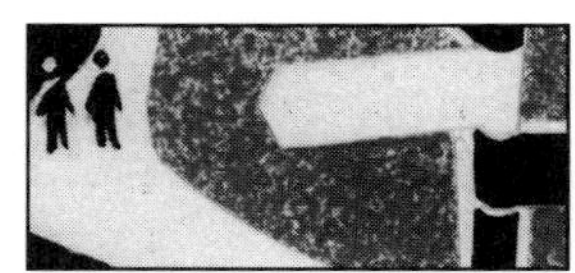

OBJECTIVES

To encourage young people to consider what kind of society they would like to be living in 20 years from now; to explore the possibilities and limitations of legislation for creating positive future change.

MATERIALS

A copy of the **Proposed laws for a future world** sheet (pages 289–90) and the **Effects matrix** sheet (page 291) for each group of three or four students; paper and pencils.

PROCEDURE

Step 1

Students are told to imagine that they are living 20 years in the future. Because of widespread global problems during this future time, an international council has been established. While nations still exist, and national governments still have the power to make laws, this imaginary council can also pass legislation.

The students are to visualise themselves as the lawmakers of the international council. They are presently considering 12 proposed new laws, and must decide if these are to take effect.

Step 2

The class is divided into groups of or three or four. Each small group receives a copy of *one* of the laws from the **Proposed laws for a future world** sheet to prepare a position on. They consider both the positive and negative effects of this proposed law, on both industrialised and developing countries. They use the **Effects matrix** to summarise their thinking, and to decide on whether or not this law should be put into effect.

Students have the option to rewrite the law if they feel this would make it more beneficial to all concerned.

Step 3

Each small group presents its opinion on the law they considered to the whole class.

Law No. 4

This law probably won't affect developing countries that much, since not as many people own cars as here. But it could be very damaging to countries that produce a lot of oil.

A lot of people in industrialised countries would object. It could be very harmful to the auto industry and people might lose their jobs.

More railways would have to be built. Traffic and pollution would be reduced.

A law like this doesn't really make sense, because the real problem is that we need to build cars with better pollution controls. It should be rewritten to require the auto industry to invent better pollution controls. It should have a way to encourage people to use public transport, but not force them to use it.

One group's reaction to a proposed law for the future

Step 4

A vote is then taken on whether or not to pass this law. (The teacher should anticipate that a range of viewpoints will exist in the class. The proposed laws are designed to promote discussion of these viewpoints. There is no correct or incorrect result of the voting process.)

Step 5

When all the laws have been voted on, the class discusses what was learned from the activity, addressing these questions:

- Which laws were easy to decide on? Which were difficult to decide on? Why?
- What kind of vision do you have of the Earth in 20 years? How did this affect the way you voted?
- Are any laws such as these currently being discussed in your own country? If so, how do you feel about them?
- Should global concerns be considered when national laws are passed, or should national interests take priority?
- Do you think it would be a good idea to have an international council? Why or why not?
- If there was an international council, what issues might it have jurisdiction over? What issues should it *not* have jurisdiction over?

VARIATIONS

1 The number of laws used can be reduced, depending on the age and ability level of the class.

2 Laws which were defeated can be considered a second time. Is there some way to rewrite this law to make it of benefit to the world's population?

FOLLOW-UP

Small groups research the functions of the United Nations. What types of issues, events, or decisions can it influence, and how?

IN THE CURRICULUM

The activity requires imagination, divergent thinking, anticipation of consequences, evaluation and decision-making. It would be appropriate in a humanities class on government or the role of the United Nations. It could also be used in an English class after reading literature on futuristic themes.

Proposed laws for a future world (1)

worksheet

1 Because of problems caused by people moving across national boundaries to escape regional conflicts and find better economic opportunities, a law has been proposed that would stop all immigration and emigration for five years.

2 In order to conserve our dwindling natural resources, a law has been proposed that would require all electric power companies to invest 35 per cent of their profits in research into solar and wind power.

3 In order to rebuild the health of the world's populations, a law has been proposed that would require all national governments to provide free health care to all their citizens.

4 In the interests of preventing further pollution of our fragile planet, a law has been proposed that would require all people who travel more than 20 miles to their place of work to use public transport.

5 Because our increasingly technological society requires a high level of education from its citizens, a law has been proposed that would require all young people to stay in school until they are 18 years old.

6 To relieve the long-standing problems of world hunger, a law has been proposed that would require all countries that produce an agricultural surplus to donate 40 per cent of it to countries in which hunger is a serious problem.

worksheet

Proposed laws for a future world (2)

7 In order to prevent the needless and wasteful deaths of our young children, a law has been proposed that would require all parents to vaccinate their children, or pay a substantial fine.

8 A law has been proposed that would require any country that starts an armed conflict against any other country to pay to the country it has attacked the full value of all property destroyed, as well as a sum in compensation for each human life lost.

9 In order to eliminate hatred between ethnic and racial groups, a law has been proposed that would require all countries to prohibit citizens from forming or joining organisations that discriminate against particular racial and ethnic groups, or act in any way to promote conflict or discrimination between groups.

10 Due to the urgent problems caused by overpopulation, a law has been proposed that would restrict all parents to having no more than two children.

11 A law has been proposed that would require all laws and customs that limit the rights and freedoms of women in any way to be abolished.

12 A law has been proposed that would require all car manufacturers to produce cars which do not use petroleum fuels in five years' time.

Effects matrix

The proposed law for a new world that we considered was:		
	Positive effects	*Negative effects*
For developing countries		
For industrialised countries		

Our recommendation on this law is: ______________________________

____

(Optional) We would need this additional information to make a decision on this law: ______________________________

____

____

(Optional) We would rewrite this law in the following way: ____________

____

____

worksheet

Activity 57

The futures tree

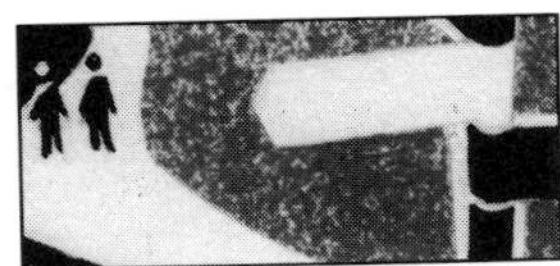

Age level 3: 16–18 years

OBJECTIVES

To introduce students to a technique which allows them to consider in depth the possible future impacts of a particular change.

MATERIALS

Large sheets of paper and felt-tip pens for each group of three; blank index cards in three colours, preferably blue, green and yellow.

PROCEDURE

Step 1

Explain to the class that it will be creating a futures tree to explore the impact of a change on various groups in society. Lead a brainstorming session on some current changes that are taking place locally, nationally or globally. Examples might be:

- an increase in the number of women working at what were once considered men's jobs;
- increasing racial and ethnic diversity in society;
- the reduction of the ozone layer;
- the rising incidence of AIDS among young people;
- the expansion of computer technology;
- the development of inexpensive solar and wind generators for electricity;
- funding cuts for education.

Ask the class to select one change to be the subject of their futures tree.

Step 2

Brainstorm with the class the various groups of people who might be directly affected by the change the class has chosen to focus on. Depending on the nature of this change, those groups might include:

children
parents
teachers
elected officials
police
business people
religious leaders
local media producers
health care personnel
social workers

Ask students to select four of these impact groups to include in the futures tree.

Step 3

Working in groups of three, students begin creating a futures tree diagram. They draw a tree trunk, which they label with a brief description of the change they are focusing on.

They then draw four short branches radiating from the trunk of their tree, and write the name of one of the four impact groups they selected on each branch.

Step 4

Each small group is given 12 green index cards. Ask students to focus on *one* impact group at a time and think of at least one, or as many as three, *immediate* consequences of the change for that group. Stress that the consequences can be either positive, negative or neutral. When this is done, the cards should be placed on the paper at the end of the appropriate branch.

> A futures tree is a complex activity to describe and carry out. Use the sample **Futures tree** diagram (page 296) to help explain the activity. This shows a diagram that was created by a group of teenagers on the topic of increasing numbers of women in traditionally male-dominated jobs. They decided that the four most important impact groups would be women, men, children and employers.
>
> The diagram may be reproduced and given to young people as a model, drawn on a blackboard or large paper for the whole group to see, or placed on an overhead transparency.

Step 5

Blue cards are then given to each small group. Students look at each immediate consequence (the green cards) and decide on at least one *secondary* consequence that would arise from it. Each secondary consequence is written on a blue card. The blue cards are then laid on the paper with a branching line connecting them to the corresponding green cards.

Step 6

Once this is done, the yellow cards are distributed. These represent *third order* consequences. Students follow the same procedure, this time looking at each blue card, deciding on a third order consequence which could arise from it, and laying it on the tree with a branching line connecting it to a blue card.

Step 7

At this point, the small groups take time to reflect on and discuss their **Futures trees**. They may stick down their cards with glue if each group member is satisfied with the arrangement. They may draw dotted lines between consequences from different branches that seem to be related to each other.

Step 8

Students move around the room to look at other groups' futures trees.

Step 9

Finally, the class discusses the following questions:

- Were there differences between the futures trees? If so, why?
- Were most of the anticipated effects positive or negative? Why might this be so?
- Did creating the diagram help you to think of effects of this change that you had not been aware of before? If so, what were they?

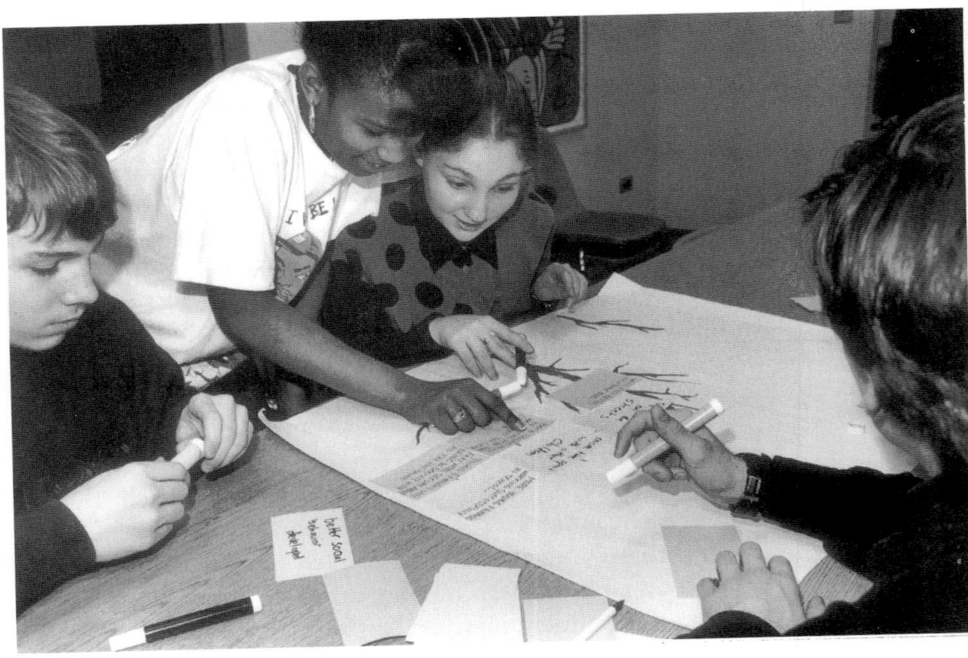

Anticipating the effects of change with a Futures tree

VARIATIONS

1 Small groups are assigned only *one* branch of the tree (women, men, children or employers, in the example) to work on. Groups can then combine their work to make one large collaborative planning tree.

2 The number of branches on the tree need not be limited to four.

3 If index cards are in short supply, young people simply draw the consequences on to the large paper.

FOLLOW-UP

1 The futures tree can extend indefinitely beyond three levels of consequences.

2 Students select an article from a newspaper and create a short-term **Futures tree** around it. They then follow the outcome of the event, and compare it to their futures tree to see how accurate their predictions were, and why.

3 Students can use a futures tree to help them plan an action project that they will carry out. A description of the project is placed on the trunk of the tree, and the impact of the project on various groups of people charted.

IN THE CURRICULUM

The activity requires skills in analysis, divergent thinking, anticipating consequences and sequencing. It can be used in a history class to examine the impact of a particular event. It could also be used in literature to examine the ramifications of events in literature. It would be useful in science classes for examining the impact of new inventions or technologies.

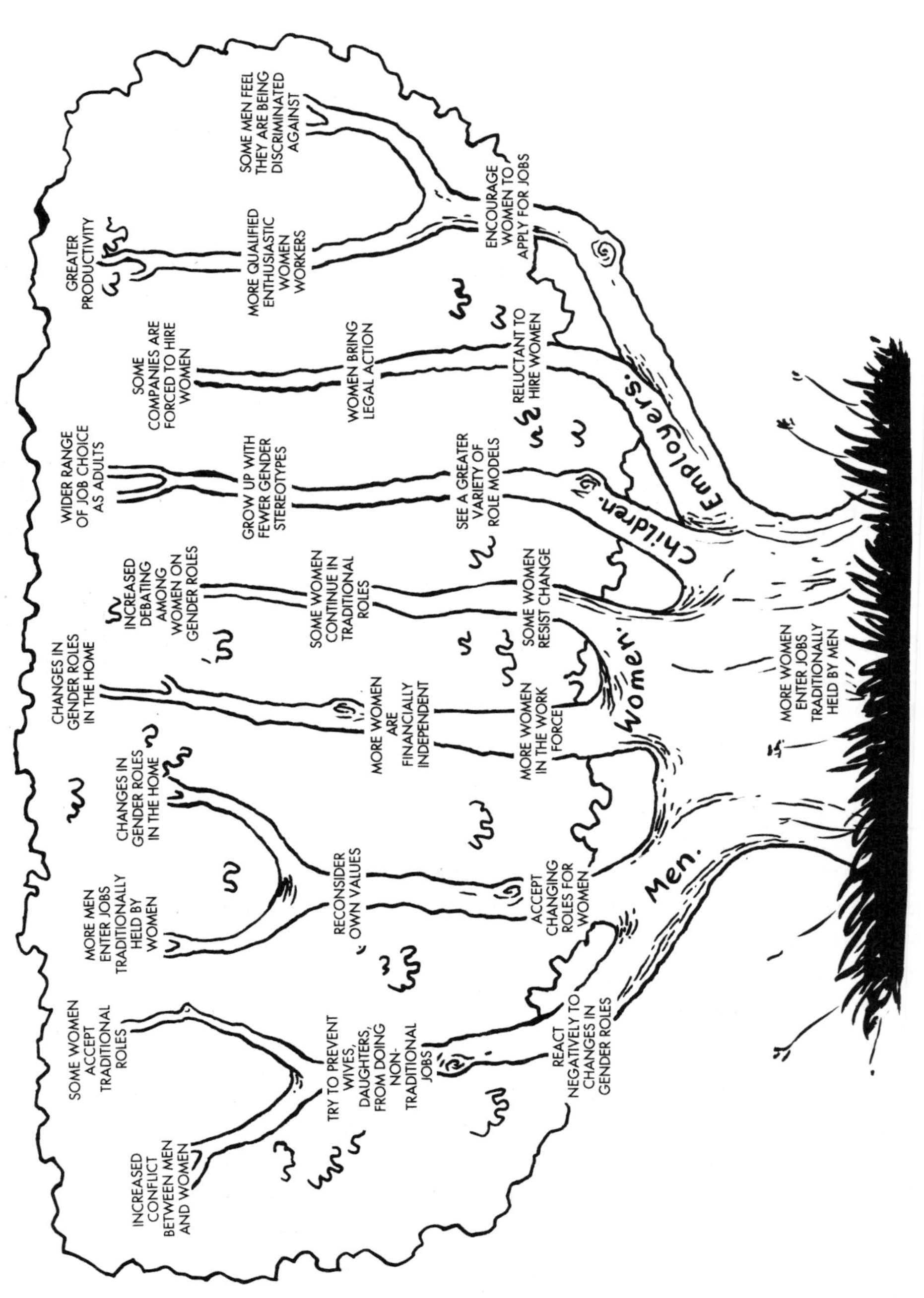

Futures tree – an example

The learning process in Education for Development involves more than a set of classroom activities and strategies. Taking practical action on global issues is a way for students to extend their knowledge, and practise the skills and attitudes necessary for global citizenship. Too often, teachers feel that taking action on global issues must mean that children attend international conferences or address gatherings of world leaders. In fact, the most exciting and significant action projects are usually ones that children carry out in their own communities.

Action projects can be more than just the culmination of a unit of study. They can serve as the rationale for gaining further knowledge on an issue. They can become the force which impels students to integrate learning from the various subject areas in a meaningful way.

The skills and attitudes required to take constructive action, whether on a local, national, or global level, must be developed over time. They cannot be expected to emerge full-blown in students who have never in the course of their education had the chance to plan and carry out action projects, any more than the skills of reading can be expected to develop in children who have never had the opportunity to read a book.

But not all projects are equally effective at extending students' knowledge, skills and attitudes. This is because action projects that are designed by teachers often vary widely in the level of participation they demand from students.

Levels of participation

There are many ways in which children can become involved in working for change, both locally and globally, but not all of these constitute participation in its fullest sense. The **Ladder of participation** diagram (on page 298) illustrates eight levels of participation. The degree of educational value increases as one climbs the rungs of the ladder.

Projects which correspond to the lowest three levels of the ladder cannot be considered truly participatory. **Manipulation** occurs when adults use children to promote a cause that they feel strongly about, but do not help children to understand that cause. When children are used as **Decoration**, they are often asked to dress in a certain way and perform to support an adult agenda, usually with the aim of prompting an emotional response on the part of adult viewers. **Tokenism** describes situations in which children are asked to speak before conferences or groups of elected representatives, but without learning anything substantative about the issue, determining their own position, or consulting with the other children who, it is claimed, they represent.

The next five rungs of the ladder designate increasing levels of real participation, and learning potential. Each may be appropriate for children at various times in the progressive development of their participatory skills.

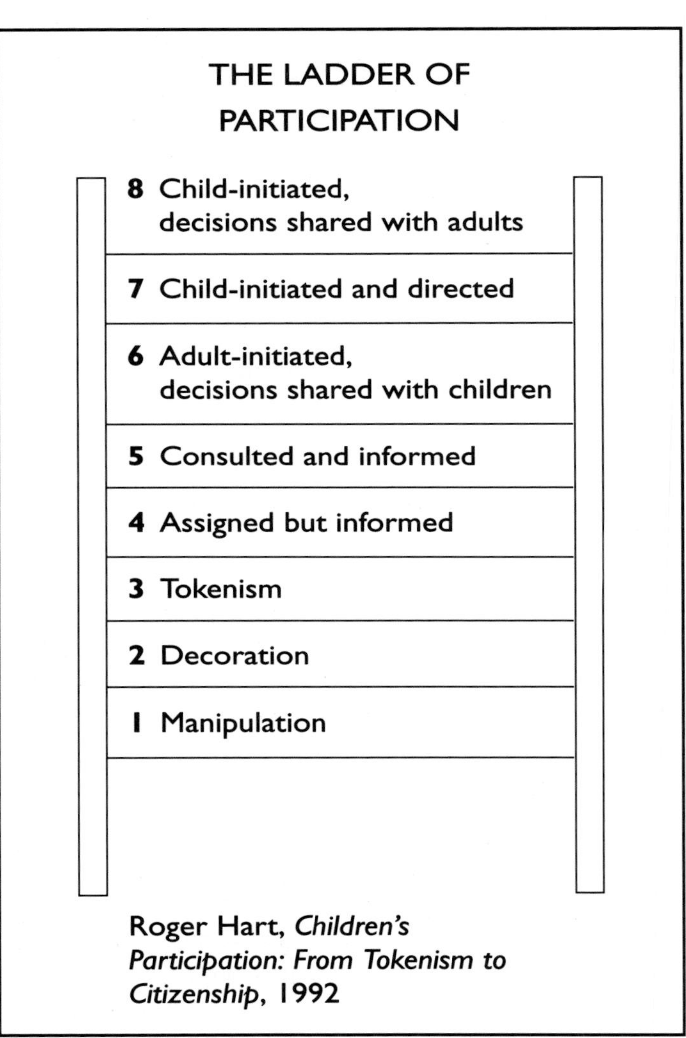

Roger Hart, *Children's Participation: From Tokenism to Citizenship*, 1992

Assigned but informed indicates that although the children's participation is decided for them, they understand the aims of the project, who decided that they should be involved, and why. At the level **Consulted and informed**, the project is designed by adults, but children's opinions are taken seriously in any decision-making processes. In projects which are **Adult-initiated, decisions shared with children**, children now have an integral role in making decisions, rather than a consultative status.

Child-initiated and directed projects are infrequently seen, because few adults are willing to relinquish complete control to children. Because of the lack of adult involvement, such projects often fail to become a true community concern, remaining somewhat marginalised. Projects which are **Child-initiated, decisions shared with adults**, however, involve adults as facilitators for the goals of the children, directing them to needed resources, providing support in developing necessary skills, and helping them to evaluate. This type of relationship enhances learning for the children, builds a sense of community ownership of the project, and provides adults with the opportunity to learn from the enthusiasm and creativity of the children.

Planning and implementing an action project

For teachers or youth group leaders undertaking an action project with young people, the guidelines suggested below will help to maximise the development of knowledge, skills, and attitudes essential to global citizenship. (These guidelines are adapted from material taken from *Taking Part*, Educators for Social Responsibility, 1987.)

IDENTIFY AN ISSUE AND CLARIFY AIMS

Sometimes a significant issue will emerge from classroom work. At other times, an issue will arise spontaneously – and unexpectedly – from an event in the community, nation, or the wider world. Young people can be encouraged to clarify their aims, and to make them as concrete as possible. It is often best for them to work for change in their own community, rather than to focus on issues that are ocurring in places where they can have little impact.

BRAINSTORM POSSIBLE COURSES OF ACTION

Students should be encouraged to think creatively and divergently about possible ways of achieving their aims. No suggestion should be criticised, as ideas that might at first seem unrealistic often inspire fresh ideas that turn out to be practical.

WAYS OF TAKING ACTION

- Writing letters to elected representatives to express a point of view on a local or global issue;
- Volunteering to work for an organisation that deals with an issue of concern;
- Fund-raising for organisations that are working for environmental quality, social and economic justice, conflict resolution;
- Becoming involved in neighbourhood clean-up projects;
- Writing letters to the editor of the school or local newspaper;
- Participating in voter registration drives, and campaigns to encourage people to vote.

IDENTIFY ANY OBSTACLES TO THESE COURSES OF ACTION

After brainstorming, students can begin to think more realistically about their suggestions. They should discuss any obstacles that would prevent them from carrying out a particular course of action, and consider what resources would be available to them to help them overcome those challenges. An obstacle need not be a reason for abandoning a possible project, as it may be a source of valuable learning experiences. But some types of obstacles – excess cost, distance, physical danger – can become reasons to eliminate certain options for action.

MORE WAYS OF TAKING ACTION

- Carrying out research or conducting local surveys on issues of concern;
- Presenting the results of such research or surveys at school assemblies, community group meetings, or town council meetings;
- Boycotting products that are environmentally unsound, or that are produced under circumstances that violate human rights;
- Inviting speakers to present opposing perspectives on a controversial issue;
- Persuading family members to adopt more environmentally sound practices in the home.

SELECT A PROJECT

After some possible courses of action have been eliminated as impractical, students select one which they feel will best meet their goals. The group can consider whether the project addresses an immediate, short-term problem or a more underlying, long-term problem. Either type of project can provide opportunities for learning, and in some cases, a short-term response may be the only one which is practical. It is important, however, for the children to learn to distinguish between solutions which deal with symptoms of a problem as opposed to ones which deal with the root causes.

IDENTIFY KEY PEOPLE, RESOURCES, AND SKILLS NEEDED

Students should spend some time thinking about the key people they will need to consider in carrying out the plan. Which people are in a decision-making capacity with regard to the issues selected – representatives, local business people, school officials, or members of community groups? What resistance to change might they have, and how might students enlist their interest and support?

Who will be affected by the project – other children, parents, residents of a particular neighbourhood, local businesses, or certain disempowered groups? What role will they have in the planning and evaluation process?

What resources – money, equipment, or consumable supplies – will the project require? Will these be borrowed or donated? Will the students have to fundraise? If so, how?

Will the project require students to develop new skills – writing business letters, speaking in public, conducting interviews or surveys? Who can be called upon to teach these skills?

DRAW UP A DETAILED PLAN

It is often helpful to think of the plan as a time line (see page 266). This helps young people see the sequence of steps necessary to achieve the goal. It can also be helpful to examine the plan with a futures tree (see page 292), in order to evaluate its possible effects.

If the project is a complex one, it may be helpful to have the class divide into smaller teams to work on different tasks.

CARRY OUT THE PLAN

The teacher's role during this phase is to trust the students to manage the project with as little interference as possible, allowing them to develop a sense of empowerment and responsibility. The teacher can act as a facilitator, pointing out actions that are working effectively, drawing links between the project and material covered in class, helping students anticipate unexpected consequences, and serving as a resource person.

A record of the project should be kept – diaries, journals, drawings, photographs, audiotapes, or videotapes. These can serve not only as a basis for reflection and evaluation, but as a way of communicating about the project to the school, the community, and the media.

EVALUATE

Whether an action project has a definite end, or becomes an on-going activity, students need to take the time to evaluate. This will help them consolidate their learning, and prepare them to take more effective action in the future. They could consider:

- What was successful about the project? Did it achieve its goals? Did it create any lasting changes?
- Was anything about the project unsuccessful? Did it inadvertently create new problems? Were any failures experienced due to inadequate planning, or to factors beyond the group's control?
- If you were to repeat this project, what would you do differently?
- How effectively did the group work together? Did everyone have a sense of participation? Were decisions and responsibilities truly shared by the group?

In Switzerland, nine-year-olds prepare an assembly for the whole school on the importance of recycling. They provide each classroom with boxes to collect recyclable materials. Once a week, they take the contents of the boxes to a nearby recycling centre.

In Brazil, teenaged girls who once made their living on the streets produce dramas about AIDS, drug abuse, housing and unemployment. They perform in locations where they can reach other girls at risk. They write and distribute a pamphlet on AIDS prevention to distribute to girls who are forced to support themselves by prostitution.

In Norway, children around the country write letters expressing their hopes and concerns about the environment. From these, a 'Children's Appeal to World Leaders' is drawn up. Ten young people aged 12 to 15 present this appeal in a public Children's Hearing to top government leaders. The young people are working on making the hearing an annual event.

Handling controversial issues

Controversy is inevitable in dealing with global issues, and may arise during the course of an action project. Controversy in the classroom can be looked upon as a problem to be avoided, or as an opportunity for communication, insight, and change. The guidelines below suggest ways in which discussion of controversial issues can be made less threatening, and more educational.

- Create a safe classroom environment. Students need to feel that it is acceptable to examine problems for which there are no easy solutions, and that everyone's perspective will be respected.
- Correct misinformation in an age-appropriate way, and find out what students need to know to more fully understand the issue. Help them do research, write or talk to persons involved in the issue, invite speakers to the class, conduct surveys, or hold debates.
- Be prepared to support students for whom controversial issues may raise strong feelings. Allow them to express their emotions in an appropriate way. Reassure them that many adults care about and are working on these issues, even if they do not always agree on solutions.
- Decide whether it is appropriate to state a personal position. The teacher's primary focus should be on helping students develop their own response to the issue, not finding 'right' or 'wrong' answers. This may involve looking at many points of view, including those that differ from the teacher's. If a teacher decides it is appropriate to express a personal position, she should make it clear to the students that it is an opinion, not a fact or an absolute truth.
- The raising of controversial issues in the classroom may prompt criticism that a particular set of values is being promoted. It can be helpful to remember that all education has to do with the transmission of certain values, and can never be an entirely neutral, value-free process. Education that aims to encourage attitudes of global citizenship must deal explicitly with questions of values.
- Focus on problem-solving. Once students have explored a range of opinions on an issue, help them determine if there is something constructive they can do about the problem, in their own locality. This will encourage a sense of personal empowerment, rather than discouragement or despair.

In the Czech Republic, young people from 500 schools do practical research on air pollution, including determining the ozone concentration in the ground layer of the atmosphere. Their collected results will be published and used for further environmental research.

In India, a group of street children aged ten to 17 open a restaurant in a bus terminal. They learn the skills of cooking, looking after customers, and book-keeping. Their work ensures that they eat nutritious meals every day. And they donate food they prepare to other local street children.

In Colombia, classes of secondary school students work in low-income neighbourhoods, educating families about hygiene, basic health care, sanitation, and the need for immunisation against common diseases.

In Sri Lanka, children of all ages work in a plant nursery, caring for tree seedlings. When the seedlings are large enough, the children help to plant them on a previously deforested hilltop near their village.

Other issues to consider

For some teachers, involving students in action projects will represent a departure from the familiar curriculum. They enter an area of education in which the outcomes cannot always be foreseen. Teachers need to be aware of the kinds of issues which action projects may raise, and to be prepared to handle them. Some of the kinds of questions or concerns which could arise are discussed below.

HOW CAN THE CONCERNS OF SCHOOL ADMINISTRATORS BE DEALT WITH?

Informing administrators in advance of plans to carry out an action project can forestall potential objections. Try to use administrators as resource people, and incorporate their suggestions whenever possible. Be clear with administrators about the educational aims of the project, and the ways in which it fits in with the goals of the school or youth group. Emphasise the fact that a variety of possible projects will be brainstormed by the students and that a predetermined point of view on the issue in question will not be imposed on the group. Make administrators aware of how parents will be kept informed of the project. A supportive administration can be of enormous benefit, as some action projects will require trips off the school grounds, and adjustments to daily schedules.

WHAT CAN BE DONE IF SOME PARENTS OBJECT TO THE PROJECT?

Projects should be planned with respect for issues which may be sensitive among the parents. Boycotting a local business, for example, can be disastrous if some of the students' parents are employed there.

Informing parents in advance of the project, and keeping them informed about its progress is the best way to prevent objections. Parents may worry that the project is taking time away from students' basic school work. Ensure that they understand the types of skills which are being developed by the project. If necessary, plan a parent meeting, or a regular newsletter about the project, produced by the students, to keep them informed.

Actively involving parents in the project is an excellent way of letting them see for themselves what their children are learning. Parents may have skills or resources they can share with the group. They may be able to help with transportation, accompanying children on house-to-house surveys, or supervising small group work.

In Uganda, a group of primary school children work to clean and fence the local well, which has become contaminated from use by livestock. They create dramatic presentations to educate adults and younger children about the risks of water-borne diseases.

In Bosnia and Herzegovina, children aged ten to 13 produce a radio programme for their peers. Working with adult editors, they design segments that address the special needs of children in war zones. The programme provides educational material for children who no longer have a school to go to.

In the United Kingdom, a class of seven-year-olds review library books, examining them for racist and sexist text and illustrations. They write letters to publishers suggesting changes to books they find unacceptable. They rewrite and illustrate library books for younger children.

In Java, a group of Scouts constructs pipelines leading to four different villages. The pipes provide safe, clean drinking water for the people of the villages. The water is also used for irrigating crops.

IS MEDIA COVERAGE OF CHILDREN'S ACTION PROJECTS APPROPRIATE?

An interesting action project will often attract the attention of newspaper and television reporters. Media involvement can help educate the community, mobilise others to become involved, and teach students how news is created.

Contact with the media should not be used as a reward for the brightest, most articulate, or most photogenic students. If only a few students can appear in a photograph or on a television programme, let the class determine the criteria for selecting who will appear.

Media producers may have different aims in reporting on the project than the class does! They may want an entertaining story, when the class wants to emphasise the seriousness of an issue. Inform representatives of the media as to the purposes of the project *before* filming or interviewing, and ask to read or view any reports before they are published or broadcast.

HOW CAN CHILDREN BE HELPED TO DEAL WITH THEIR FEELINGS IF AN ACTION PROJECT FAILS?

Teachers can help students avoid action projects that 'fail' by encouraging realistic expectations of what can be achieved. Students should not expect, for example, that a letter to the town council will bring about overnight change on a multi-faceted development issue!

Some projects which are apparent 'failures' may only be undergoing temporary setbacks. Much can be learned from such projects, and from the challenge of having to adapt a plan to unforeseen circumstances.

But not all action projects will ultimately achieve their aims. Despite careful planning, projects can be influenced by events beyond the control of the students.

If this happens, allow time for students to express their feelings – anger, resentment, sadness, disappointment, frustration. Then encourage them to discuss the reasons for the difficulties encountered, distinguishing between those which were due to outside events and those which might have been prevented.

Focus on any positive outcomes of the project. What did they learn that they did not know before? What things can they do that they did not know how to do before? What new ideas and insights could they bring to their next action project? Record these ideas for future reference.

In Peru, a group of urban street workers in their teens set up an organisation that provides a forum for street children to express their needs to international agencies. They provide financial and emergency assistance to their members, and survey their local areas on issues such as health, education, work, recreation, and children's hopes for the future.

In the United States, six teenagers make a video on unequal funding for schools in their city. The video compares the lives and hopes of two students, one who attends a well-equipped middle class school, and one who attends a working class school with few resources and poorly trained teachers. The teenagers screen the video with parent groups, and on national television, sparking debate on ways to reform the school funding process.

In Belgium, a group of children draws up a petition against the manufacture and sale of war toys. They circulate it in a number of communities and collect signatures. They then draw up a proposal for a law to ban the advertising and sale of war toys, and meet with elected representatives to urge its passage.

WHAT SHOULD BE DONE IF THE CHILDREN'S PARTICIPATION EXPANDS BEYOND THE ORIGINAL PROJECT PLAN?

A project which is 'too successful' can be problematic for some teachers! Children who set up a thriving recycling project in their classroom may want to extend it to the whole school. Students who volunteer to spend a set number of hours working in a programme for children with disabilities may be reluctant to break off relationships they have formed, and wish to continue their involvement.

Some projects may be continued after school, or incorporated into the work of youth groups or clubs. Interested parents or community groups may wish to become involved and can take over from teachers much of the responsibility for supervising the project. In some cases, it may be possible to negotiate with school administrators for secondary school students to receive academic credit for community participation.

Whenever possible within the time constraints of the curriculum, longer-term project commitments should be encouraged. Inviting other classes in the school to collaborate can both expand the project, and relieve the time demands on one class. The project can be integrated into other subject areas which are being taught, so as to ease concerns about time being taken away from the curriculum. Children running the recycling project could practise mathematical skills by weighing and measuring the scrap materials they collect each week, for example; students working with disabled children could use their experiences as the basis for writing assignments. In other words, a whole school approach to action projects can expand their educational potential.

Education for Development content and methodology

Cohen, E, *Designing Groupwork*, 1986, Teachers College Press, New York and London. Combines the theory of small group cooperative work with suggestions for practical applications across the grade levels.

Comite Español del UNICEF, *Manual de Educación para el Desarrollo*, 1985. A summary of the basic principles of Education for Development, with a number of suggested activities and ideas for action projects.

Convention on the Rights of the Child, 1989. This comprehensive document is the first legally binding code of children's rights in history. It was adopted by the United Nations General Assembly in 1989. Copies are available from the Centre for Human Rights, New York and Geneva, and UNICEF, New York and Geneva.

Educators for Social Responsibility, *Making History*, 1987, Cambridge, Massachusetts, USA. A detailed guide to helping young people design and carry out action projects, for secondary schools.

Educators for Social Responsibility, *Taking Part*, 1991, Cambridge, Massachusetts, USA. A practical manual for primary teachers outlining a vision of what an 'empowering classroom' would look like, and describing a number of decision-making strategies.

Fisher, S, and Hicks, D, *World Studies 8–13*, 1985, Oliver and Boyd, Edinburgh and New York. A thorough introduction to World Studies, with clear explanations of classroom activities.

Fountain, S, *Learning Together: Global Education 4–7*, 1990, Stanley Thornes, Cheltenham, England. An exploration of social skills that can be developed in the early school years, which form a foundation for Education for Development; many classroom activities.

Greig, S, Pike, G, and Selby, D, *Earthrights: Education as if the Planet Really Mattered*, 1987, WWF and Kogan Page, London. A brief, readable survey of critical global issues; examines the inter-relationships between a number of educational initiatives, such as peace education, development education, environmental education, and human rights education.

Hanvey, R, *An Attainable Global Perspective*, 1982, Global Perspectives in Education, New York. A thoughtful discussion of the central aims of education with a global perspective.

Hart, Roger, *Children's Participation: From Tokenism to Citizenship*, 1992, UNICEF International Child Development Centre, Florence, Italy. A fascinating paper which draws the distinctions between action projects which use students manipulatively, and those which provide the opportunity for genuine learning experiences and authentic community participation.

Inter-Agency Commission, WCEFA, *Final Report: World Conference on Education for All*, 1990. A summary of the educational priorities set forth at the World Conference on Education for All, useful for placing Education for Development in a global context.

Italian Committee for UNICEF, *Introducción a Un Encuentro Con America Latina*, 1987. Contains not only a summary of major development issues, but suggestions for activities which are applicable to a number of topics in Education for Development.

Jacobs, H H, ed., *Interdisciplinary Curriculum: Design and Implementation*, 1989, Assocation for Supervision and Curriculum Development. A short but clear reference work on the theory and practice of interdisciplinary curriculum planning.

Johnson, D W, and Johnson, R T, *Learning Together and Alone*, 1975, Prentice-Hall, New Jersey. An extensive summary of research on cooperatively-structured learning, with guidelines for classroom practice.

Johnson, D W, and Johnson, R T, *The Socialization and Achievement Crisis: Are Cooperative Learning Experiences the Solution?*, 1983, Sage Publications. An important monograph summarising research on the academic and social effects of cooperative learning.

Lewis, Barbara A, *The Kid's Guide to Social Action*, 1991, Free Spirit Publishing, Minneapolis, Minnesota, USA. A highly practical book which teaches skills such as telephoning, letter-writing, interviewing, conducting surveys, creating petitions, fundraising, advertising and writing grant proposals. Although examples are drawn mainly from the experiences of US students, the many case studies provide abundant inspiration for action projects.

Pike, G, and Selby, D, *Global Teacher, Global Learner*, 1988, Hodder and Stoughton, London. An extensive work on the theory of global education, with many chapters full of classroom activities.

UNICEF, *The Future Role of UNICEF External Relations*, 1990, UNICEF, New York. A policy paper describing the objectives, priorities, organisation, and activities of UNICEF external relations.

UNICEF, 'Annual Report', 1990, UNICEF, New York. An annual summary of progress on issues of child survival and development.

UNICEF, 'Education for Development: Report of the Consultation, Thonon-les-Bains, France', 1991. This report details the basic concepts and learning process of Education for Development.

UNICEF, 'Education for Development', E/ICEF/1992/L.8. This paper, presented to the 1992 session of the UNICEF Executive Board, defines Education for Development, and sets out its role in industrialised and developing countries.

UNICEF, *The State of the World's Children*, 1989, UNICEF and Oxford University Press, Oxford. An annual report which provides useful statistics on a number of issues relevant to child survival and development. The 1989 edition includes a useful summary of issues which have failed to be taken into consideration in many development planning processes.

Interdependence

Cole, M, *Dialogue for Development*, Book 1 (1983) and Book 2 (1985), Trocaire, Dublin. Contains a wealth of information and statistics for teachers on development issues and North-South relationships, in a lively and readable format.

Cooke, D, *et al*, *Teaching Development Issues*, 1986, Development Education Project, Manchester, UK. An excellent series providing background information for teachers and student activities in the following areas: colonialism, food, population changes, work, aid and development.

Eccles, P, *et al*, eds, *75:25 – Ireland in a Still Unequal World*, 1991, Congood, Dublin, Ireland. Background material for teachers on development issues, with charts, statistics, case studies, and cartoons.

Johnson, J, and Benegar, J, *Global Issues in the Intermediate Classroom*, 1981, Social Science Education Consortium/Global Perspectives in Education, Boulder, Colorado, USA. Contains a section of interdependence activities for students aged ten to 14, including the simulation game **Who's got the batteries?**

Lamy, S, *et al*, *Teaching Global Awareness with Simulations and Games*, 1980, Center for Teaching International Relations, Denver, USA. Contains a number of interactive approaches to teaching about aspects of interdependence, for students aged 12 to 18.

Population Reference Bureau, *World Population Data Sheet*, 1993, Washington DC, USA. An annual summary of significant demographic data for each country and region of the world.

World Bank, *World Development Report*, 1993, Oxford University Press, UK. An annual report containing current data on social and economic development in more than 180 countries.

Images and perceptions

Derman-Sparks, Louise, *Anti-Bias Curriculum*, 1989, National Association for the Education of Young Children, Washington DC, USA. Though intended for early childhood teachers, this book presents a superb rationale for helping children counteract bias; the philosophy and approach are appropriate for teachers of all age groups. Specific examples tend to focus on American minority groups, but teachers and youth leaders will be able to adapt it for their own situations.

Development Education Centre, *Get The Picture!*, 1990, DEC, Birmingham, UK. A practical handbook full of classroom ideas and background information for introducing primary school children to visual literacy and media education.

Fountain, Susan, *Gender Issues – An Activity File*, 1991, Stanley Thornes,

UK. A handbook of classroom activities for teachers of children aged eight to 13 to raise awareness of gender stereotyping and its effects.

Hicks, David, *Images of the World: An Introduction to Bias in Teaching Materials*, 1980, University of London Institute of Education, London, UK. An excellent survey of the types of images of developing countries found in British textbooks.

Milner, David, *Children and Race*, 1983, Ward Lock Educational, London, UK. A useful compilation of research on the development of children's racial identity and prejudices.

Prieswerk, R, *The Slant of the Pen: Racism in Children's Books*, 1980, World Council of Churches, Geneva, Switzerland. A thorough overview of the ways in which racist attitudes are perpetuated in children's literature.

Social justice

Fountain, Susan, *It's Only Right!*, 1993, UNICEF, New York, USA. A practical guide for learning about the Convention on the Rights of the Child. A series of activities for students aged 13 to 18 helps young people become familiar with the articles of the Convention, understand its relevance to their own lives, and make realistic plans for taking action on children's rights issues.

Hicks, D, and Steiner, M, *Making Global Connections*, 1990, Oliver and Boyd, Edinburgh, Scotland, UK. A handbook for teachers which shows how to put the principles of the World Studies 8–13 Project into practice.

Joyce, Kathy, *Drama for Justice*, 1987, Christian Aid, London, UK. A collection of seven topics which can be explored by secondary students through drama, simulation, and role play. Topics include refugees, student labour, access to clean water, problems created by tourism, etc.

Lister, Ian, *Teaching and Learning About Human Rights*, 1984, School Education Division, Council of Europe, Strasbourg, France. A clear discussion of human rights education, particularly useful for its recommendations concerning methodology and the 'human rights school'.

Office on Global Education/Center for Teaching International Relations, *Students Hungering for Justice*, 1991, USA. Three teaching packs – for primary, middle, and secondary school students – on justice, children's rights, and the issue of world hunger. Contains a section on suggestions for ways students can take action.

Schniedewind, Nancy and Davidson, Ellen, *Open Minds to Equality*, 1983, Prentice-Hall, USA. Interactive teaching strategies for raising students' awareness of justice and injustice, especially with regard to race, sex, class, age, and disability. While some of the content is specific to situations in the United States, most of the formats used are easily adaptable to other countries.

Tuvilla Rayo, Jose, *Derechos Humanos*, 1990, Junta de Andalucia, Consejeria de Educacion y Ciencia, Spain. A theoretical discussion of the links between justice, peace, and human rights, with guidelines for teaching strategies. A section on classroom activities uses literature to illustrate these concepts, as well as interactive small group exercises.

UNICEF Canada, *Within Our Reach*, 1988. A collection of cooperatively-structured activities that help students understand concepts of justice as applied to issues such as health, food, and education.

United Nations, *Teaching Human Rights*, 1989, New York, USA. A useful introduction to teaching about rights issues, with particular reference to the Universal Declaration of Human Rights. Contains suggestions for encouraging a classroom climate which promotes rights, as well as suggestions for practical activities which link justice with development, the environment, peace, discrimination, etc.

Conflict and conflict resolution

Adams, D *et al*, 'The Seville Statement on Violence', *American Psychologist*, October 1990, Vol. 45, No 10, pp. 1167–68. This document was drafted by twenty scholars from around the world at the 6th International Colloquium on Brain and Aggression, at the University of Seville, Spain, in 1986. It makes a strong case for the fact that aggressive behaviour is learned, not inborn.

Asociación Pro Derechos Humanos/Centro de Investigación para la Paz, *Educar para la Paz: Una Propuesta Posible*, 1990, Madrid, Spain. A concise and practical summary of issues relating to peace education, with suggestions for its integration into all areas of the curriculum.

Hicks, David W, *Education for Peace: Issues, Dilemmas and Alternatives*, 1985, Occasional paper No 9, Centre for Peace Studies, St Martin's College, Lancaster, UK. A useful summary of the theoretical reasons for having peace education in schools; it addresses a number of frequently-heard criticisms of the approach.

Joint Peace Programme of The Irish Commission for Justice and Peace and The Irish Council of Churches, *Power To Hurt: Exploring Violence*, 1991, Belfast, Northern Ireland and Dublin, Ireland. An excellent handbook for teaching about conflict and violence, for secondary schools. Some activities refer specifically to Irish issues, but are adaptable to situations in other countries.

Kreidler, William J, *Creative Conflict Resolution*, 1984, Scott, Foresman and Company, Glenview, Illinois, USA, and London, UK. A comprehensive guide to introducing peacemaking skills, including cooperation, communication, and awareness of stereotyping, with over 200 classroom activities for the primary grades.

Kreidler, William J, *Elementary Perspectives 1: Teaching Concepts of Peace and Conflict*, 1990, Educators for Social Responsibility, Cambridge, Massachusetts, USA. Nearly 100 activities for primary schools, helping children link personal conflict resolution strategies to issues in the wider world.

Prutzman, Priscilla, *et al*, *The Friendly Classroom for a Small Planet*, 1988, New Society Publishers, Philadelphia, Pennsylvania, USA. Also available as *Repuesta Creativa Al Conflicto*, CEPPA, San Jose, Costa Rica, South America. Activities for the primary years which build self-esteem, communication and cooperation, as well as strategies for developing conflict resolution skills.

Reardon, Betty, *Comprehensive Peace Education*, 1988, Teachers College Press, Columbia University, New York, USA, and London, UK. A scholarly review of the history and development of peace education, its key concepts and goals.

Richardson, Robin, *Culture, race and peace: Tasks and Tensions in the Classroom*, 1982, Occasional Paper No 2, Centre for Peace Studies, St Martin's College, Lancaster, UK. A brief summary of the necessity of forging links between peace education and other areas such as multicultural education and development education.

Change and the future

Fisher, S, and Hicks, D, *World Studies 8–13*, 1985, Oliver and Boyd, Edinburgh, Scotland, UK. Contains a chapter on 'The World Tomorrow' which provides a readable theoretical background for teaching about the future, as well as a number of classroom activities.

Pike, G, and Selby, D, *Global Teacher, Global Learner*, 1988, Hodder and Stoughton, London. A section on 'The Temporal Dimension' gives a framework for seeing past, present, and future in a global perspective; many classroom activities are suggested as well.

Robertson, *The Sane Alternative*, 1983, River Basin Publishing Co, St Paul, Minnesota, USA. An exploration of the concept of alternative futures.

Slaughter, R, *Futures Tools and Techniques*, 1987, University of Lancaster, UK. A clear and thorough exploration of the rationale for futures education, with a number of techniques which are usable in the classroom.

Zola, J, and Sieck, R, *Teaching About Conflict, Nuclear War and The Future*, 1984, Center for Teaching International Relations, University of Denver, USA. Contains a chapter on teaching about the future which suggests a variety of classroom activities; student materials are included.

Index